Work Transformation

David

Thanks for your
comments, support
+ encouragement

Ken

To my parents

Weston and Priscilla

For their faith in me

To my wife

Judith

*For her understanding, support,
and encouragement*

Work Transformation

Planning and Implementing the New Workplace

Ken Robertson

KLR Consulting Inc.
Vancouver, British Columbia
Canada

HNB Publishing   •   NEW YORK

ISBN: 0-9664286-0-9

Cover design by Jennifer Morris

This book is printed on acid-free paper.

The publisher offers discounts on this book when ordered in bulk quantities.

HNB Publishing
250 West 78th St., # 3FF
New York, NY 10024
hnbpub.com

Current printing (last digit):

10 9 8 7 6 5 4 3 2 1

PRINTED IN THE UNITED STATES OF AMERICA

Foreword

A regular part of my youth in the late 1950s and early 1960s was watching the "Ed Sullivan Show" on Sunday evening. As those of you who grew up during that time (or who watched the reruns on cable) know, Sullivan assembled all kinds of acts for his variety show. He always seemed to include some kind of juggler or similar performer who stunned the audience with the amazing ability to make various (and multiple) objects defy gravity as they remained airborne or suspended.

I remember in particular an act featuring someone who'd come on stage with a set of long, thin poles and a supply of dinner plates. One by one, he'd start each plate spinning on top of a pole and would then somehow extend the pole upwards—eventually winding up with several poles erected, each with a plate spinning on top.

That's when the fun began—fun for us viewers, but impending panic for the performer, I suspect. His task was to give each one of those poles just enough of a nudge to keep the plate spinning at the right speed. If the plate's speed slowed down, it would teeter and eventually come crashing down to the stage and break. I guess if he broke too many plates, he didn't get invited back again.

The audience was obviously supposed to concentrate on those plates wiggling and wobbling atop the poles; that's where the cameras were usually focused. But I seem to remember more about the performer than the spun plates: he was obsessed with watching the poles and plates and figuring out just how to tweak each pole at the right time so the plate would spin and not crash.

The image of that performer trying to keep those poles moving and plates spinning has stuck in my mind over the years, and it continues to strike me as an excellent metaphor for much that goes on in organizational life. In fact, it pretty much describes *my* corporate years. The big difference between the plate spinner and me, however, is that I broke a lot more plates than he did. And most of the plates I tried to keep in motion were loaded with various kinds of steaming-hot, smelly, or otherwise dangerous or objectionable items. If the wobble wasn't just right, some of that stuff would come spilling down all over me—and the plates would crash at my feet.

As I read this book by Ken Robertson, the image of that Ed Sullivan–era plate spinner came instantly to mind. Picture this: your organization is represented by just three of those poles—one for people, one for technology, and one for facilities. That's about all there is—*who* does the work, what *tools* they use to do it, and *where* they do it. Now, imagine that three somewhat burly and aggressive jugglers (oops—"managers") are on stage (oops—"at the office") trying to do everything possible to keep their own pole (oops—"areas of responsibility") in motion so that they don't let the plate crash (oops—"projects fail" or "results suffer").

Each of the three can do a reasonably good job keeping his or her one pole moving just right, but the real challenge begins as they start moving closer to each other because the stage is getting smaller (oops—"budgets are being cut" or "competitive pressures are increasing"). They're each trying to look out for the other two people who are starting to encroach on their territory, while keeping the plate spinning and not letting the pole fall. Soon, the three begin bumping into each other—the poles start to shake dangerously, the plates start to wobble, and . . . well, you can imagine how this little corporate performance ends.

Robertson's approach to work transformation addresses the very fundamental problem alluded to in that scenario: with limited room to navigate and increased pressures, how can the traditional singular, function-specific approach to organizational performance succeed?

That is, can we still expect to optimize the individual results with people, technology, and facilities if we treat each as a separate entity? More important, can the organization perform satisfactorily if we insist on seeing those three functions as individual and perhaps competing parts of the organization? The answer to both questions, quite clearly, is a resounding "no"—spoken with the same noise level as the sound of three big dinner plates crashing on the floor at once. We simply can no longer pretend that these three pivotal organizational functions can be managed independently—and I'm not sure they ever could.

This book is subtitled *Planning and Implementing the New Workplace*, and it is very much a new workplace that we are facing today, as we turn the corner on a new century. It is a workplace in which the fundamentals of this book will prevail. Smart organizations will finally realize, accept, and act on the fact that:

- We no longer need to bring all the office workers to the office, just because we brought all the farm workers to the farm or factory workers to the factory. Thus, we have much more flexibility in *place* than ever before;
- We no longer need to bring all the officer workers to the office at the same time, even if they are "collaborating" or "team members" or otherwise expected to work together. We have much more flexibility in *time* because knowledge workers can work together (at least some of the time) without physically being together;
- We are in the middle of—and perhaps at times overwhelmed by—the most powerful application of technology to office work that we've ever seen. Computing and telecommunications—individually and together—have, quite simply, fundamentally changed *how* we do what we do as knowledge workers;
- We are recognizing—albeit slowly—that office workers are not constitutionally guaranteed their 120 ft² of cubicle space and that a "one size fits all" approach to uniformity and "standards" in office design makes about as much sense as "one size fits all" underwear. To borrow from Star Trek, office space truly is the last frontier in organizational life.

I'm not aware of any other book intended for practicing managers that incorporates these realities as well, or that does such a good job of forcing the reader to think in terms of integrating people, technology, and facilities. And you'll do more than "think" as you read this book, because it is written with as much emphasis on *doing* as on thinking about the issues. The conceptual underpinnings of the book mesh nicely with a very through implementation guide. It's not always easy reading, and the steps and processes Robertson suggests aren't simple or simplistic. But neither are they impractical or impossible. If you invest some attention to the book, the payback in organizational effectiveness will be tremendous.

By the time you get through this book, you may be tired of seeing Robertson's model of how these factors relate to each other and to business objectives. If you find yourself tiring of that diagram, go back and read the last few pages again—because the diagram appears every time the author wants to remind us just how important it is to keep those three factors linked in our minds and in practice.

Besides, a triangle with its three linked sides is *infinitely* more stable than three independent, wobbly poles.

Gil Gordon
President, Gil Gordon Associates
Editor, Telecommuting Review

Preface

The concept of work transformation is created by integrating human resources, facilities management and information technology strategies together in new and creative ways to deliver business value to an organization. Work transformation involves rethinking the way we work, where we work from, and the environment we work in.

This book describes how an organization can break out of its traditional definition of work and move forward to an environment that is more flexible, empowering, communicative, and pleasing. One of the ways this is accomplished is by implementing alternative work arrangements such as teleworking, work at home, part-time work, modified work weeks, and phased retirement. These new work arrangements help employees balance work and family while delivering significant business benefits to the organization.

The second element of work transformation is the implementation of alternative space arrangements. This concept requires organizations to rethink the way space is structured. The new space strategies include concepts such as space sharing, hoteling, team spaces, casual meeting areas, and meditation zones. The new space arrangements create more of a community feel to the office environment as opposed to the rabbit-warren cubicles so many employees work in today. Alternative space arrangements also provide direct bottom-line business benefits in terms of reduced space requirements, reduced churn costs, and more effective utilization of space.

The third element of work transformation is the effective use of enabling technologies. The information technology solutions make it possible to support employees working from home, in shared spaces in the traditional office, in distributed work centers, and on the road. The information technology available today can enable the implementation of alternative work arrangements and alternative space arrangements.

This book has been structured to give readers an overview of these concepts. It is different from other books in this field in that the focus is not just on human resources, facilities management, or information technology. Instead the focus is on *integrating* these concepts, as shown below.

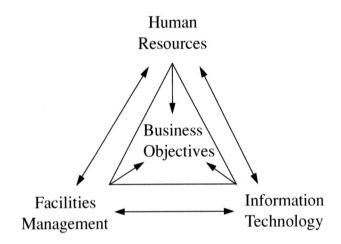

This diagram is used throughout the book to stress how critical the integration of these three key elements is to successfully implementing work transformation. I have been researching and implementing these concepts for the past eight years and realize that the common thread of all successful implementations is their integration of these concepts with a strong focus on creating business value.

This book is designed to take the reader from concept to theory to implementation. Chapters 1–2 introduce the concepts of work transformation. Chapters 3–5 review the theory of the human resources, facilities management, and information technology components. Chapters 6–8 describe how to implement a work transformation program. Chapter 9 provides a detailed case study along with a summary of several actual implementations. Finally, Chapter 10 provides a brief glimpse into the future to show how work transformation is just a stepping stone towards even greater changes down the road.

Ken Robertson

Acknowledgments

Writing a book on a topic that is truly leading-edge such as work transformation requires enormous support. I would like to quickly acknowledge some of the people and organizations that have helped in the evolution of this material.

My interest in the subject evolved from my research on telework at Simon Fraser University in Burnaby, British Columbia. My thesis advisor, Dr. John Richards, helped to teach me the fundamentals of researching a topic to the fullest extent. The long and arduous hours of producing this thesis were rewarded when telework started to become an integral part of my consulting practice.

I learned to evolve the concepts of telework through my early work with clients in this area. All of these clients were prepared to pioneer some of these new concepts and to go out on a limb based on the assumption that some business value would be derived. During this period, I have been able to learn more about the inner workings of how and where people work, how to best deliver business value, and, most importantly, how to get people thinking outside of the box. To all of these clients, my most sincere thanks for letting my firm, KLR Consulting Inc., be a part of your pioneering efforts.

In the past few years, several of my clients have provided opportunities for me to test out the materials presented in this book. This has given me the chance to tune the concepts to the point where they could be documented, as presented here. I should also stress that this learning process is not over, we are still learning more and more about the concept of work transformation. My thanks to all of these organizations that, in many cases, took a leap of faith on these concepts and in our ability to transform their work environment.

I am not by trade an interior designer; in fact, many who have seen me draw up an office interior cringe at my drawing skills. I am therefore greatly indebted to my friend and colleague Peter Selnar at OfficeWorks, who has constantly provided me with information on interior design and whose staff has been kind enough to take my scribbles and turn them into well-designed CAD drawings.

Finally, the creation of any book requires an unbelievable amount of support from one's family. My wife, Judith, has lived through the creation of two books in the past three years, which is a challenge for anyone. Her incredible ability to edit my many articles, newsletter issues, and these books has always amazed me.

Thanks.

Ken

Contents

Chapter 3
Human Resources   **36**

Chapter 4
Facilities Management   **64**

Figures

1

Introduction

We are living in a time of tremendous change that is forcing employees and organizations to create new and innovative ways to stay competitive in the emerging global marketplace.

The rapid pace of change today is clearly illustrated by Bill Fields, CEO of Blockbuster Entertainment, as quoted in *Fortune* magazine in November 1996.

When the rate of external change exceeds the rate of internal change, disaster is imminent.[1]

Changes within the organization must occur at a faster rate than changes outside of the organization. If this does not occur, then the organization's competitive position is lost. Nula Beck, a Canadian economist, suggests that companies that do not adapt and change will find themselves working in a broom-closet.[2]

Fields and Beck are advising that the old steady and true approach is not going to make it in today's economy. To be successful, organizations must revisit some of the traditional ways of doing business and look for new and creative ways to expand or, at a minimum, maintain their market share. If an organization is not changing as fast as other organizations changing around it, then it may have to seriously consider its future role in the marketplace, which may be much smaller than today's role if it exists at all.

In the midst of all these changes is the *way* work is performed and *where* it is performed from. Most organizations are still using the same 1950s model of structuring work arrangements. This involves having employees working fixed schedules (typically 8:00 or 9:00 A.M. to 5:00 P.M., Monday to Friday) and working out of an office facility that really has not changed much in the past 50 years. Organizations need to think about the speed of change in these areas and whether they can afford to continue to function within these traditional models.

To determine whether an organization should be looking at redefining how and where employees work, it is necessary to understand the external changes. Key external changes include changes in the global economy, organizational changes, personal changes, and changes in technology.

GLOBAL ECONOMY

The concept of a global economy has been discussed for a long time. The impact of the evolving global economy is starting to take hold in many North American companies.

Twenty years ago, very few companies were affected by changes in other parts of the world. Today, through the use of technology, the world has become a much smaller place. Competition is no longer limited to within a city, state/province, region, or country but truly is pervasive in the developed and developing world. The global marketplace has emerged and is becoming more predominant every year.

Many companies are now competing with off-shore organizations that may be able to produce the same products or services at a lower cost and/or higher quality and/or with a higher level of customer service. Many of these off-shore organizations can utilize basic telecommunications technology to service customers in another organizations backyard. And they can do it by paying wages that are commensurate with the standard of living in the country of origin. This can be a severe challenge for traditional companies that now must become much more creative in their approach to competing in the marketplace.

The global marketplace is a two-way street. Not only can companies from other countries start competing in your marketplace, but your organization can start to expand its sales into other countries. The technology available today and that which will become available in the next decade will make the geographic distance between producer and consumer less and less important.

ORGANIZATIONAL CHANGES

There have also been significant changes in traditionally stable organizations. Many so-called blue-chip companies have made dramatic changes in the way they operate. Some companies such as IBM have seen their marketplace change and have had to make dramatic changes to stay competitive. Others such as

Smith Corona, which was one of the world leaders in manufacturing typewriters, are now out of business. Smith Corona stuck to its typewriter market with diminishing demand as customers migrated to word processing on their personal computers.

Corporate changes have affected public- and private-sector organizations of all sizes. Many organizations grew uncontrollably during the 1980s. When changes in market conditions forced these organizations to cut costs, the cost cutting usually included re-engineering business processes, downsizing, reducing operating costs, selling corporate assets, and moving to strategies to make the organization more flexible.

Public-sector organizations, which in many cases have been insulated from economic changes, are also feeling the pressures to downsize and reduce the costs of government. These organizations are struggling under the debt load they have established over the past 50 years and are having great difficulty in paying their basic operating costs and interest on debt. In addition, taxpayers are now starting to organize and force the public sector to reduce costs.

All organizations seem to fall into the same set of basic challenges. Figure 1-1 shows a conceptual view of an organization in terms of the products and services it produces, the business practices and processes required to deliver the

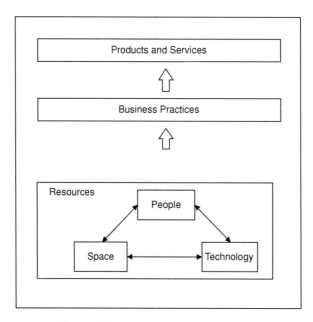

Figure 1-1 Generic business model.

products and services, and the key resources available to the organization to make it all happen. In the diagram, the three key resources (people, technology, and space) are shown in a triangle, each one interdependent.

The pressures for change are everywhere and are driven by changing customer expectations, new government mandates, new competitors, and replacement products. The marketplace for all organizations (public and private sectors) is in the midst of tremendous change.

Organizations are reacting to these changes by reengineering their business processes and, in many cases, downsizing their organizations. These changes have put tremendous strain on the resources available, often pushing them to their limits. To get more for less, the organization must rethink how the resources are utilized.

Luckily, there is hope for revitalizing these scarce resources. New technologies help employees do their jobs more effectively. Alternative work arrangements, supported by technology, are providing employees with more personal choices while still supporting key business objectives.

The final dimension of the resource triangle is space. For many years, organizations have ignored space, choosing to fit employees into the traditional space planning parameters. During this time, space has grown to become the second largest cost for most organizations (after employee wages and benefits). Now, with the introduction of alternative space arrangements, organizations can begin to use space as more of a business tool.

The result is a new model of resources, as shown in Figure 1-2, where some reengineering of people, space, and technology is delivering significant business value to organizations.

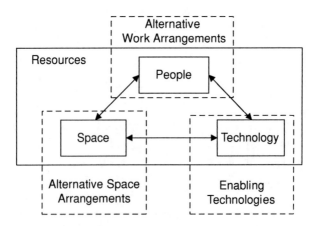

Figure I-2 New resourcing strategies.

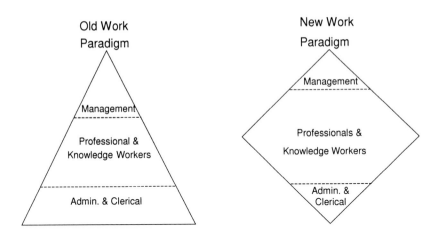

Figure 1-3 Human resources paradigm shift.

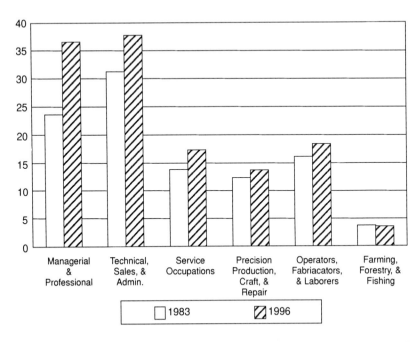

Figure 1-4 U.S. workers by occupation 1983–1996). (Source: U.S. Bureau of the Census.)

It is also interesting to notice the paradigm shift occurring with human resources. Figure 1-3 shows the reduction in management by flattening the organizational structure, the equally dramatic reduction in the number of clerical and administrative staff through the use of technology, and the emergence of a large number of workers in the professional/knowledge worker category. The knowledge workers are probably the most critical to any organization's success, and they are also the ones who will likely be most receptive to alternative ways of working.

Figure 1-4 shows the shift to knowledge workers in the United States by occupation.[3] These data are even more dramatic when analyzed in terms of the incremental change by occupation between 1983 and 1996. Figure 1-5 shows this analysis, comparing the percentage change by occupation for this period (during which there was overall a 25.7% increase in the work force). Clearly, the professional ranks are growing while all the other occupational groups are growing at a rate that is slower than that of the rest of the work force.

This shift in the type of workers has also been documented by Statistics Canada. Figure 1-6 shows that the blue collar work force has diminished from 61% of all jobs in 1948 to 29% in 1995 and a projected 20% in 2020. During the same period professional work has grown from 6% in 1948 to 19% in 1995 to a projected 22% in 2020.[4] If you are skeptical about the extent to which this

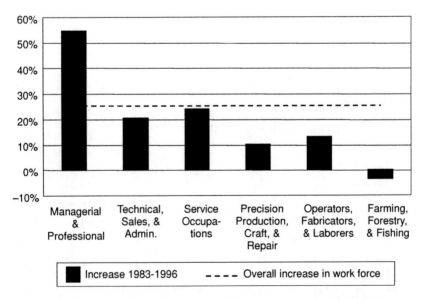

Figure 1-5   Percentage of change in work force by occupation (1983–1996).

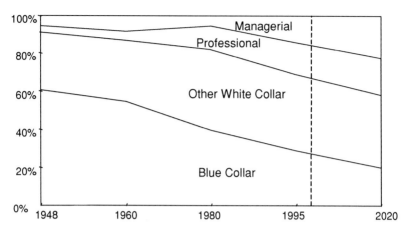

Figure 1-6 Employment breakdown by occupation in Canada since 1948 and projected through 2020. (Source: Statistics Canada.)

dramatic work shift is occurring, think about some of the jobs people are doing today. How many of your friends are working in a factory? How many secretarial jobs are in your organization today versus 10 years ago? Does your organization still have a typing pool? Are professionals now responsible for their own word processing?

Also, think of the shift in professional jobs. Consider the early days of commercial airlines, when all flight attendants had to be registered nurses. Today this is no longer a requirement. Or consider hospital nurses, who are seeing technology replace portions of their work and the use of lower paid nursing assistants to run these machines. Along the same lines, we are also seeing how nurse practitioners and registered nurses are now starting to take on some activities previously restricted to physicians.

Indeed organizations and their employees are changing.

PERSONAL CHANGES

Today's workers are also changing. They are experiencing both changes in demographics and in lifestyle choices.

The demographics of today's worker reveals a telling story of change. A quick analysis of Canadian and American statistics shows a dramatic increase in the number of women in the work force over the last 25 years.

This increasing number of women in the work force means that employers must be cognizant of the requirements of these working women. Women who are single parents or part of a two-income family with children are looking for flexible alternatives to manage their work and home lives. As an increasing number of women reach management and executive-level positions, it is critical that employers provide some flexibility to retain those who are highly qualified but who may not want to be in the central office five days a week.

Of course, men are not excluded from this equation. There is a growing number of men who are now single parents or taking a much more active role in raising their children or are part of a two-income family with children. These employees also are looking for flexible alternatives to help them balance work and family.

Changes have also occurred in the traditional family structure. In the 1960s, the typical family structure was referred to as the nuclear family. The nuclear family consisted of a father who worked and a mother who stayed home to care for the children. The nuclear family is nearing extinction today. American and Canadian census data clearly show a very dramatic increase in the number of two-income families in the last 25 years.[5] In 1961, the percentage of families in which both spouses worked was 17%; this percentage increased to 33% in 1971, 50% in 1980, and 58% by 1986. For many families, this is not just a lifestyle choice—it may be the only way to economically survive.

In the modern family model of the 1990s, mother and father work while the children are often in some type of day care. Consider a family living in the suburbs with both parents working in an office in the central core of a city that is an hours drive away. Given a typical 7.5-hour work day, a 1-hour lunch break, and a 2-hour commute, each employee spends at least 10.5 hours away from the family. Even when children are in school, they may remain unattended for at least four hours a day. A lot of employees are looking for better ways of balancing work and family. Alternative work arrangements may allow employees to significantly increase the amount of time they spend with their families.

In the United States, in 1960, 18.6% of married women with children under 6 years of age were in the work force; by 1996, the percentage was 62.7%, representing almost a 250% increase in participation (Figure 1-7).[6] During the *me generation* of the 1970s and 1980s, many individuals were guided by their desire to do whatever was best for them. The business world today is very volatile; many people see the basic family and community values as one of the few areas of stability. Today, people are trying to re-establish basic family values by reconnecting with their families and their neighborhoods. Employers

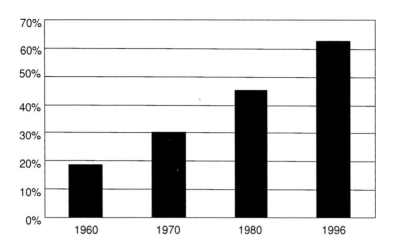

Figure 1-7 Percentage of maried women with children under 6 years old in work force. (Source: U.S. Bureau of Census.)

need to recognize this trend and position their programs to allow employees to reach a reasonable balance between work and family.

TECHNOLOGICAL CHANGES

The availability of electronic technology at dramatically lower cost is making possible a large number of changes. The computer industry has consistently lowered the cost of hardware while providing more features, power, and capability. This has allowed users of the technology to increase their personal productivity.

In the 1970s, many organizations were developing large computerized business systems to handle the bread and butter applications such as general ledger, accounts payable, inventory management, and payroll. Although these applications dramatically changed the way organizations operated, they were at the same time limited because they could be accessed only through large central computer processors.

Advances in technology now allow tasks previously limited to large central computers to be performed more economically on smaller computers. This advancement has lowered the economies of scale previously associated with central computers, shifting the emphasis of corporate computing towards the use of distributed computers.

Many companies are now investing in technology to make their employees more productive, while reducing their operating costs and providing more and better services to their customers. To utilize the technology, companies have invested heavily in the development of new integrated applications that attempt to store critical corporate data such that it can be easily accessed by authorized employees in an efficient and effective way. In using technology in this fashion, companies have now realized that many of their employees are information workers; they depend on the information that is stored on the computer for much of their job. In addition, jobs that need access to this stored information are now portable. It is no longer necessary to be at the location where the paper records are stored, when this information can retrieved via computer from any location.

The technology explosion is not limited to corporations. One of the fastest-growing components of the technology environment is the use of technology at home. Figure 1-8 shows the consumer electronics sales for home computers from 1985 to 1996.[7] This represents almost a 600% increase over an 11-year period. In 1995, Statistics Canada estimated that 25% of Canadian households had a personal computer (PC). Many experts expect that Bill Gates's strategy of getting a PC into every home will likely come close to reality by the end of the millennium. In essence, the average North American household will include a telephone, television set, and some sort of computing device.

The Internet has had a significant impact on the way work is performed. In the past few years the Internet has taken off to become a key component in many corporate technology strategies. The Internet is bringing an entirely new range of applications to the corporate portfolio which will transform (yet again)

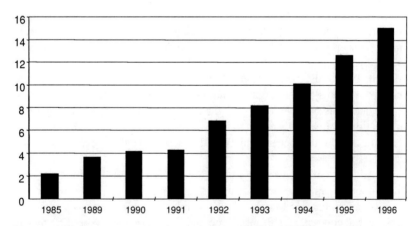

Figure 1-8 Consumer electronics sales for home computers in the United States. (Source: Electronics Industries Association, Wahington, D.C.)

the way business is delivered. For example, Hallmark Cards has a website (www.hallmarkreminder.com) that allows customers to record key dates into the database allowing Hallmark to send them an e-mail a week before the event to remind them to buy a card—hopefully, a Hallmark card. Tide laundry detergent has a site with information on how to remove stains using Tide products (www.tide.com/stainDet/indx.html). These are but two examples that show how the Internet is creating an entirely new information-sharing medium.

Other new Internet applications are integrating distributed processing with real-time information. The American Automobile Association (AAA) offers a CD ROM–based application called Map 'n Go (www.delorme.com/mapngo/). To use this application, the user enters the city where travel is to begin and the one he or she will be traveling to. The local application shows a map of the shortest driving distance between the two locations. The application also automatically connects with the Internet and picks up real-time weather and traffic information for the chosen route.

Technology is enabling major changes in organizations and in the lives of employees. Organizations in the new economy that ignore the far-reaching implications of change are courting disaster for themselves and their employees.

THE TIME TO CHANGE IS NOW!

Economic, organizational, personal, and technological changes are making companies sit up and take notice of how they can creatively reduce costs, increase revenues, compete globally, meet their employees desire to better balance their work and home lives while gaining the maximum business value from their technology investment. This is not an easy task, but it certainly represents an exciting opportunity.

The solution to business problems used to be a lot easier: develop a reasonable product, market it locally, hire local people, manage the organization, and gradually expand within state/province or country. Because today's marketplace is changing at such a rapid pace, survival will go to those who can adapt quickly and effectively to these changes. This point is strongly made in the 1995 best seller *Competing for the Future*, in which authors Gary Hamel and C. K. Prahalad of Harvard University suggest, "The future is to be found in the intersection of changes in technology, lifestyles, regulation, demographics, and geopolitics."[8]

Hamel and Prahalad add that it is critical to create our own future to remain competitive. They conclude that

> A firm's strategic architecture must be based on a deep and creative understanding of industry discontinuities, of the firm's core competen-

cies, and of potential new customer needs. Industry foresight must be well grounded. It must point the company in the direction of genuine opportunities. At the same time it must not put an arbitrary limit on just how far and fast the company can travel on the road to the future. Unless senior management is willing to commit to a goal that lies outside the planning horizon, there can be no strategic intent. The future will be discovered by someone else.[9]

Like Fields and Beck, these Harvard researchers are clear on this point: keep up with the changes or be prepared to loose your marketplace.

THE NEED TO CHANGE OUR WORK ENVIRONMENT

Given the premise that it is necessary to ensure that internal change exceeds external change, then it is time to question some of the traditional office values. For instance, why are people still working in the same work environment created over 50 years ago? This is a question that innovative executives, managers, and employees should be asking themselves today.

The traditional office environment is built around the concept that people should congregate at the central location, be assigned a specific type of space based on their status in the organization, and work specified hours. This traditional work environment served organizations effectively in the past, but is it the way of the future? In the past, all employees had to gather together because their jobs were very paper intensive, communications devices were extremely limited, and the prevailing management philosophy was designed around the armed forces command and control model. In the 1950s, this was the way to go. Now, as we approach the year 2000, we must question why.

Why do employees have to congregate at a central location? Is this necessary for everyone? Would some employees be better off working closer to their customers? Could employees do some of their heads-down work from locations which are quieter?

Why is it that when an employee becomes a manager, she or he gets an office with a closed door and more square feet? Does this make sense? What if employees were to utilize the type of office space based on what they *needed to do today*? For example, a senior analyst who plans to be interviewing could book an enclosed office with a door for privacy for a few days. Or, an employee who is developing a multimedia presentation could use the space that houses a high-speed computer graphics workstation.

Why do employees have to work specific hours of the day and specific days of the week? If an employee works out of the New York office supporting customers in Germany, it might make more sense to start work at 4:00 A.M. to more effectively service customers during working hours in Germany. What if an employee's spouse works in the retail industry and has to work the weekends while the employee's job is Monday to Friday. Could the organization be more creative and give the employee Monday and Tuesday off and let the employee work Wednesday to Sunday?

These questions are extremely realistic. They represent the issues many companies and employees are dealing with today. The key to survival in this changing world is to move with the changes. Those who start to think outside of the lines and break some of our long-held traditional beliefs will likely come out ahead in tomorrow's economy.

SOLUTIONS TO TODAY'S CHALLENGES

There is no one solution to all of today's challenges. Instead, there is a broad range of potential solutions that companies need to consider and select from to meet their business objectives. The optimal solution may be a combination or hybrid of strategies.

One such set of solutions lies in the concept of work transformation. Work transformation is the concept of integrating alternative work and space arrangements with enabling technologies to meet the changing business environment.

Alternative work arrangements (AWAs) include creative ways for employees to perform their jobs while meeting business objectives and helping employees to create an effective balance between the quality of their work and their personal lives. Alternative space arrangements (ASAs) involve changing the landscape of the traditional office to accommodate both traditional workers and those using alternative work arrangements.

Work transformation is not a single-function concept. Figure 1-9 shows work transformation as the integration of facilities management, human re-

Figure 1-9 Integration of key strategies to support work transformation.

sources, and information technology. Those who attempt to implement work transformation without integrating all of these concepts will usually fail to achieve the full benefits of this new concept. On the other hand, those who treat work transformation as a cross-functional project should be able to maximize the business value from these new concepts.

OBJECTIVES OF THE BOOK

The intention of this book is to show individuals and organizations how work transformation can deliver significant business value to an organization.

This book will help managers and employees better understand both the theory and the practical application of work transformation concepts. The materials presented provide the knowledge needed to evaluate the appropriateness of work transformation and implement these strategies within an organization.

The book does not present a cookbook formula for work transformation; instead, it takes the realistic approach of providing the knowledge to apply within an organization. The focus is on the three key resource strategies: human resources, facilities, and technology. The strategies presented for consideration can be applied to business cases, feasibility studies, or internal research.

It should be noted that an entire book could be written on each of these three strategies. This book presents a high-level overview of each area, thus providing managers who are considering work transformation with the basic knowledge required to make sound business decisions.

The move towards work transformation is an evolutionary journey. It is unlikely that an organization will implement all of these ideas in one big bang. A key to success is to continue to change and evolve the way the organization manages people, space, and technology to maximize business value.

The book ends with a glimpse into the future, providing some ideas for how these concepts can be extended to open up a broad array of new and exciting opportunities.

NOTES

1. *Fortune*, November 25, 1996.
2. Beck, Nula. Speech entitled Thriving in the New Economy, presented at the Call Center 2000 Conference in Vancouver, B.C., on January 29, 1997.
3. U.S. Bureau of Census. Statistical Abstract of the United States: 117th Edition. Washington, DC, 1997, pp. 410–412.

4. Kettle, John. Make Way for Managers and Professionals, *Globe and Mail*, February 5, 1997.

5. Statistics Canada. Population and Dwelling characteristics: Families, Part 2, Catalogue 93-107. Census of Canada 1986, March 1989.

6. U.S. Bureau of Census. Statistical Abstract of the United States: 117th Edition. Washington, DC, 1997, p. 392.

7. U.S. Bureau of Census. Statistical Abstract of the United States: 117th Edition. Washington, DC, 1997, p. 760.

8. Hamel, Gary, and Prahalad, C. K. *Competing for the Future: Breakthrough Strategies for Seizing Control of Your Industry and Creating the Markets of Tomorrow.* Harvard Business School Press, Boston, MA, 1994, p. 95.

9. Ibid, p. 146.

2

New Opportunities

Organizations are constantly striving for more new and creative ways to increase productivity, reduce costs, enhance competitiveness, and improve the bottom line. Every organization has a bottom line which must be addressed. Private-sector organizations are clearly focused on profitability. For nonprofit and government organizations, a comparable incentive is to improve levels of customer service and program delivery.

Organizations, regardless of industry and profit or nonprofit status, possess the common goal of improving overall effectiveness in today's marketplace. Many organizations have attempted to improve through the utilization of business reengineering. Business reengineering, coined by Harvard professor Dr. Michael Hammer, is the fundamental rethinking and radical redesign of business processes to achieve dramatic improvements in critical, contemporary measures of performance, such as cost, quality, service and speed.[1]

Reengineering involves reviewing current business processes and practices, questioning the actual need for them, and, if required, determining how they can be streamlined. Many who have gone through the reengineering process find that the most significant returns may be achieved by questioning the most basic assumptions they have made in the past.

Hammer's description of the Ford Motor Company's accounts payable reengineering is now a classic example of reengineering. In the early 1980s, Ford was trying to reduce costs in its accounts payable area. After an initial study, it was determined that by automating some functions the contingent of accounts payable staff could be reduced by 20%, bringing the number of clerks down to 400 (a reduction of 100 employees). This solution seemed pretty impressive to the Ford executives until they visited Mazda, where the accounts payable function was handled by 5 people. Even this difference—a ratio of 80:1—was too great to ignore. Ford was forced to go back and reengineer its procurement practices. The net result was a new process that eliminated vendor invoices, replacing them with a computer system that is used by the shipper who receives the goods. If the goods match the purchase order, then the system is updated and a check is automatically cut; if not, the goods are sent back to the vendor. This reengineered process resulted in a 75% reduction in staffing in accounts payable (down to 125 employees).

The Ford reengineering story provides a very important lesson. Organizations must be prepared to rethink traditional definitions if they are to move forward and achieve the maximum benefit. An excellent example of this entrenched position can be found in the traditional definitions of work and office. The average person might define these terms in the following manner:

- *Wor*k
  - What I do to make money
  - Usually performed full-time—Monday to Friday, 9:00 A.M. to 5:00 P.M.
  - What I do when I'm in the office
- *Offic*e
  - Where I go to work
  - Space that has been assigned to me
  - Space that is assigned based on my position within the organization

Many people are quick to describe work and office in the fashion above, as they have grown up within these rather limiting definitions. The real opportunities lie in rethinking the traditional definitions of work and looking for new and creative ways of reengineering jobs, and rethinking *how* the work is performed and *where* it is performed from.

This chapter describes some of the new opportunities to help change these current definitions and to help organizations get the most value from new ways of working. The goal is to transform how and where work is performed by considering the potential of alternative work arrangements, alternative space arrangements, and enabling technologies.

ALTERNATIVE WORK ARRANGEMENTS

Many organizations are implementing alternative work arrangements (AWAs) as a way of achieving key business objectives while providing an opportunity for employees to better balance their work and personal lives, thereby improving their overall quality of life (at work and at home).

The following are a few of the common alternative work arrangements.

Variable Work Hours (Flextime)

A variable work hours system, also known as flextime, allows employees some choice in deciding when they will work. These work hours are governed by established core hours (hours during which the employee must be available).

Regular Part-Time

Regular part-time includes workers who work less than the regular 35 to 40 hours per week as part of their regular employment arrangement.

Modified Work Week

Employees working a modified work week are able to schedule their hours of work such that they work longer hours each day (paid at regular rate) while working fewer work days over a defined work cycle (e.g., working 9 hours per day for 9 days every 2 weeks).

Phased Retirement

Phased retirement is a way for individuals to retire gradually by reducing their full-time employment commitment over a set period of years. Many organizations are starting to utilize this work option to help soon-to-be retired workers break out of the rut of working every day at the traditional office. Some employers are also contemplating this work option to entice valued older workers to stay in the work force longer.

Job Sharing

Job sharing is the concept of two employees with similar skills and experience sharing the same job. This work option is usually dependent on one employee being able to find another employee who also wants to job share and who has the appropriate skills for the job. Some companies have set up job sharing databases by which employees who want to job share can find another employee with the same or complementary skills who is also seeking a job share opportunity—in essence, a job sharing matchmaking service.

Telework

Telework, also known as telecommuting, is the concept of employees performing some portion of their regular job from a remote location. These employees use basic voice and data communications technology to stay connected to their traditional work location and their customers. The remote locations used by a teleworkers can be their own home (most common), a company-sponsored telework center (close to the employee's neighborhood), or a shared neighborhood telework center (shared by multiple employers).

Teleworkers usually work remotely 2–3 days per week on a regular basis. These employees are able to perform their heads-down work in the quiet of their remote location and return to the traditional office location 2–3 days per week for meetings, group work, and so forth.

Work at Home

Work-at-home employees work remotely from their own home 5 days per week all year long. These employees only come into the traditional office on an occasional basis for meetings with their manager. Work at home is ideal for employees who are physically challenged and cannot easily make it into the traditional office. Employees who are physically able to commute to the traditional office find this form of telework to be difficult in that they tend to become isolated from the rest of the organization.

Mobile Work

Mobile workers are employees who work from multiple work locations, often spread across some geographic distance. These employees are typically equipped with cellular phones, portable technology and cellular modems. The mobile worker's job is performed at multiple work locations, so having a traditional office space is not practical. Typical examples of mobile workers are employees in sales, on-site customer service/maintenance, auditors, and consultants.

Most alternative work arrangements are voluntary. The mobile working arrangement is usually considered a critical aspect of the job and is most likely a mandatory component of the job. For example, a sales person who needs to meet customers face to face at the customer's location would have to be a mobile worker to perform his or her job.

There is a tendency to try to classify organizations into those that can benefit most from AWAs and those that will benefit least. This is a difficult problem, as virtually all organizations have some components that could be applied to AWAs. For example, employees who work on the manufacturing floor are highly unlikely to be able to telework, but these same employees may be able to work modified work weeks.

As with many things today, there are no hard and fast rules. Managers must be open to looking at the entire organization to find the areas where some of the AWA components could be applied. The key is to be open minded about the concepts while also being realistic about the business impact.

ALTERNATIVE SPACE ARRANGEMENTS

Alternative work arrangements present various alternatives to the traditional definition of work. Alternative space arrangements (ASAs), however, redefine the traditional office altogether. Alternative space arrangements are best categorized as those arrangements that are applied in the regular office (on-premises options) and those that are applied to space that is external to the regular office location (off-premises options).

On-Premises Options

Alternative space arrangements available within the office facility include the following.

Teaming Space

Teaming space is simply the space shared by a team. This space is usually an open area where team communication and collaboration can flourish. The space is also usually characterized by moveable furniture which can be adjusted to meet the team's specific needs.

Shared Office

A shared office means that two or more employees sharing a single, assigned workspace. Employees must consult with each other to determine when the space can be used.

Group Space

Group space refers to an area assigned to a designated group or team. Employees who are part of the group negotiate with their fellow employees regarding when the space can be used.

Nonterritorial Office

The nonterritorial office works on the concept that no one is permanently attached to any single workspace. The nonterritorial office is structured around just-in-time concepts, which have employees selecting the workspace that meets their specific requirements at the time they need it.

Off-Premises Options

The alternative space arrangements available outside of the regular office facility include:

Mobile Offices

Mobile offices are used by employees who spend the majority of their work time on the road. These employees are equipped with portable computers (notebooks) and cellular phones and modems. In some cases, the base station for a mobile worker is the employee's home.

Telework Centers

Telework centers are facilities that are located in the neighborhoods of the employees. Employees work from a telework center part of the week and from the regular office the rest of the week. These facilities are typically for the use of only a single organization, although there are now some centers that are shared by multiple organizations.

Guest Space

Guest space is similar to a telework center, except that it is not a stand-alone facility. Guesting involves using someone else's facility as the remote work center. For example, an employee may be located full-time at a customer's location for the duration of a project.

Home Office

The home office is space that is utilized by both teleworkers (work at home 13 days per week) and work-at-home employees (work at home full-time).

ENABLING TECHNOLOGIES

Technology has changed at a rapid pace over the past 20 years. In this time, the technology has evolved from multi-million dollar mainframe computers of the 1970s, which had less computing power than desktop computers today, to extremely powerful notebook computers, which can be carried from location to location. This change in computing power has dramatically changed the cost/benefit ratio of using technology. No longer is technology limited to those few workers who would be given access to the mainframe. Today technology is on nearly every desktop in organizations throughout North America.

The telecommunications technology has also come a long way. The 1970s saw the introduction of portable terminal devices that allowed users to dial into a mainframe. These devices utilized what were then such high-tech devices as paper feed and acoustic couplers. Those who used the first portable devices were thrilled with the ability to connect to a central computer at speeds of up to 300 bits per second. Today, the modern teleworker can use a notebook PC with a color screen connecting multiple computers through a wide area network at speeds of at least 56,000 bits per second.

Technology is becoming smaller and more portable. Advances in technology are occurring to the point where technology can now be attached directly to an employee. For example, aircraft mechanics are now experimenting with new technology that allows them to access engineering drawings and maintenance specification from any location and to display the results on a screen that is projected onto a special pair of video goggles. This allows the mechanic who has climbed into the wheel carriage of an airplane to access the drawings and instructions necessary to perform a repair without having to climb out of the airplane to access a tethered terminal or traditional paper documents.

Technology is clearly changing the world of work. The key, however, is not to implement technology for the sake of technology but rather to utilize the technology to gain business value. In the private sector, this means using technology to gain a competitive advantage or at least to maintain an organizations competitive position. In public-sector and nonprofit organizations, this would correspond to improving program delivery and the level of customer service, and making the most efficient use of budgeted resources.

Some of the most important technologies are familiar; others are only beginning to achieve widespread penetration.

The Internet

The acceptance and use of the Internet will probably be recorded as the most significant technological event in the 1990s. The Internet was created in 1969 by the U.S. Defense Department's Advanced Research Projects Administration as a modest packet-switching network called ARPAnet. John Quarterman of Matrix Information and Directory Services Inc. (MIDS) of Austin, Texas, has been tracking the growth of the Internet for several years. Figure 2-1 shows the MIDS data from a start of the Internet, when it linked four host computers in California and Utah, to 16 million worldwide hosts in 1997.

Electronic Mail (e-mail)

Electronic mail, or e-mail as it is commonly known, is absolutely essential in today's organization. e-mail allows employees to communicate without concern for time or location. For example, an employee on a modified work week can communicate with a work-at-home employee even though the two are not working at the same time or in the same location.

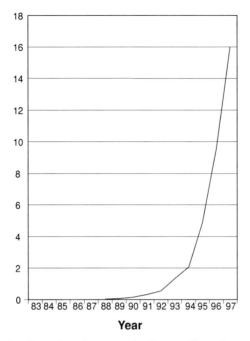

Figure 2-1 Growth in Internet (millions of hosts) worldwide.

Voice Mail

Voice mail is becoming another essential service in today's organization. Like e-mail, voice mail provides a quick and easy method of sharing information with other employees. Remote workers find that voice mail is a mandatory communications tool. The coming integration of voice mail and e-mail will help to further enhance productivity and communication.

Local Area Networks/Wide Area Networks/ Metropolitan Area Networks

Most organizations have implemented local area networks (LANs) and are interconnecting these local networks into wide area networks (WANs). These networks allow users of personal computers to share files, access software that resides on other computers, and facilitate workgroup, workflow, and scheduling solutions. The metropolitan area network (MAN) is typically a fiber optic–based network that is quickly becoming the next step in linking geographically dispersed sites and employees at speeds that are the same as the LAN.

Scheduling Tools

With employees working a broader range of hours and days and from a variety of locations, the use of scheduling tools becomes extremely important. These tools are required to book meetings with employees and to book space (meeting rooms, quiet office space, an open workstation, etc.).

Workgroup Computing

Workgroup, or collaborative, computing is a category of computing that supports the activities of people working in groups to achieve a defined business purpose. This technology helps people work together more effectively to facilitate information sharing, organize information into actionable knowledge, and productively interact with others.

Wireless Voice and Data

The mobile worker requires the use of cellular or digital technology in the form of a portable telephone and modem. This technology allows the employee to be in touch with the organization from any location. Wireless voice solutions may also be considered for use within the nonterritorial office design. Wireless telephones can be assigned to employees, who then take them to whatever workstation they have chosen within the central office.

Remote Access

Remote workers need data access to their LAN/WAN/MAN and the computers that are attached to them. This requires the use of some form of remote access capability to support this connection. The connection can be used for electronic file transfers, sending and retrieving e-mail, running computer applications, and so forth.

Flexible Technology

Flexible technology is required to support the nonterritorial and shared office concepts. The strategy should be to attach the technology to the person and not to the physical location. This requires the use of portable personal computers, a network that allows any user to log on and be instantly recognized, and follow-me telephones.

Conferencing

Conferencing solutions help to remove any geographic gap that may exist among employees. The three most common types of conferencing are audio, document, and video. Audio conferencing allows two or more people to participate in the same telephone conversation. Document conferencing allows two or more people to share a document, allowing them to jointly mark it up and see the document evolve in real time. Video conferencing allows two or more people to communicate visually by seeing each other and sharing images (documents, drawings, etc.) or video clips (e.g., videotape of a work issue). Document and video conferencing tools are now penetrating the marketplace. These tools will be of great help to remote workers. Video conferencing is also now available for the personal computer. This technology allows users to open a window on their computer and use an inexpensive fixed-distance camera (typically either built into the monitor or on top of it) to participate in the video conference from their own desk. Some experts expect this level of technology to be a standard offering for personal computers in the next few years.

High-Speed Telecommunications

Key to the above-mentioned tools and technologies is the overall telecommunications infrastructure. Many will work only with adequate high-speed communications.

One of the greatest challenges of working remotely is the use of high-speed telecommunications facilities. A critical limiting factor in many solutions is the amount of bandwidth available. This is being addressed through telephone company products such as ADSL (asymmetric digital subscriber line), which downloads data at 2.2 megabits per second, ISDN (integrated switched digital network), which allows the sharing of voice and data traffic at 128,000 bits per second (128 kbps), and Switched 56, which offers service at 64 kbps. The cable companies are also expanding their networks to carry data traffic.

POTENTIAL BUSINESS BENEFITS

Work transformation is accomplished by integrating alternative work arrangements, alternative space arrangements, and enabling technologies. There are many benefits an organization can derive from the implementation of work transformation.

Increased Human Resources Flexibility

Work transformation assists in increasing the flexibility of an organization's work force. The work transformation environment forces managers to be more results oriented, managing more on output than on visual presence. Employees also become more focused on delivering specific results due to this change in management style. The net result is an improvement in the overall flexibility and adaptability of staff.

Enhanced Job Performance

Job performance (productivity, quality, and timeliness) can be difficult to measure for many jobs. However, most work transformation pilots have demonstrated improvements in job performance either empirically or intuitively. For teleworkers, the productivity improvements are typically 15–20%. Most teleworkers also experience improvements in quality of work by being able to concentrate on specific tasks for longer periods of uninterrupted time. Improvement in quality, however, is most difficult to quantify and is, therefore, commonly based on qualitative analysis. The timeliness component of job performance relates to the employee's ability to complete tasks in a timely fashion. This can be analyzed in terms of elapsed time required to complete specific tasks.

Fostering a Flexible Work Culture

Work transformation introduces the concept of flexibility to the work environment. To continue to be successful, organizations must continually improve and be as flexible as possible. It is impossible to accurately predict the future; however, by fostering a flexible work culture, an organization can reposition the company's work force to handle market, technology, or policy changes that may occur.

More Effective Communication

One of the challenges of work transformation is maintaining communications. Some of the traditional methods of communicating, such as wandering by an employee's desk, will not work as effectively. However, many organizations have found that the implementation of work transformation forces employees and managers to come up with more creative ways to communicate and that the net result is an overall improvement in communications. For example, organizations will enhance the use of e-mail and the corporate Intranet for communications. Others have used work group computing software to enhance communication across the organization. Many employees working at home should be as easy to reach as on their regular in-office days.

Enhanced Focus on Results

A key component of work transformation is switching from visual management to management by results. When employees and managers understand the end deliverables, they are able to be more focused on attaining these outputs. Typically, the result is improved productivity in terms of throughput, quality, and timeliness. The focus on results for employees also helps the manager to improve his or her skills in being results oriented. When the manager and the employee work in partnership towards the end result, the effect is to make the overall organization more competitive and effective.

Reduced Office Space Cost

Employees who are teleworkers, mobile workers, or part-timers are, in most cases, able to work from smaller or shared office space at the regular office. This should result in a reduction of office space costs. For example, five teleworkers could share three workstations by coordinating their telework and traditional office days. This scenario would free up two workstations for every five teleworkers.

The implementation of new space designs will also likely reduce the amount of space required. The new designs typically include smaller workstations, better use of common areas, and an overall reduction in the total space required.

Improved Job Satisfaction

The new work environment is usually perceived by many employees as a way of allowing them to better integrate the needs of the organization with their own personal needs. This means giving the employee more personal freedom, which generally equates with greater employee satisfaction. Many studies have shown that increases in employee morale typically translate into greater productivity and improved quality.

Supporting Positive Employee Relations Environment

Work transformation is most successful in an environment of trust and respect among the organization, the manager, and the individual employee. The new arrangements can be used to reinforce the trust and respect already in place or to shore up an environment where trust and respect is being rebuilt.

Supporting Improved Business Processes

Many organizations have experienced reengineering initiatives. Work transformation concepts can be incorporated into business transformation plans to further improve certain processes. For example, those departments that work with staff or clients in other time zones may be able to increase the business effectiveness of the department by having some employees working from home during nontraditional hours or through working variable work hours or extended hours per day.

Environmental Responsibility

Virtually all organizations want to be environmentally responsible but have great difficulty in truly delivering on this goal. Organizations that utilize telework and work-at-home employees are able to enhance their level of environmental responsibility by reducing the number of commuters who are affecting the environment every work day.

Reduced Absenteeism

The level of absenteeism among teleworkers is usually lower than the company average. Employees who are equipped to work at home are able to work on days they do not feel well enough to make the commute, days they are still contagious, or days when their children are home from school/day care due to illness and require parental attention. The impact of the increasing amount of eldercare responsibilities many employees are now facing can also be minimized through telework. Current American and Canadian statistics show that 7–12% of employees have eldercare responsibilities; this percentage is expected growth to 33% by 2020.

Improved Recruiting and Retention

The recruiting ability of an organization improves if AWAs are formalized. Many potential employees value the opportunity to select from a range of AWAs and are likely to view organizations offering AWAs as being progressive, caring about people, and more focused on results than traditional processes. Organizations also find that a larger number of applicants apply when AWAs are taken into consideration. For example, a qualified candidate currently living in Seattle may consider applying for a job in Portland knowing that he or she may be able to telework three days a week, thereby making the long commute more acceptable.

Organizations with work transformation programs also find that they have less turnover. Employees who utilize work arrangements that allow them to balance work and family are unlikely to switch jobs to work for employers who do not offer the same arrangements. Also, in the event of a job transfer that would normally entail relocating, employees with the option of teleworking may be able to retain their job without having to move. Conversely, an organization that has provisions for AWAs may be able to retain the services of an employee if it is the employee who is obliged to relocate—say, the employee's spouse, who does not work for a company that offers AWAs, is transferred to another city.

Ability to Attract/Utilize People with Disabilities

Telework can be used as a way of easing some of the barriers that exist for people who have a mobility limitation. Physically challenged individuals can often work from home when it would be either cumbersome or impossible to commute to a traditional office on a daily basis. Telework also allows organizations to recruit a greater number of disabled workers.

Improved Customer Service

Work transformation provides improvements to the level of service provided to customers. These improvements can be in the form of better access to staff in facilities that are closer to the customers, expanded hours of operation provided by staff working from home, or through enhanced communication between team members in an open team space, which usually directly improves the level of customer service.

Leverage from New Technologies

The telecommunications and computing technologies available today make the implementation of work transformation possible. Notebook computers can easily be transported to any location where the employee is working; data communications can take place over the regular telephone system; and emerging technologies such as desktop video conferencing and workgroup computing software can bring remote workers together to maintain the dynamics of the team environment. The net result is a higher return on investment for the organization.

Improved Quality of Work Life

The work transformation concepts take into account the desire to improve the quality of work life for employees. The telework concepts allow employees to reduce the amount of time they spend commuting to and from work. The employees also benefit from improved productivity and customer service and from the knowledge that they are helping to improve the profitability and efficiency of the organization. These work and personal benefits help to improve the overall morale of staff and the quality of work life for all employees.

Ability to Stay Competitive

Many organizations are positioning themselves to improve effectiveness and reduce costs. Private-sector organizations see this as a fundamental component of business survival. Although the public sector does not feel competitive pressure in the same sense, it is accountable to budgets, which relate directly to the cost per unit of goods or services produced. In short, every organization is under pressure to remain competitive—the use of work transformation concepts can, in many cases, either provide the opportunity to gain a competitive advantage or be required to remain competitive with peer organizations.

Facilitation of Enhancing or Supporting Cultural Change

Enhancing or supporting cultural change is an often overlooked benefit. Many organizations use work transformation to help reinforce changes to corporate culture. This can be a powerful benefit. For example, when a company wants to change its philosophy to being more open and communicative, it might change its office design from separate, closed offices to having people work in open team spaces, with casual meeting areas available for employee interaction. The new space will speak volumes more about the changes than changing just the organization's mission statement.

Figure 2-2 shows the tangible and intangible business benefits described above. Many of the intangibles could easily become tangible benefits in some organizations. For example, an intangible benefit such as fostering a more

Intangible Benefits	Tangible Benefits

• **Organizational Rewards**
  • Increased human resources flexibility
  • More effective communication
  • Support for improved business processes
	• **Bottom-Line Rewards**
	  • Reduced office space costs
	  • Reduced absenteeism
	  • Reduced recruiting/<R>retention costs

• **Employee Relations**
  • Improved job satisfaction
  • Positive employee relations environment
  • Improved quality of work life
	• **Soft Tangibles**
	  • Enhanced job performance
	  • Improved customer service

• **Cultural Rewards**
  • Fostering of a flexible work culture
  • Support of cultural change
	• **Good Corporate Citizenship**
	  • Environmental responsibility
	  • Way to attract/utilize people with
	    disabilities

Figure 2-2 Intangible and tangible business benefits of work transformation.

flexible work culture could have a significant impact on the bottom line if the organization needs to quickly change work practices/processes to meet changing market demands. Instilling a sense of flexibility in the organization would likely make such as transition less costly. The tangibles have a direct bottom-line impact. For example, the implementation of space sharing at a ratio of 2.5 employees per desk will produce a 60% savings in the costs of leasing space, providing furniture, and so on, for each of these employees.

POTENTIAL EMPLOYEE BENEFITS

Employees can benefit significantly from work transformation. A few of the common benefits include the following.

Reduced Stress

Employees who telework or work modified work weeks often have less stress in their lives than those who must commute to their regular office every working day. Employees who work in the traditional office also experience high levels of stress from trying to handle a large workload solely from the traditional office, with all its inherent distractions. Teleworkers can reduce this stress by commuting to the traditional office fewer days each week and by working in quiet, uninterrupted workspace at home, where they can be more productive and effective at performing some tasks.

Many employees find that their current space causes stress. This is typically true for employees who are trying to do concentrated work in an environment with ongoing interruptions and distractions or those who are trying to hold small meetings in workspaces designed for one person. The new space strategies relieve some of this stress and provide employees with a workspace that support their requirements in a just-in-time mode.

Balancing Work and Family

Employees utilizing new work arrangements realize that they can be more effective at balancing the pressures of work and family. Employees who tele-work save time from their daily commute and can return all or some portion of this time to their families. Employees who job share or work part-time find that they can better balance their personal and work lives by not having to work full-time. This can be particularly helpful at specific times in an individual's life (e.g., when caring for small children or preparing for retirement).

Greater Freedom, Control, and Enjoyment

Employees who utilize alternative work arrangements find that they have greater freedom, control, and enjoyment in their personal lives. They accomplish this by working the hours that they are personally most productive and being able to more effectively and creatively integrate their work and personal lives. Employees in these arrangements are empowered to make decisions that allow them to meet their work and personal objectives.

Managing Dependent Care Responsibilities More Effectively

Many employees choose new work arrangements to better handle their dependent care responsibilities. Today, dependent care is not limited to children; it also includes eldercare and partner care.

Working from home part-time doe not eliminate the need for dependent care. However, it provides employees with more options to meet their dependent care responsibilities. This might include reducing the number of hours a child is in day care on telework days; working variable work hours to accommodate day-care hours; or working modified work weeks to allow the employee to deal with eldercare responsibilities (e.g., driving them to appointments).

Reduced Conflicts Between Work and Personal Schedules

Many employees find that it is difficult to balance their work schedule with their own personal schedule. Without flexibility, it may be impossible to make their daughter's 5:30 P.M. baseball game or attend their son's 3:00 P.M. school play. The use of new work arrangements can assist employees by providing them with greater flexibility to meet *some* of these scheduling challenges while still meeting the business objectives of the position. For example, many people who telework start their days very early in the morning (getting up at the same time they would if they drove to work) and then are able to either take some time off during the day or finish their day early in the afternoon while maintaining the same number of hours of work. On these telework days, employees can still get their work accomplished and attend to personal matters.

Work Hours Better Coordinated with Partner to Share Family Responsibilities

Today everyone leads busy lives. Employees have commitments at work, with their children, partner, and quite often extended family. Often, the biggest challenge is trying to coordinate all of these activities. Employees and their partners who utilize new work arrangements find that they can accommodate these commitments more effectively by organizing their schedules. This might involve one partner working early morning variable hours and coming home in the midafternoon to deal with the children while the other partner works later, variable hours and is responsible for breakfast and getting the children off to school. This opens an entire new set of opportunities for solving personal scheduling challenges. Work transformation also helps single parents, who tend to have a more difficult time in solving personal scheduling challenges.

Cost Savings

Many of the new work arrangements actually save employees out-of-pocket costs. For example, teleworkers and those on modified work weeks are typically able to realize tangible savings in their gas, food, parking, and clothing expenses when working at home part-time or by working a reduced number of days per week.

Ability to Work During Personal Peak Performance Times

Not everyone is at ones personal best from 8:00 A.M. to 5:00 P.M. Some people are better in the morning, others later in the day. Everyone has some idea as to when one is most productive. Work transformation can allow employees the flexibility to work during their personal peak performance time. This is better for the overall productivity and allows employees to relax during the times when they feel less energetic and to work during their peak periods.

Improved Employee Morale

Most of the work transformation concepts result in improvements to employee morale. Work transformation can provide employees with more options to manage their work and personal lives. The net result is a happier employee who recognizes the benefit of working for a progressive employer.

Equal Access to Space

Assigning space based on status or rank is always a controversy in an organization. Employees often fuss over why someone has more space or a different type of workstation. These concerns can be eliminated by assigning space based on need, not rank.

Enhance Opportunities for Communications and Learning

Many of the traditional office designs do not effectively support opportunities for communication with other employees and the associated personal learning experience. Alternative space arrangements include small, quiet spaces for desk

Intangible Benefits	Tangible Benefits
• **Work Related** • Work during personal peak times • Improved morale • Equal access to space • Enhanced opportunities for communication and learning • **Personal** • Reduced stress • Greater freedom, control, and enjoyment • Reduced conflict between work and personal lives	• **Financial** • Cost savings • **Family** • Balance between work and family • Management of dependent care • Schedule coordination with partner

Figure 2-3   Intangible and tangible employee benefits of work transformation.

work; open spaces for team communications; and spaces to accommodate ad hoc communication in the hallways, at the coffee bar, or in a soft seating area. Employees benefit by the enhanced opportunities for communications and learning.

Figure 2-3 summarizes the employee benefits into several categories. As with the business benefits, the employee benefits offer a broad range of solutions to staff. For most employees, the intangible benefits far outweigh the tangible cost savings.

INTEGRATION OF HUMAN RESOURCES, FACILITIES MANAGEMENT, AND INFORMATION TECHNOLOGY

The key to successfully implementing work transformation is to integrate human resources, facilities management, and information technology strategies, as shown in the Figure 2-4.

Work transformation is most successful when all three strategies operate together. The goal should be to present an integrated work transformation strategy that focuses on the business objectives of the organization.

Many organizations have tried to implement work transformation concepts by using only one or two of these three components. In most cases, these initiatives either fail completely or their success is limited to very small groups. Problems arise when each of these service groups is perceived as having special

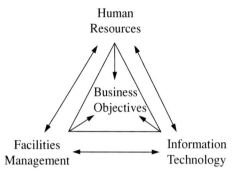

Figure 2-4 Strategies to support work transformation.

interests in introducing the concepts. The facilities management group is perceived as trying only to reduce facility costs by dramatically reducing the number of ft² of office space per person. The human resources group is perceived as presenting yet another change that is focused on employee well-being, with limited bottom-line return. The information technology group is accused of implementing these concepts just to use some of the new technology—whether or not it is needed.

Although these perceptions may not be valid, they are, nevertheless, very common in many organizations. This is why management must develop a cross-functional strategy that shows how each of these disciplines can be brought together to produce the desired result. This consolidated strategy must be focused on the organizations business objectives. If it is not, the senior executives and managers will have tremendous difficulty in trying to buy into the concepts.

The next three chapters describe the issues involved in each of these three key areas.

NOTES

1. Hammer, Michael, and Champy, James. *Reengineering the Corporation: A Manifesto for Business Revolution.* New York: HarperCollins, 1993, p. 32.
2. Quarterman, John S. Matrix Information Services Inc. Austin, Texas, 1996. website: www.mids.org/growth/internet/index.html

3

Human Resources

A critical element of work transformation is the implementation of alternative work arrangements (AWAs). Alternate work arrangements represent new forms of how work can be performed. The traditional method of performing work is to travel to the office and work eight hours a day, five days a week—a way of working that is still valid for many jobs and employees. However, some employees and organizations are looking for creative ways to assist the organization in meeting its business objectives while satisfying the growing need of employees to improve their overall quality of life (work and personal).

In essence, AWAs allow the manager and the employee to customize the way they work to meet the specific needs of the job, the organization, and the individual employees. These arrangements are usually employee initiated and manager approved, although in some circumstances the arrangements may be a condition of employment.

WHY ORGANIZATIONS ARE FORMALIZING ALTERNATIVE WORK ARRANGEMENT PROGRAMS

Today, most organizations understand that the world of work is changing. These changes are occurring at all levels: to support expanded customer and shareholder expectations, to gain the maximum value from enabling technologies, and to support employee expectations of better balancing work and family. For many organizations, the implementation of AWAs is merely an extension of an organization-wide continuous improvement program.

The key to success for organizations is to formalize these new ways of working. This formalization allows organizations to increase employee and management awareness of the concepts and to ensure that business and personal objectives are being met. The formalization effort creates an environment in which employees have equal access to opportunities. However, equal access does not always mean treating everyone the same. Most AWA programs are designed to encourage creativity and flexibility while remaining focused on achieving the expected business and personal objectives.

Organizations must recognize the degree of change associated with AWAs for both employees and managers. A critical key to success is to empower employees and managers to make effective business decisions. This may involve breaking through barriers such as the perception that "visibility equates to productivity"—the notion that the manager must see the employee in the office to have confidence that the employee is working. The AWA theme is for employees to deliver results, regardless of work location or hours of work.

IMPACT ON THE WAY WE WORK

The implementation of alternative work arrangements will have a profound impact on the way we work today. The AWA concepts challenge the fundamental standards of how and where we work. The traditional model of working 8:00 or 9:00 A.M. to 5:00 P.M. in the regular office is now only one of many work alternatives available.

To successfully make the transition to a more flexible series of work options, managers and employees need to understand the degree of change being undertaken. This change is not limited to just the organization; it will also impact families and neighbors. Remember, we are changing some pretty fundamental cultural concepts—this change will occur, but it will take some effort.

A few of the key impacts to be considered include the cultural change, the way employees are managed, and the change in the office environment.

The cultural change is less significant for those who choose to use variable work hours or modified work weeks. It is most significant for those who choose telework, job sharing, or regular part-time. These latter employees are breaking out of the traditional definition of a job and need to consider the financial implications of some of these alternatives (e.g., job sharing and regular part-time). Those who telework need to think about the how their families will adjust to their working from home 2–3 days a week. Teleworkers also need to think about how their neighbors will react, remembering that in the past, the home was viewed as a relaxing refuge, not as a place to perform work activities.

Managing employees will also change with the introduction of AWAs. Managers who are most comfortable with a "seeing is believing" management style are very uncomfortable when people work outside of their visual territory or during hours when they are not in the office. All managers will have to adjust their management style to being more output driven and results oriented. Managers must learn to work in partnership with their employees to determine what the outputs should be and when they can be delivered. This may require a significant change in management style for some managers.

The concept of using alternative work arrangements also creates an opportunity to utilize alternative space arrangements. Those employees who telework, job share, or work part-time will be able to share space during the days they are in the regular office. The concept of not having a dedicated office space is disturbing for some employees. The key again is to recognize the change, understand the rationale, and implement creative solutions.

Bob Johansen and Rob Swigart addressed many of these issues in their excellent book *Upsizing the Individual in the Downsized Organization: Managing in the Wake of Reengineering, Globalization and Overwhelming Technological Change.* Johansen and Swigart describe a new organizational strategy, what they call the fishnet organization.

> Imagine a net laid out on a dock. If you grab a node and lift, the rest of the net lattices nicely under it. A temporary hierarchy appears as long as you hold up the node, with layers consistent with how high you lift the node and the width of the mesh. The hierarchy disappears when you lay the net down. Pick up another node, another soft hierarchy appears.[1]

Johansen and Swigart see the move to virtual offices and the complete redefinition of work. They explain that

> As we get closer to the millennium, Americans will think of companies less as buildings and more as processes and products. Not only will business managers work in new spaces away from traditional office buildings, but they will work at any time, not just during the traditional eight-hour business day. This is the brave new world of remote work.[2]

DEGREE OF CHANGE

Different AWAs represent different degrees of change in terms of work environment and the office space that is required.

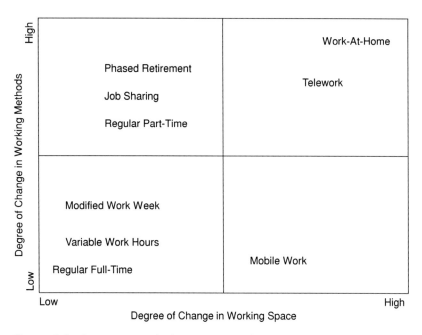

Figure 3-1 Positioning of alternative work arrangements in terms of change.

Figure 3-1 shows that the implementation of variable work hours and modified work weeks will have only a minimal impact on working methods and in the office space requirements. As we move along the scale Degree of Change in Working Methods, we find that regular part-time, job sharing, and phased retirement will require greater changes in the way work is performed. This quadrant also represents the greatest degree of change for employees who will be working part-time and receiving part-time pay and benefits.

The mobile work option is shown in the low degree of change with regard to work methods and a higher degree of change in working space. The low change in work methods is because most mobile workers typically are expected to be mobile as part of their job. Becoming a mobile worker is not typically voluntary but rather is an expected requirement of the job. For example, a sales person who is calling on external customers will not be in the office during sales calls. Many of these employees are forced to come into the regular office at some point during the day to file reports, access their mail, make phone calls, and so on. By recognizing these individuals as mobile workers and providing them with mobile technology, the organization can significantly improve their productivity and sales output without making any significant changes in the work that is being performed.

The upper right quadrant represents the greatest change in the method of work and the working space required. The AWAs in this quadrant include telework and work at home. Both of these work options require major changes in the way employees schedule and perform their work and in the way their immediate supervisor manages them. The work-at-home arrangement represents the greatest change, as the employee will rarely be in the regular office and face-to-face communications will be extremely limited. Extra effort is required by employees, managers, and coworkers to make these arrangements work. But, as with many situations, this extra effort can be rewarded with the most significant return on the expected benefits, so the effort is definitely worthwhile.

The challenge for any organization is to determine the extent of change it is able to absorb and sustain. Some organizations take the strategy of allowing only alternatives within the Low/Low quadrant to minimize the risk. These organizations often become disenchanted with AWAs, as they end up seeing only limited business benefits. Other organizations want to maximize the business benefits so immediately concentrate on the High/High quadrant. These high-risk takers often fail, as they do not have a balanced program.

The best solution to maximize business benefits is to function in all four quadrants. The organization should be implementing AWAs across the entire spectrum to ensure that each employee and each department is able to gain the best return on their AWA investment. Those that take this strategy also clearly demonstrate a responsible risk-taking philosophy that shows employees the commitment to new ways of working while still achieving the necessary business returns.

WHO CAN PARTICIPATE?

All employees should be eligible to consider AWAs. However, to be successful, they must have (1) a job that is suitable for the option being considered and (2) the support of their manager and their team.

To determine the AWA potential for a given job, it is best to start by breaking down the job into tasks. Employees may find that some portions of their job could be done anytime and anywhere, making them a potential candidate for telework, modified work week, or variable work hours. Employees do need to apply some basic logic as to situations where AWAs are realistically applicable. For example, heavy equipment mechanics will not be repairing dump trucks in their backyard just because they would like to telework.

Some organizations try to restrict the use of AWAs to certain groups of employees. Research in this area has shown that AWAs can be applied to 80–90% of an organization's jobs. The organization should not assume that these concepts apply only to knowledge workers, clerical staff, or administrative staff but should recognize that they are also very effective with managers and executives.

Duncan B. Sutherland, Jr., who has studied the white-collar productivity paradox, advises that giving any employee the opportunity to work in a nontraditional setting may be the most important way of improving productivity. In a 1992 paper, Sutherland describes the opportunity to allow employees to do the "mind's best work."[3] Sutherland suggests that we should allow employees to work when, where, and with the people they want to—that we need to use technology to allow people to do their mind's best work. In essence, allow people to shape the workplace, not the workplace shaping the people.

Sutherland's comments are valid when considering the amount of work that someone can accomplish by coming to the office early, staying late, or taking work home. In all of these cases, employees can usually operate at a much higher level of productivity because of the lack of interruptions. Imagine what it would be like if a manager or an executive could work from home one day a week—they would be able to free themselves from the operational jungle of meetings and issues to focus on key strategic initiatives. These employees would certainly enjoy the opportunity to have the time to do their mind's best work—so why not let them?

IMPACT ON EMPLOYEES

Alternative work arrangements will impact employees. Obviously, implementing AWAs will impact those who are successful in getting an AWA approved for themselves. However, it will also affect those who work with employees who are using an AWA. Employees who work with those on AWAs find that their job is sometimes changed; the flow of work in the team is impacted and scheduling meetings is problematic. These impacts are very realistic and to be successful, employees and managers must develop creative solutions.

Teams with members who utilize AWAs must learn to use alternative forms of communications to reach workers who are either remote or working different schedules. They must also establish processes and guidelines that will allow the team to maintain an orderly flow of work and to ensure tha meetings are held during times that will accommodate those who are on a different time and/or place schedule.

IMPACT ON MANAGERS

Managers are impacted by the implementation of AWAs. The necessary tasks are evaluating AWA requests, communicating with employees who are utilizing an AWA, and adjusting management styles to accommodate this broader range of work options.

To be effective, the manager needs to understand AWA concepts and the potential business benefits. In some cases, the manager may choose to have the work team decide on the AWA request. This requires the manager to facilitate the discussion and team resolution.

A major challenge for the manager is in interacting with employees who are utilizing an AWA. Managers have to develop communication practices that allow them to stay in touch with their employees. These practices include greater use of e-mail, telephone conversations, and scheduled manager–employee meetings.

The biggest challenge for the manager is to adjust his or her management style to accommodate this broader range of work options. This usually means having to make adjustments to being more focused on the end result and less on visual management. Managers need to work in partnership with their employees to create an effective method of managing those who choose to work outside of the normal hours and/or office space. Some managers may feel that they are losing control if they allow AWAs. These managers need to move past this fear and recognize the opportunity for developing new and creative working solutions that will deliver the expected benefits to the organization and its employees.

EXAMPLES OF SUCCESSFUL ALTERNATIVE WORK ARRANGEMENTS

DuPont

Many organizations have implemented AWAs in the past 10 years. These organizations are leading the charge towards redefining the way employees work. One of the leaders in AWAs has been E. I. du Pont de Nemours & Company (DuPont) in Wilmington, Delaware.

DuPont developed a workplace flexibility program to enhance its ability to retain employees. Joan Gardner, vice president of management resources says, "If we don't have programs that will encourage our people to stay, then somebody else is going to invent the next breakthrough product." Joan's comments are echoed by Ed Woolard, ex-CEO of DuPont. "When I started working at DuPont, I was told 'leave your personal life at home and your work life at the office.' Well, we've learned that's impossible."[4]

DuPont researched work and family issues from 1985 to 1995. The company has produced 10 years of data indicating that the use of flexible options is a good business practice in and of itself. While establishing its workplace flexibility programs, the company has been emphatic that business needs must be met before all other considerations.

In October, 1995, DuPont released a study documenting the correlation between employee commitment to business success and the company's workplace flexibility programs. This research covered 18,000 employees from nearly 20 business units and provides a 10-year comparison of results. John A. Krol, President and CEO of DuPont, concluded that "the results of the study clearly indicate that work/life programs are a powerful tool to motivate people and encourage commitment to achieving business objectives."[5]

The survey showed employees using or aware of the DuPont workplace flexibility program to be the most committed employees in the company and the least likely to feel overwhelmed or burnt out. They were 45% more likely than those not using the services to strongly agree that they expend extra effort on the company's behalf. An additional 33% were more likely to report feeling supported by the company. Respondents reported an average work week of 47 hours (55 hours for managers), and the study found no difference in work hours reported between those with and without dependent-care responsibilities.

The survey also found that 41% of DuPont's employees have used flexible hours, 6% have worked as telecommuters, 4% have used family leave, and 3% have reduced their hours. But employees are still making tradeoffs to achieve a balance between work and family obligations: 34% will not accept relocation; 24% would refuse jobs with increased travel; 21% would refuse jobs with more stress or overtime; and 12% have refused promotions.

Deloitte & Touche

Another corporate leader in alternative work arrangements is the "big six" accounting firm of Deloitte & Touche LLP in Wilton, Connecticut. Jim Wall, National Director, Human Resources, explains that "our only competitive advantage is having talented people, so we need to keep them."[6]

Deloitte & Touche started to consider AWAs, as it was concerned about the high attrition rate among the firm's female accountants. Interviews with employees, including some who had left the organization, led to a flexible workplace program that solved the problem.

At Deloitte & Touche, time is money, as consultants bill their clients by the hour. Employees must be willing to be flexible about flexibility; if an employee working a four-day week has to work on a Friday that is normally taken off, the time is made up elsewhere. Wall explains that "we used to measure productivity by input rather than output."[7] This transition is critical to the success of AWAs. Employers need to recognize that measuring the work product, rather than the time somebody spends in the workstations, requires a change in mindset that may take some managers longer than others.

Bell Atlantic

Bell Atlantic (formerly NYNEX) of White Plains, New York, provides phone service for the northeastern United States. The company feels that flexible work arrangements are critical to its operation. Robyn Phillips, Director of Corporate Culture Initiatives, explains that "although women have shown a much stronger willingness to request flexible arrangements that require approval, men use full-time flexible options as often as do women."[8]

Bell Atlantic has found that some feel that employees using the flexible work arrangements are less committed, less loyal, and less hard working. This, unfortunately, is a common attitude about AWAs within many organizations. Bell Atlantic's Phillips has looked at ways to combat this defeatist mentality. "When we find groups of employees who have an environment where flexibility can work, we discuss it with them and promote it by giving examples of success from within the company."[9]

The companies described above show how they have connected the alternate work arrangements directly back to the business benefits. This is critical to ensuring that the decision and support for AWAs is kept at a business level. This approach helps to keep everyone involved focused on the business rationale for AWAs and keeps the discussion of this topic away from a personal and sometimes emotional level. The last thing an organization wants to do is to decide who is eligible for AWAs based on the degree of personal hardship or the emotional attitude of the individual manager towards AWAs. The business approach brings all decisions to a level playing field and will usually result in win–win situations where most will feel that they have been treated fairly.

UNION AND OTHER LABOR CONCERNS

Unions often raise concerns about changing the traditional definition of where and when work is performed. Many unions are supportive of minor changes to the standard work definition (e.g., job sharing, variable work hours, modified work weeks) but become very concerned about more dramatic changes (e.g., telework, work at home).

The remote work arrangements (telework and work at home) are clearly the most contentious. Each union will have its own concerns, but there are a few that are common to almost every situation.

Employee Status, Salary, and Benefits

There are numerous reasons cited for concerns over the implementation of remote work arrangements, including moving to "piece-rate" work and wages. Many union leaders fear that employees will be forced to work at home, that management will be concerned solely with output, and that employees will be only a step away from being paid on a per-output basis–essentially becoming contingent workers. Many unions argue that the move to telework is a resurrection of the old garment industry, only that now the setting is the "electronic sweatshop."

Although remote work is most successful when managers switch to managing by output rather than by the amount of time worked, it does not follow that employees will be switched to piece-rate compensation. Unfortunately, the union concern over piece-rate work is well founded. A classic example was an organization that began having staff work from home to take unsolicited customer orders. Instead of paying per hour, the company paid per order. The result was that many of the employees had to work two to three additional hours a day to make the same salary they had when they worked in the office.

Labor concerns about AWAs should be addressed in a common forum between union and management. Most successful organizations with remote work practices have guidelines about paying remote workers the same wages and benefits as those who come to the traditional office every day. These companies may manage by output, but they pay based on the same scale and formula regardless of location.

Most telework programs in place today are voluntary, and this seems to solve the problem of employees being forced to work from home. If managers are wondering why this is a problem, then consider the following scenarios in which an employee clearly would *not* want to be forced to work at home:

- The employee is living in a small, one-room apartment. The employee would, obviously, prefer not to spend the majority of the day in the same room.
- The employee has two children under the age of six. A baby-sitter comes to the home every work day to care for the children. Until both of the children are in school, the employee may find it too noisy to work from home.
- The employee is in an unhealthy relationship at home. Going to work is a sanity break the employee does not want to spend any more time at home than necessary.

These examples are not exhaustive, but they illustrate how not every employee might want to work at home.

Another common concern is who will pay for the required technology and facilities to work remotely. There are a broad range of solutions to this situation. Most unionized organizations provide equipment such as a computer, modem, telephone, and separate phone line to remote workers. Today, most employers expect employees to provide their own furniture and space in their home. Many unions express a desire to have the employer pay the incremental utility costs (heat, electricity, etc.) for those who work at home. Most employers do not pay this, as they feel the personal savings achieved by the teleworkers (food, gasoline, parking, etc.) more than offset the incremental utility cost.

Women's Concerns and Child Care

Several unions have also expressed concerns about the additional burdens telework places on women. Theresa Johnson, a telework researcher for the Public Service Alliance of Canada (PSAC), which represents all federal government employees in Canada, describes what she calls the women's double burden.[10]

Johnson explains that since the 1970s, mothers have entered the labor market in increasing numbers. In 1991, 68% of women with children at home were in the labor force. This figure is up from 52% in 1981. And economic necessity has kept them there. Without two incomes, many families slip below the poverty level. Families cope as best they can, getting parents to work and children to school and day care five days a week. There has been as intensification of life both in the home and at the office.

This is particularly the case for many women, especially mothers, working outside the home. A Statistics Canada survey reports that women assume responsibility for 78% of housework and child care and men assume 78% responsibility for repairs, maintenance, and yard work. The women's tasks took 2½ times the number of hours that the men's tasks required. These data clearly show that women continue to bear the larger responsibility for unpaid domestic labor and child care.

Johnson concludes that it is not surprising that any work option is well-received if it offers increased time for family responsibilities. She believes that only one truly new option is available to relieve pressure, and that option is telework. Telework offers some relief from a major symptom of the '90s—too much work, too many demands, and not enough time.

Johnson is concerned that telework does not tackle the underlying problems many workers, particularly women workers, face. It fails to shorten the work week, and it does not address the fact that women carry the larger share of domestic labor and child care. In fact, telework may exacerbate some of these problems. Teleworking women often report assuming a larger share of household tasks because they are generally perceived by their families as "at home" and therefore available to take on extra household duties.

Johnson is also concerned about the impact on child care. There continues to be a perception that child care savings can be enjoyed with telework. Popular wisdom persists in this belief despite research pointing out that child care and paid labor are *not* compatible activities.

Most employers are extremely uncomfortable with employees mixing telework and child care. Johnson's point is reflective of the view many union leaders have regarding this issue. It is, however, critical that employers structure their telework programs to avoid this problem. Johnson's concern about the distribution of "home responsibilities" is a reality of our society today. Many studies have concluded that women do a larger percentage of the total household work than men. Making this a more equitable arrangement is not within the realm of reality for most employers. The challenge is a societal one, though it appears that this trend is slowly starting to shift.

Labor Solidarity and Collective Agreements

The primary concern of unions is one that is rarely discussed. It is the perceived loss of control by the union executives. In most situations, the union members are fully supportive of the alternative work arrangements but the union executives create an obstacle to implementation. Most unions are structured around being able to have some control over the dissemination of union information and the ability to quickly reach and contact employees with the potential of securing some form of job action. When teleworkers are included in the equation, this ability to rally employees becomes problematic for union leaders.

Employers must recognize the unions concern regarding communicating with and having access to their members. Some organizations have met these requirements by ensuring that union bulletin boards are available on-line and by ensuring that union leaders have e-mail access to their members. This approach can actually improve the level of communication and access.

In 1992, the BC Systems Corporation in Victoria, British Columbia, was one of the first unionized organizations in Canada to adopt a formal telework program. Mona Sykes, Staff Representative with the British Columbia Government Employees' Union (BCGEU) in Victoria, was the primary union contact involved in the negotiations with the BC Systems.

Sykes explained that there were several concerns that BCGEU had regarding telework, all of which had to be adequately addressed prior to signing a memorandum of agreement. One of the key concerns was the status of teleworkers—were they employees, contractors or piece-workers? The only acceptable position was for teleworkers to be employees—individuals who would receive the same pay and benefits regardless of their location of work. Other key areas of concern were insurance, liability, and ownership of equipment. In the BC Systems situation, it was agreed that the employer would supply the technology and the employee would provide the desk and chair. The decision to have the employer supply the equipment made the resolution of insurance and liability issues much easier.

Sykes suggests that if any organization is considering telework, then the collective agreement should be updated to provide for this provision. Sykes suggests that the collective agreement should include a clause that states "If telework is to be used as a work option, the union and the employer must agree to negotiate an agreement to facilitate this arrangement."[11] This clause, according to Sykes, will create an environment in which the union is working with the employer right from the beginning to ensure that the bargaining unit members' rights are protected.

Sykes believes that "most employees like the concept of telework at first glance but it is the responsibility of the union to ensure that all aspects of this arrangement are examined carefully."[12] The first step in starting up a telework program should be to involve the union as early as possible in the process. This way union representatives can express their views and make suggestions to improve the implementation.

Sykes believes that there are mandatory elements of a telework program:[13]

- Telework is a voluntary arrangement.
- Selection of teleworkers is fair and equitable
- Telework be limited to a maximum of 3 days per week.
- The employer must supply the technology
- The union must have electronic access to the telecommuters.

The key to success in unionized organizations is to include the union representatives in the planning and implementation of alternative work arrangements. The issues of remote workers are fairly common and should be addressed by a joint union–management task force to reach a common understanding. These discussions should be constructive in nature and should *not* become part of an overall bargaining situation. Although the implementation of AWAs is usually strongly supported by employees, it is critical that management and the union stay focused on making it work for all involved.

INSURANCE

The implementation of some AWAs (especially for teleworkers and work-at-home employees) may have an impact on corporate insurance. Organizations must review their current insurance policies as they relate to general liability, theft, loss of corporate records, and workers compensation to determine the impact of having employees work from home.

In most larger organizations, theft and loss of corporate records is self-insured meaning that these organizations absorb the loss internally rather then looking for compensation from an insurance company. Some organizations have asked employees to place a rider on their personal insurance policies to cover theft of corporate assets from the employee's home. Typically these riders are relatively inexpensive and provide coverage for stolen equipment.

Coverage for workers compensation [WC (USA)/WCB (Canada)] is another challenge for teleworkers and work-at-home employees. Although all WC/WCB jurisdictions have their own rules, it is generally applicable that the employee's home office on telework days is recognized as the employee's place of work as long as the employer has a formal agreement with the employee sanctioning the telework/work-at-home arrangement. The Occupational Safety and Health Administration [(OSHA) in the United States] and WCB also want to ensure that organizations are taking appropriate steps to ensure that the home office is a "relatively safe" place to work. OSHA/WCB expect that minimal occupational health and safety standards be followed at the home office (i.e., no extension cords running across the middle of the office space, no papers piled up to extent that they create a fire hazard, employees are not working from their coffee tables, etc.). Most organizations train their teleworkers on how to meet these basic safety guidelines and some even provide yearly home inspections.

The insurance issue is really one of managing risk. Organizations must determine the level of risk they are prepared to take and to acquire the appropriate amount of coverage. All organizations that are implementing these AWAs should contact their insurance companies and OSHA or local WCB agency for further information on this topic.

BENEFITS

The implementation of some AWAs (part-time, job sharing and phased retirement) has an impact on benefits. The organization needs to develop appropriate policies on how benefits will be handled for these employees before these AWAs are made broadly available.

Some organizations prorate employee benefits based on the number of hours they work per week. For instance, an employee who goes to part-time 20 hours/week (from full-time—35–40 hours/week) could expect the benefits to be reduced by 50%. This will affect vacation, pension, medical, and so on. Other organizations reduce only the vacation benefit and leave all the other benefits the same. Still others do not offer benefits to part-time workers. Each organization has to decide on what route to take, given the applicable local and national labor laws. Those who choose to go with no benefits may find that this reduces the number of full-time employees who will consider using AWAs.

The issue of benefits for part-time workers has been a major issue with unions in both Canada and the United States in the past decade. Any unionized organizations should initiate discussions with union representatives regarding this issue if the AWAs that include part-time are to be offered.

OPPORTUNITIES FOR DISABLED WORKERS

The use of some AWAs also creates opportunities to utilize disabled workers who may have been previously excluded from the workplace. Some employees who are physically challenged find that a work-at-home arrangement allows them to become a part of the work force without having to endure the commute from home, a commute that may be unbearable for some disabled people.

The use of work-at-home and telework arrangements can also be particularly effective for employees who have been injured on the job and are not able to return to their previous job. One interesting example is Art Erickson, an employee of Telus (a telecommunications provider in Alberta), who was disabled due to a work-related injury. In 1992, Art started working out of his home. Art explains that

> Telework also holds great promise for those with disabilities. The time, effort and stress of commuting is reduced, if not eliminated. As well, working at home allows the disabled to adjust work hours and to make up time lost on days when working is physically impossible. My position with Internal Communications is well suited to telecommuting as my work activities are easily conducted in the home-office environment using e-mail, a phone and a fax. I still suffer frequent spasms as a result of a work-related accident, so having privacy during major attacks is, for me (and no doubt my coworkers), a bonus.[14]

Disabled people who work from home will likely require a greater investment in capital equipment than other teleworkers, depending on the type and extent of the disability. These costs may include customized computers, special desk accommodations, special telecommunications equipment, and so forth. The initial costs are usually more than offset by the incredible benefit this arrangement brings to the employee and the organization.

In July 1990, the Americans with Disabilities Act (ADA) was signed into law in the United States. The ADA legislation is intended to make American society more accessible for people with disabilities. The employment section of the act (Title I) states that business must provide reasonable accommodations to protect the rights of individuals with disabilities in all aspects of employment. This could require changes to job functions, altering the layout of workstations, or modifying equipment. American-based companies should carefully study the ADA legislation and look for opportunities to ensure that the proposed work transformation program will support and enhance the ADA rules.

WORK AND FAMILY

Alternative work arrangements are a critical element of any corporate attempt to help employees balance work and family. In their December, 1992, report "Balancing Work and Family: A Study of Canadian Private Sector Employees," Dr. Christopher Higgins, University of Western Ontario; Dr. Linda Duxbury, Carleton University; and Dr. Catherine Lee, University of Ottawa studied over 14,000 employees in over 30 private-sector companies from more than 400 cities, towns, and villages across Canada.

The authors of the report describe the labor force of the 1990s and beyond as being dominated by employees who share at least some responsibility for the care of family dependents (i.e., children or elderly parents or relatives). They cite that this is due to a number of factors including "demographic shifts in the composition of the labor force; changing sex-role norms; different living patterns, changes in attitudes and values; increased education and opportunity for women; the trend towards smaller families; the rise in divorce rates; and a shift from a manufacturing-based society to a computerized information-based service economy."[15] The myth that one's work role is separate from (and is more important than) one's family role is no longer valid.

The changes in work force demographics have created a new emphasis on the balance between work and family life. Conflict and stress generated between work and family life impair performance both at work and at home. The researchers note that organizations cannot afford to ignore the issue of balancing work and family demands. Therefore, to help employees balance the work/family interface, the following six recommendations were made by the researchers:[16]

1. Provide greater work-time flexibility to result in enhanced recruitment/retention, increased productivity, heightened morale, and commitment to the organization.

2. Provide greater work-location flexibility. One option is to encourage working at home. The employee can select the most efficient hours and locale according to work style, the demands of other family members, and scheduling of leisure activities. In addition, the elimination of commuting can add substantially to the time available for the family.
3. Educate employees on the issues of work–family conflict. Those companies that are responsive to the work–family issue will be in a better position to recruit high-quality individuals.
4. Make a commitment to promote women. It would help to break the male-dominated cycle that persists in North American organizations and to provide role models and mentors for other women in the organization.
5. Provide flexible and complete benefit packages. Providing a shopping basket of benefits would be attractive to existing and future employees, particularly those who are part of dual-income families.
6. Educate managers. [The researchers indicate that it is not organizational policies that are at fault for many of the problems experienced by women, but the outdated attitudes of male managers.]

WORKPLACE WELLNESS

A 1994 study by the Canadian Mental Health Association confirms the work and family observations described above. This study concluded that balancing work and family is the second most important workplace wellness issue—the first is managing stress.[17]

Alternative work arrangements clearly have a role in managing stress and assisting employees in better balancing work and family. Figure 3-2 shows the major sources of stress and the consequences of this stress.

The figure show how the organization can add to the stress levels of employees, and the business consequences of stress. The implementation of work transformation is not the sole solution to these stress-related challenges, but it certainly can address some of the concerns.

The *American Journal of Health Promotion* suggests that

Organizations must consider a broad range of programs and initiatives to create a comprehensive health promotion program. Organizations can enhance the physical environment by making the workstations ergonomically sound, provide healthy food in the cafeteria and vending machines, provide quality equipment to staff and consider fitness facilities. Organizational policies can also be enhanced to include flexible working arrangements, flexible benefits and policies to support work and family.[18]

Major Sources of Stress

Personal	Environmental	Organizational
Poor self-esteem	Light	Too much to do
Poor interpersonal communications	Noise	Too little to do
Lack of connections	Temperature	Role ambiguity
Disruptive relationships	Humidity	Role conflict
Health status changes	Job hazards/risk	Too much responsibility
Monetary problems	Job demands (physical, time, and mental pressures)	Accountability
Burnout/boredom	Improper equipment	Overqualified/underqualified personnel
Risk-taking behaviors	Improper interface between people and machines	Uncertain future
Substance abuse	Techno-stress	Management style
Status dissatisfaction		Lack of control
Values/attitudes/beliefs		
Coping mechanisms		

Consequences of Stress

Physical Effects	Psychological Effects	Behavioral Effects	Organizational Effects
Headaches	Depression	Smoking	Absenteeism
Migraines	Apathy	Alcohol abuse	Turnover
Backaches	Boredom	Drug abuse	Poor industrial relations
Asthma	Irritability	Eating disorders	Health insurance claims
Ulcers	Anxiety	Accident proneness	Workplace accidents
Diabetes mellitus	Low self-esteem	Violent outbursts	Low productivity
Hypertension	Difficulty with decision making		Low morale
Heart disease	Hypersensitivity to criticism		Job dissatisfaction
Amenorrhea	Sleep disorders		Diminished performance
	Conversion reactions		
	Sexual dysfunction		
	Burnout		

Figure 3-2 Major sources and consequences of stress. (Source: Modified from *American Journal of Health Promotion*, Fall, 1986, pp. 6–10; May–June, 1990, pp. 333–337.)

ALTERNATIVE WORK ARRANGEMENT GUIDELINES

All formal AWA programs require some definition in terms of organizational policies, procedures, and guidelines. The following represent some of the common guidelines organizations may consider in implementing AWAs. Each organization will want to implement guidelines in the style that is most familiar and comfortable. The goal of all organizations should be to develop alternative working arrangement practices that are acceptable to management and to the mutual benefit of the organization and the individual employee.

In general, the following are the basic principles of most alternative work arrangements:

- *AWA Fundamentals*
  - Not appropriate for all employees
  - Not a universal employee benefit
  - Not a condition of employment
  - Participation strictly voluntary
- *AWA Eligibility*
  - Employees must not be on any type of performance improvement process (i.e., not on probation after a poor performance review).
  - Employee and his or her manager must complete the appropriate self-evaluation questionnaires and, where appropriate, produce a business case (see below).
  - Arrangement must have the complete support of the manager and the team.
- *Operational Issues*
  - Formal agreements should be signed by the employee and his or her manager.
  - Employee and his or her manager must agree on an appropriate schedule
  - Manager may revise the schedule to meet operational needs
  - Employee may request changes to the schedule but must obtain his or her manager's approval prior to making any changes
  - Those who are job sharing, working regular part-time, or teleworking must be prepared to utilize shared or smaller office facilities when they are working at their regular work location.
  - Appropriate security and safety precautions must be taken by remote workers.
- *Cancellation*
  - The AWA agreements for variable work hours, modified work week, or telework can be canceled by either the manager or the employee on two weeks' advance written notice.
  - The AWA agreements for job sharing, regular part-time, and phased retirement represent an entirely new employment agreement. Cancellation of these agreements by either the manager or the employee will require two weeks advance written notice.

ALTERNATIVE WORK ARRANGEMENT ASSESSMENT PROCESS

Employee Self-Evaluation

The concept of empowering employees has become common in many organizations today. This same concept should be applied to the selection of individuals to participate in AWAs.

The purpose of the self-evaluation is to have the employee go through the basic analysis of determining the appropriateness of an AWA for the job, personality, and work environment. This concept is particularly valuable for employees who must weigh the potential benefits and negative consequences of AWAs. Many organizations use a self-evaluation questionnaire that employees can complete to determine how the proposed work arrangement will work for them.

Each organization will probably want to develop its own self-evaluation questionnaire to reflect its specific culture and situation. The questionnaire should include a series of questions and statements related to the AWA(s) being considered. For example, a telework questionnaire should include questions regarding the ability to perform the job remotely, the amount of unscheduled interaction, personal characteristics that are best suited to remote work, structure of the home office, and basic technology requirements. A questionnaire for job sharing will focus more on the ability to share responsibility and credit with another employee, how the job can be split, etc.

The self-evaluation questionnaire should be easily completed by staff and should elicit answers using check boxes instead of long open-ended responses. At the end of the questionnaire, the employee should be encouraged to honestly and realistically evaluate the appropriateness of the new work arrangement.

The self-evaluation questionnaire must be a thought-provoking process to trigger the analysis of appropriateness. It should not be scored like a "magazine quiz," with facile pigeonhole categories describing the degree of appropriateness. The decision on whether to implement AWAs should not be trivialized.

If the questionnaire is structured correctly, employees will not only be able to determine the appropriateness of the work option for their particular situation, but they will also learn about the work option. Over the past several years, I have seen many employees use self-evaluation tools. In at least 20% of the cases, employees complete the process, expand their knowledge of the work option, and decide that it is not appropriate for them at that point in time. It is much better for employees to come to this conclusion on their own rather than have the manager tell them that a proposed AWA is not appropriate.

Manager's Input

Once employees have completed their self-evaluation, generally they will know whether or not an AWA is appropriate. At this stage, an employee can present the self-evaluation information to the manager and affected team members for review and approval if the employee is a suitable candidate.

The manager should review the materials and meet with the employee to discuss the advantages and disadvantages. The goal is to come to a consensus on the appropriateness of the preferred alternative work arrangement being proposed. Figure 3-3 shows the decision-making process for an application to remote work.

Task Analysis

Review the employee's tasks to determine how he or she will be impacted by the chosen AWA. For example, if teleworking is chosen, the employee and his or her manager need to determine which tasks can be done on telework days and which must be performed in the office. For remote workers, managers need to objectively evaluate whether or not a task needs to be done from the regular office.

Impact Analysis

The employee and the manager should discuss what impact the chosen alternative will have on coworkers, customers, and the manager. Will it increase the workload of coworkers? Will there be an improvement in the level of customer service?

The review of impacts should include a discussion of potential solutions to minimize negative impacts and maximize positive impacts.

Business Benefits

The business benefits should be identified and quantified, wherever possible (e.g., increased productivity, space saving, proximity to customer).

Cost/Benefit Analysis

The implementation of most of the AWAs will not have a direct cost. However, the remote work arrangements will likely include a one-time investment in technology and an ongoing operating cost for telephone lines, support, and so forth. The costs and the quantified benefits should be consolidated into a cost/benefit analysis.

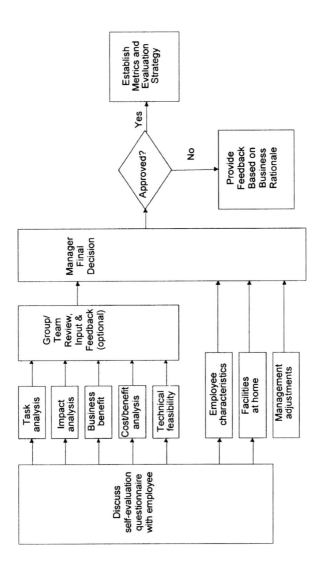

Figure 3-3 Decision-making process for request to work remotely.

Technical Feasibility

The implementation of remote work normally requires access to technology in terms of e-mail, fax, voice mail, desktop applications, shared files, and corporate applications. The manager and the employee (or small groups of employees) should meet with the information technology group to determine the technical feasibility of teleworking.

Employee Characteristics

The manager and the employee should review the employee's characteristics (as identified in the AWA self-evaluation questionnaire [see also p. 183]) to ensure that they will be successful with the selected work arrangement.

Facilities at Home

For teleworkers and work-at-home employees, the manager needs to review the proposed home office environment with the employee to ensure that it will be safe and productive. Many organizations have their internal occupational health and safety group set up guidelines for home offices.

Management Adjustments

Managers considering AWA requests must honestly analyze their own management style and determine whether or not they will be able to effectively function with these new arrangements. Typically, this will involve establishing basic criteria for output by the employee and managing by results. Although this may be "business as usual" for some managers, it will represent a significant change for others.

If the manager's style does not readily accommodate teleworkers (see Adjusting Management Style to Accommodate Alternative Work Arrangements, p. 59), then the manager should contact the human resources group to attain the appropriate training to be successful in a "managing by results" environment.

Group/Team Review

Managers may choose to review the employee's AWA request with their work team or group. This process should be performed to gain input and feedback from the group. The areas of coworker and customer impact should be emphasized in this review.

Final Decision

Each AWA request should be evaluated on an individual basis, although it may be appropriate to group requests together to help avoid making decisions on a first-come, first-served basis.

The final decision is up to the manager. The manager should carefully review the information available and make the final decision based on sound business rationale. Managers must not make their final decision based on the personal needs of the employee. If they do, they will not be applying these applications equitably within their workgroup.

If the application is refused, the manager must meet with the employee to provide feedback. This feedback should include reviewing the business reasons for turning down the application. Where appropriate, the manager may also want to suggest how and when the application may be reconsidered in the future.

If the application is approved, the manager must meet with the employee to establish methods of communications, work schedules, specific metrics for measuring the expected business benefits, and a time for reviewing the overall success of the implementation.

ADJUSTING MANAGEMENT STYLE TO ACCOMMODATE ALTERNATIVE WORK ARRANGEMENTS

The implementation of an AWA often requires adjustments in the manager's communication methods and management style. These adjustments are minor, in some cases, but are critical to improving the chances of attaining the expected business benefits from the AWA.

Communication Methods

Managers will have to alter their communication methods to ensure that they are effectively communicating with those employees who are not working exclusively during regular hours or at the regular office location. These changes will include greater use of e-mail, the telephone, and scheduled face-to-face meetings to communicate with employees. Enhanced communication will also involve ensuring that remote employees are included in impromptu group meetings or when new opportunities are available. The old phrase "out of sight, out of mind" will not be acceptable. The manager must take the necessary communication steps to ensure that employees using AWAs are not overlooked.

Management Style

Every manager has his or her own management style. For some managers, the adjustments required to work with employees on AWAs will be minor; for others, the necessary changes will be more significant. The key change for many managers will be to shift away from "visual management" to management by results. Visual management is a common management trap whereby managers feel confident that work is being performed only if they can see their employees working. This may not be possible when managing employees using certain AWAs. The employee teleworking from home three days per week will be visible only 40% of the time. It would be rash to assume that the employee is working only 40% of the time.

The move to management by results forces managers and employees to be more specific on the outcomes or deliverables of the job. The goal is for the manager to work in partnership with the employee, to document the expected results, and to put in place mechanisms to manage the delivery of these results. This approach allows the manager to become more focused on the end result and less concerned about where and when the employee performs the work. This change is beneficial not only for AWAs but also for the manager's entire workgroup.

Managers should not underestimate the effort that will be required to make these management adjustments. They represent fundamental changes in the way many managers have operated in the past and will take time and energy to change. Managers should ask their employees who are utilizing AWAs to provide feedback on the effectiveness of the changes and fine-tune them accordingly.

It is important to gather feedback at an appropriate time. For example, the first 2–4 weeks is an adjustment period for all involved—the feedback gathered at this point may be more reflective of a reluctance to change than a true operational problem. Typically, after 3 months, the impact of the alternative work arrangement has settled in for the employee and his or her coworkers, customers, and managers. This is a good time to gather feedback. The AWAs should also be reviewed on an annual basis thereafter.

This point is brought home by Marcia Kropf, Vice-President of Research and Advisory Services, at New York–based Catalyst, a nonprofit organization dedicated to effecting change for women. "If employees, especially managers, view the workplace flexibility program as an accommodation for people with special needs, they will not accept it as just another way of working."[19] We must remember that establishing programs is not enough to change culture change. Employees must know about policies and be comfortable using the options.

MONITORING AND EVALUATING

To maintain continuous improvement, the organization must continually monitor, evaluate, and fine-tune its program. Managers need to determine methods of monitoring the key business benefits that are expected from the AWA. These benefits should be tracked and evaluated on a regular basis with the intention of fine-tuning the AWA to maximize the business return.

Managers also need to track the performance of employees using AWAs. This will involve integrating the AWA performance measures into the employees regular performance management program. The manager and the employee need to work together to monitor and evaluate these specific measures.

Alternative work arrangements should be reviewed on a regular basis to ensure that they are still meeting the business benefits and the personal expectations of the employee. Some of the arrangements such as part-time, phased retirement, and job sharing are difficult to discontinue. In these situations, the employee must re-apply for available full-time jobs in order to be brought back into the office full-time. The other arrangements are easier to change or reverse, if required.

When an AWA does not work out, the manager, employee, and the team should use the unsuccessful arrangement as a learning experience. The manager should analyze why it did not work and what can be done to ensure that future experiences are more positive. The manager should add the learning experience to their AWA knowledge base and not use the failure as an excuse for automatically rejecting all future requests.

Managers and employees should also recognize that changes in the job or in the employee's personal life may require cancellation of the AWA. For example, an employee who is currently teleworking and receives a promotion to a position where remote work is not possible will have to stop teleworking. Similarly, employees who receive new jobs often come back into the office for a period of time to learn the new job before starting up their AWA again. Changes in the employee's personal life have the same affect. An employee who has been teleworking may want to stop the arrangement if they now have a baby in the house, which would make working from home difficult. This employee may choose to return to teleworking when the child is able to go to day care on the employee's telework days.

SUMMARY

The human resources issues associated with work transformation are not insignificant. They represent a broad range of challenges that need to be addressed.

Organizations should position their work transformation program such that it includes a broad range of options that will provide choices for employees while maximizing the business value to the organization. Managers need to open up the work transformation program to all staff using a formal set of policies, guidelines, and procedures to ensure success. The program must be established such that it addresses work and family, workplace wellness, and equity issues.

If the organization has an organized work force, then it must involve the union as early as possible to ensure that the union and management can work together towards the same goals. The strategy of having union and management on the "same page" seems simplistic enough, but in reality this will be a major challenge. Both parties have to agree to the business objectives and then work together to accomplish the business goals while protecting the rights of the employees.

Finally, the organization needs to address the challenge of changing the way management manages employees. This will involve the shift from visual management practices that many managers are most comfortable with to managing by results. The shift of senior management will likely be accomplished by getting them to buy into the vision of work transformation. The shift of middle managers will be more difficult. The success of the work transformation program will very much depend on the ability of middle managers to make these adjustments.

NOTES

1. Johansen, Robert, and Swigart, Rob. *Upsizing the Individual in the Downsized Organization: Managing in the Wake of Reengineering, Globalization and Overwhelming Technological Change.* Reading, MA: Addison-Wesley, 1994, p. 15.
2. Ibid, p. 23.
3. Sutherland, Duncan B., Jr. Technology and White-Collar Productivity: Time, Tools and the Minds Best Work, in *Knowledge Infrastructure Engineering: An Emerging Community of Practice in Knowledge-Intensive Organizations* (H. Parunak, ed.). Ann Arbor, MI: Industrial Technology Institute, 1992.
4. Sheley, Elizabeth. Flexible Work Options: Beyond 9 to 5, *HR Magazine*, February, 1996, pp. 53–58.
5. Ibid, p. 54.
6. Ibid, p. 55.
7. Ibid, p. 57.
8. Ibid, p. 58.
9. Ibid, p. 58.

10. Johnson, Th resa. Women's Issues Related to Telework. *Telework International,* *3*(1 [Spring]), 1995.
11. Robertson, Ken. Telecommuting—A Union Perspective. *Telework Canada, 1*(1 [Spring]), 1993.
12. Ibid.
13. Ibid.
14. Gobal, Kathy. Telecommuting at Alberta Government Telephones. *Telework Canada, 1*(1 [Spring]), 1993.
15. Higgins, Christopher, Duxbury, Linda, and Lee, Catherine. Balancing Work and Family: A Study of Canadian Private Sector Employees—National Centre for Management Research and Development, Western Business School, University of Western Ontario.
16. Ibid.
17. Canadian Mental Health Association. *Mental Health Promotion in the Workplace.* February, 1994.
18. O'Donnell, M. P. Definition of Health Promotion: Part II. Levels of Programs. *American Journal of Health Promotion,* 1986 (Fall), pp. 6–10.
19. Sheley, Elizabeth. Flexible Work Options: Beyond 9 to 5. *HR Magazine,* February, 1996, pp. 53–58.

4

Facilities Management

The facilities management function is critical to the successful implementation of work transformation. The key facilities component of work transformation is to investigate, design, and implement alternative space arrangements ASAs.

Alternative space arrangements is an umbrella term for supporting a range of approaches to assigning workspaces in nontraditional ways. These nontraditional ways include new designs for space that are focused more on the tasks performed at a particular point in time rather than on the traditional concept of a "permanently" assigned workspace.

As described in Chapter 2, ASA options are basically split into those that are implemented on premises and those that are implemented off premises. Figure 4-1 shows some of the common ASA solutions.

The ultimate flexibility in space usage is now commonly described by the phrase "work anytime/anyplace." Bob Johansen, of the Institute of the Future

On-Premises Options	Off-Premises Options
• Regular office	• Guesting space
• Teaming space	• Mobile space
• Shared space	• Telework center
• Group space	• Home office
• Nonterritorial space	

Figure 4-1 Common alternative space arrangement solutions.

in Menlo Park, CA, explains that the "boundary between the office and home is thinning to transparency in the information era."[1] The degree of flexibility is something that organizations and employees need to be constantly aware of. Johansen advises that the anytime/anyplace office, once a vision of hope for many over-worked managers of the eighties, can turn into "the all-the-time, every place office, a vision of hell rapidly taking form in the real world."[2]

For some employees, work transformation equates to working at home. Johansen's comments reinforce the need to know when to stop working and how to separate work and home environments. This sentiment was echoed by Gil Gordon, a telecommuting consultant, who at his annual telecommuting conference in 1994 presented each participant with a button reminding people to know when to "turn it [computer] off and get a life."[3]

SAMPLE ALTERNATIVE SPACE ARRANGEMENT SCENARIOS

Perhaps the best way to define ASAs is to provide a few before and after examples:

Example #1

Work Situation

Bill is a technical writer. His job involves meeting his customers to gather information, researching his topic on the Internet and in the corporate library, writing his technical documents, and then reviewing them with his customers.

Before Work Transformation

Bill worked full-time in the regular office. He was assigned a standard 125 ft² open-plan office. In analyzing his actual space utilization, he discovered that he is in his office only 50% of the time, with the rest of his time in meetings or doing research. Bill has also commented that his open-plan office is not the best for enabling him to achieve the level of concentration he needs for his writing.

After Work Transformation

Bill now works in an alternative work environment. He does not have a dedicated full-time workstation. He is part of a technical communications team that has a dedicated teaming space. Bill's new space has small meeting facilities, which are effective for the meetings with customers. On days when Bill is planning on being in meetings or doing research, he works out of a small library carrel where he can plug in his laptop to access his e-mail and use his telephone.

During periods when Bill will be writing, he uses a small, enclosed workspace, which enables him to achieve the level of concentration he needs to get his writing accomplished.

Example #2

Work Situation

Joan is a customer service representative. Her job is to provide direct customer support and marketing services to a range of clients throughout the Bay Area of San Francisco. To do this, Joan spends a large portion of her time at her clients locations or in transit between clients. When Joan is in the office, she is usually in meetings with other support staff to ensure that her customers requirements are being effectively communicated.

Before Work Transformation

Joan had a dedicated workspace at the regular office. Because of the level of Joan's position, she was allocated a 150 ft^2 enclosed office. When Joan tracked the actual use of her office space, she found that she was in the office building only two days per week, and during these periods she was in her office only 25% of the time (an effective space utilization of 10%). The time in her office was primarily to make phone calls, go through her in-basket, and check her e-mail.

After Work Transformation

Joan is a classic example of a mobile worker. To meet the requirements of her job, she must be out of the office at least three days a week. In the new work environment, Joan does not have a dedicated office; instead she is able to use shared space on an as-required basis. Usually when Joan comes into the office she will use a touchdown space in the casual seating area. This location provides Joan with a comfortable space to interact with her colleagues (which she misses on the days she is out of the office) while providing her a location for accessing her e-mail. Joan's work is critical and sometimes sensitive. When she has a series of calls to make (usually after a meeting) she will use a phone booth space (4 × 6 ft), where she will have complete privacy.

Example #3

Work Situation

Patrick is a financial analyst. His job involves reviewing financial information, developing reports on financial status, and reviewing these reports with his customers.

Before Work Transformation

Patrick worked full-time from the regular office. He was assigned a standard 100 ft^2 open-office workstation. In analyzing his actual space utilization, he discovered that he was in his office 75% of the time, with the rest of the time in meetings. Most of Patrick's work is "heads down" and requires a high level of concentration.

After Work Transformation

Patrick is now a teleworker. He works three days a week from home, where he does the majority of his heads down work. When he returns to the office, he uses one of three workspaces that he shares with four other teleworkers. His shared workspace is smaller than the one he had before, but it works effectively since Patrick spends half his time in the office at meetings.

These three examples show the broad range of ASA solutions. In all cases, the workspace the employee previously worked in has changed, but the changes have varying degrees of significance. For employees like Joan, who are out of the office most of the time, the change is not significant. These employees are in the office for meetings and to interact with others, not to sit in an isolated workspace.

Employees who telework from home find that they are quite prepared to share space at the regular office because they have a "dedicated" workspace at home. Employees such as Bill, who no longer has a dedicated workstation, face the most significant change. These employees are in the office every day and initially see their world turned upside-down. However, after a short period of time, most of these employees see the benefit of having the type of task-oriented space they need on an as-required basis.

The examples illustrate some of the significant changes that need to be taken into account when considering ASAs. Organizations need to make the paradigm shift from considering space as a piece of real estate assigned exclusively to an employee based on rank to treating it as several different types of workspaces which any employee can use on an as-required basis.

We must also think of the workspace options in terms of those that are available on premises (at the regular office) and those that are available off premises. Those who choose to telework may do the majority of their "desk work" at home or at a telework center. Other off-premises options use technology to make those who are already out of the office more mobile. With the use of better, more portable technology, the organization can keep these individuals in the field for longer periods of time. This opportunity should not be seen as trying to keep the person out of the office primarily to save money on facilities but rather as an opportunity to improve the level of service provided by allowing employees to spend more time with their customers.

The ASA concept is built around sharing space, using new types of spaces, and creating flexible work environments that allow employees to effectively work in the shared space. The flexibility will include the use of moveable furniture, adjustable chairs, and adjustable work surfaces. For many employees, the only fixed location they will have in the future office will be a locker and a small, moveable storage cabinet (a pedestal on wheels), which they can roll to the location they will be working from that day.

DEGREE OF CHANGE

The examples described above show that different ASAs represent varying degrees of change in terms of working methods and the office space that is required. Figure 4-2 shows that the implementation of teaming space usually represents the least amount of change in terms of working space and working methods. This implementation of teaming space usually represents the least amount of change in terms of working space This low-risk strategy is being

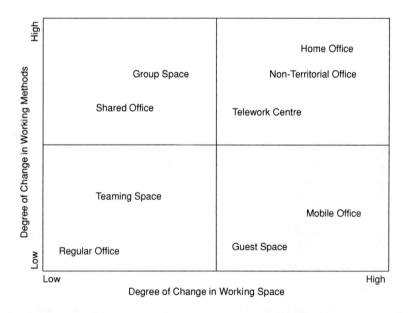

Figure 4-2 Positioning of alternative space arrangements in terms of change.

implemented by many organizations that have reengineered their business processes to be more team oriented. In these organizations, the change to employees working in a space where they are all together and can easily communicate will usually improve the level of job performance. The teaming strategy is often the starting point for introducing change to the workspace.

The use of shared space and group space requires moderate changes to the workspace and more significant changes to the employee's working methods. The shared-office concept can usually be implemented within existing space with only minor modifications. The degree of change in how the employee works is slightly more dramatic in that the employee must adjust to sharing space. Usually the shared office or group space is implemented in conjunction with alternative work arrangements (AWAs) such as regular part-time, job sharing, phased retirement, and telework.

The implementation of group space involves an even greater degree of change in terms of changes in workspace. Shared-space offices are usually limited to a small number of people sharing a series of offices. The group space involves a larger number of employees sharing the space and is more likely to require redesign of the workspace. The dynamic of involving the employees in the design and implementation of the group space adds to the level of change.

The right-hand quadrants contain solutions that require a greater level of change in the working space. The guest space and mobile office represent a different workspace from the traditional office but their use usually entails a minimal impact on the working patterns of the employees—largely because employees working in these arrangements are doing so because it is a mandatory part of their job. For example, a sales person is already likely spending much working time on the road, visiting customers. To officially make this employee a mobile worker and remove any dedicated workspace at the traditional office will mean a relatively minor change in the way the employee functions.

The upper right-hand quadrant represents the greatest degree of change, risk, and potential return. The officing solutions here include the remote locations such as an office in the employee's home, distributed telework centers, and the use of nonterritorial offices in the regular office location. The remote offices obviously represent significant change for the facilities management group in that these offices will be very different from the typical central office location. The design and implementation of home offices will vary based on whether the employee is teleworking (2–3 days per week) or on a work-at-home program (5 days per week).

The implementation of nonterritorial offices will represent a significant degree of change for the organization. The nonterritorial office strategy is based on the premises that employees will select the workspace that best meets their specific requirements on an as-required basis. This will result in the creation of a wide range of new workspace options and will require employees to change the way they interact with their space.

The best strategy to maximize business benefits is to be functioning in all four quadrants. The organization should be implementing alternative officing solutions across the entire spectrum. The solutions offered should, wherever possible, coordinate the ASA solutions with AWA offerings. This will allow the organization to truly maximize the business value associated with work transformation.

A good starting point for an organization that is uncomfortable with major change is the use of teaming space, guest space, and mobile offices. In all of these cases, the change in space will occur without significantly changing the way employees work. Once the organization is comfortable with the basic returns associated with these solutions, it should move into the upper quadrants, where the changes in working patterns are greater but where the potential business benefits are much greater, too.

EXAMPLES OF RECENT CORPORATE ALTERNATIVE SPACE ARRANGEMENTS

The arrival and acceptance of new business strategies is usually formalized when the new concept hits the front cover of *Business Week* magazine. The concept of ASAs made a splash on the front cover of the April 29, 1996, issue, announcing the legitimacy of this new way of working. The *Business Week* profile had a definite impact on North American organizations. After the cover story appeared, many consultants in this field noticed a significant increase in the interest level.

Business Week highlighted programs at several companies, including Alcoa, Procter & Gamble, and In Focus Systems Inc.

Alcoa

Alcoa (Aluminum Company of America) abandoned its traditional 31-story office tower in Pittsburgh, PA, with standard 12×15 ft private offices, for a new three-story complex on the banks of the Allegheny River, with smaller, open offices. The concept of alternative officing represents a cultural change that is occurring from the top of the organization on down. Alcoa Chief Executive Officer, Paul H. O'Neil, does not have a permanently assigned office. The executive suite has no permanent walls or doors. All of Alcoa's senior executives work in open cubicles and gather around a "communications center" with televisions, fax machines, newspapers, and tables to encourage impromptu meetings. O'Neil's own favorite hangout is the kitchen, where he and his staff nuke take-out food, huddle, and talk work. "It's like being at home in your own kitchen and sitting around the table."[4]

Alcoa downsized, reengineered, and reorganized work around teams but found that it was not able to achieve the benefits of being more responsive and competitive in its traditional office environment. It has found that the new work styles do not usually work in buildings designed for the old hierarchical organization.

Procter & Gamble

Procter & Gamble has also adopted alternative officing strategies in a major way. P&G's new $280 million, 1.3 million ft² building 20 miles north of Cincinnati has been designed to "promote product development and to use the facilities as a competitive advantage—not to focus on some trendy architectural forms or status symbols."[5]

The P&G office is designed around project teams. Staff work in open cubicles, grouped together, and are visible to each other, regardless of rank. File cases are literally on wheels, and offices are designed in "bricks" that can be reconfigured in short order if a team needs to get bigger or smaller. P&G has escalators between floors, huddle rooms throughout, lunchrooms and lounges with electronic whiteboards that can convert drawings to e-mail, and wide corridors—all designed to encourage communications.

The building opened in July 1995, and J. P. Jones, P&G's Vice President, Research and Development for Over-the-Counter Health-Care Products, explained, "I'm convinced it will deliver 20–30% productivity gains because data sharing is immediate and higher-quality decisions are made faster."[6]

It is also interesting to note that P&G has recognized the need to help dual-career families and single parents. This has included flexible working arrangements, and the inclusion of a fitness facility, dry cleaner, shoe-repair shop, and a cafeteria that prepares food that employees can take home at night. These additional amenities show an understanding of how the organization's physical plant can help employees balance work and family, which is still rare in many organizations today.

In Focus Systems

In Focus Systems Inc., a Wilsonville, OR, maker of computer projection systems, found that conventional open-office cubicles were too much of a barrier. Vice President Allan Alley was determined to shorten product-development times by trying to improve the level of communication between his engineers and marketers. Alley felt that the open cubicles were "the worst of both worlds—with no impromptu meetings and a lot of wasted space."[7]

In Focus implemented Steelcase Inc.'s Personal Harbors. Each personal "harbor" is like a small cylindrical booth with a door that can be closed, and because it is curved, it actually seems to increase the interior space. There is enough room inside for a flat work surface, PC, phone, file drawer, and other standard desk items.

The key is that the harbors are grouped around a large puzzle-like table that can be broken into several pieces. When harbor doors are open, people move in and out of the group space to talk to colleagues, participate in meetings, or just listen in. Alley explained that "people will never leave a [traditional] meeting room, but with this system they stay in a meeting just long enough to contribute and go back to work. The personal harbor creates an atmosphere where we can rapidly develop products."[8]

Gould Evans Goodman Associates

These concepts apply to a broad range of companies. Gould Evans Goodman Associates, the second largest architectural and design firm in Kansas City, MO, has been experiencing 30% annual growth over the past few years. A recent move to a new facility created the opportunity for the firm to rethink how to structured its office. Lead Interior Designer, Karen Gould, envisioned the ideal workplace: a fully mobile office that could accommodate continuous growth and constantly changing project teams with tables, computer stands, and storage units on wheels so that workers could easily move the units together for team projects and impromptu meetings.

The firm chose Haworth Inc.'s Crossings furniture, which has all components on wheels. The wheels allow Gould Evans Goodman to accommodate rapid expansion without much downtime. Gould explains that "in the past, we lost many working hours and spent a lot of money moving furniture and shuffling offices. With Crossings in our new site, we can just pack up and move on a moment's notice—mobility is the key."[9]

Gould Evans Goodman specializes in a broad range of services, and employees change roles frequently, participating in a variety of projects. "We are constantly forming and re-forming teams and working on several types of projects at once."[10] The flexible design and furnishings allow Gould Evans Goodman to have the ultimate in flexibility.

In each of these examples, the changes have a common thread—they were driven to support specific business objectives. These organizations put the effort into clearly understanding their business needs and were prepared to think *outside the box* to come up with new and creative solutions.

It is interesting to note that several of the examples involved a move to a new building. As Alcoa discovered, it is often difficult to implement radical facilities changes without moving into a new building that will support the degree of flexibility required. However, most organizations do not subscribe to the strategy of such dramatic and radical changes. They prefer instead to gradually move into these new ideas and evolve to the more extreme implementation over time. Usually, this type of strategy can still be accomplished in existing buildings and/or older buildings. Obviously, the stepping-stone approach is less costly in the short term but will likely cost more in the longer term than the radical change option.

ALTERNATIVE SPACE ARRANGEMENT CHALLENGES

The implementation of ASAs is not an insignificant change for an organization. These concepts will be successful only when they are presented in a realistic and practical fashion. The key to success is to identify the primary challenges in the organization and then to work with the each user group to break through these challenges.

Sharing Space

The most common challenge is resistance to change. Most employees are accustomed to having some type of workspace "permanently" assigned to them. Replacing this concept with the idea of shared space can make some employees feel they are losing their connectivity to the organization. Space is very personal. Most employees have personalized their workspace to the point where it becomes a very comfortable spot for the employee. In the midst of massive changes, most employees feel more secure when they are in their own personal workspace.

Organizations need to help employees be more comfortable in their remote work locations as part of the tradeoff for sharing space. This might involve providing ergonomic chairs for teleworkers or updating the technology available to mobile workers. Organizations need to show staff that they are not merely squeezing down on the amount of space; instead they are redistributing the investment in facilities and technology to better meet the business objectives of the organization.

Space by Need

The change from *space by rank* to *space by need* is another area of resistance. Employees who have worked with the organization for a long period of time and have moved up to the higher level positions often feel they have "paid their dues" and now deserve the larger workstations. For these employees, sharing space or using smaller workstations is not seen as a positive move.

This issue needs to be handled by reminding staff that they will be able to work from multiple locations within the ASA concept and that they will be able to use a larger workstation on those occasions when they have a true operational need for one.

The concept of space by need, and not rank, is a hard concept for employees to embrace, particularly if the concept is not applied throughout the organization. For example, if the organization adopts these changes for staff but there is no change at the senior manager or executive level in terms of how they use space, then it will be difficult to convince staff of the benefits.

Loss of Cubicle

Some employees will lament the loss of their beloved cubicle, especially if the option is to go to a more open team space. Employees have a love–hate relationship with their cubicles; they are highly prone to complaining about them until someone suggests taking them away.

Most employees believe that the cubicle provides them with a greater level of visual and sound privacy then being in a team space. Our studies have shown that this is a false perception. Most people in cubicles have some degree of visual privacy, but adequate sound privacy is usually not achievable. The sound of unmodulated voices readily carries through and around cubicle partitions. We have, in fact, found that more open team areas are quieter, as employees can see each other and thus become more cognizant of the tone and volume of their voice.

Loss of Office

Employees who have their own personal office sometimes become concerned about moving into a more open environment. They explain that they need the office for confidential meetings and discussions with staff, customers, and so on. The ASA concepts should include multiple small-meeting rooms that can be used by any employee. Employees who previously had offices can merely drop into one of these rooms for confidential issues and then return to their regular workspace.

Usually the concern over the loss of the office is more a concern of loss of status than of functionality. Employees who have waited a long time to get an office feel very uncomfortable in giving it up. The reality is that managers who stay in an enclosed office while their teams are in open team spaces quickly find that they are out of the loop in terms of the team interaction and discussion that will naturally occur within the team space.

Manager's Perceived Loss of Control

Managers are often concerned about a perceived loss of control from ASAs. Some managers are uncomfortable when people are not sitting in the same workstations or are not visible to the manager. Their concern is how to manage what cannot be seen. These managers need to make a few adjustments to their management style; to switch from traditional visual management practices to management by results.

Some managers also become concerned over the reduction in the floor space allocated to their group. They may feel that this reduction somehow reduces their relative power, based on their perception that power is directly related to the number of employees they manage and the size of their overall group space. This perception needs to be overcome to get managers focused on the cost savings and business benefits associated with ASAs.

These are just a few of the common challenges involved with considering ASA concepts. The ASA analyst must work with the organization to help it see past the loss of individual space and appreciate the opportunities associated with these new concepts.

DESIGNING ON-PREMISES SOLUTIONS

The process for designing ASA solutions will vary based on whether the organization is designing on-premises or off-premises solutions. Two of the North American leaders in this area are Franklin Becker and Fritz Steele, authors of *Workplace by Design: Mapping the High-Performance Workscape.*

Becker and Steele help us to think outside the box by considering new and creative ways to design the workplace. They remind us that "we don't cook, eat, sleep and entertain in the same room in our homes. Why should we always discuss a project, type a report, or read a technical article in the same workspace?"[11]

As creatures of habit, many people are stuck in the traditional definitions of an office, especially with regard to where it is located and what it should contain. Organizations need to break out of this mold to find new and creative ways to use space.

The concept of ASAs is not easily defined, although one may apply the general goal of consolidating several new space components to create a new work environment that supports the tasks to be performed by the space users.

To design the new space, the designer must first understand the range of potential space components. The following are some of the common space settings that make up the overall work environment. These spaces are intended to support the work requirements of the usersnot necessarily to reflect the rank they hold within the organization. The components may be categorized as common space or task-oriented space.

ASA Components: Common Space

Common space represents the areas that are used by all users. In traditional spaces, these areas would have limited use for delivery of tasks. The ASA approach suggests looking for creative ways to use these spaces for tasks that lend themselves to these types of areas. The following are some of the typical common areas.

Personal Storage

An important element of the ASA design is personal storage areas. ASAs are based on employees using the space available on an as-required basis. This means that they may be using any number of workspaces in a given week or even in a given day. With this degree of portability, the designer needs to establish some permanent location in which employees can store their personal items.

This storage of personal items is typically split between items requiring limited access and those requiring more frequent access. A personal locker should be established for those items that require limited access. The personal locker can be a traditional school-type locker or a lockable filing space.

Employees will also require storage for personal items that they use on a regular basis (e.g., pens, paper, current files). If employees use multiple workspaces, it is appropriate to establish moveable storage files for these items. This will allow the employee to roll the cabinet to the workspace he or she will be using. These rolling cabinets need to be small and light enough to be easily moved from location to location. Another design consideration is the placement of the "parking lot" for these cabinets. It should be located such that the distance the employee needs to move the cabinet is minimal.

Common Filing and Storage

Groups and teams will require greater use of common storage than in traditional offices. In the traditional setting, most people have a complete set of files and supplies, with limited use of common filing and storage. The new ASA concept involves minimizing the amount of personal filing and storage and increasing the use of common files. This will require a greater use of cabinets for group storage. These cabinets will likely be spread throughout the work area to minimize the distance employees need to travel to the common files.

This distributed concept of common storage should also contain reference materials that typically exist at each workstation. This will include items such as software reference manuals, procedure manuals, and dictionaries. Organizations can also reduce their physical filing requirements by utilizing a greater degree of electronic storage. This solution not only reduces the floor area required to store files but also makes the files available electronically for any location, including from home.

Mailing Areas

It is critical to establish a single mail pickup area, given that employees may not have assigned workspaces. This area will include mail slots for each employee. The mail slots should be located near the entrance to make it convenient for people to pick up mail when entering the facility. Mail dropoff areas (one of which may be integrated with the pickup area) should be located centrally to minimize the distance an employee needs to get to one.

Equipment Galley

Support equipment such as fax machines, photocopiers, and shredders should be grouped together into a common equipment area. This area should be away from the high concentration task settings to minimize disruption. The area should also be designed to support casual interaction between employees.

Lounge and Other Casual Spaces

Lounge areas are usually soft-seating-type areas for casual meetings. In most traditional offices, the only area similar to this is the front reception. The goal of the lounge is to provide an environment for casual meetings, interacting with others, and relaxing. The new work environment does not punish someone for wanting to work in a more casual setting, particularly since many effective meetings can be held in these settings.

These casual spaces could include small alcoves for impromptu "hallway meetings." A few organizations are now creating spaces where an elbow-high ledge is structured against the wall with a few bar stools and a white board. This type of space does not take up a lot of room but provides an excellent casual space for a meeting.

Another example of casual space is to create spaces with casual seating arrangements. This might be a space with soft couches and chairs, an outdoor space with a picnic table, or any other arrangement that will encourage people to interact. Some organizations have taken these casual spaces to more of an extreme by creating meditation spaces with radical seating (e.g., beanbag chairs, Adirondack chairs, wooden gliders) and soothing music, or recreational spaces with pool tables in order to stimulate employee interaction.

Library

The library space is designed as a quiet area for storing manuals, trade publications, general periodicals, and books that are specific to the function of the group. The library is seen as a quiet place where an employee may go to read, research, or perform other solitary work.

Food Spaces

The food space recognizes that people socialize and discuss business issues in environments such as restaurants, coffee bars, and so forth. The goal of the food space should be to create an attractive, appealingly lit area that will encourage employees to interact within the space. The food area could be designed with table and chairs for casual meetings, with a bar and bar stools for impromptu meetings, with whiteboards for discussion, and most importantly with quality food products that will attract the employees to the space.

Some organizations are installing high-quality café spaces. These spaces include bar level seating, traditional café tables, and some soft seating. The space is usually near the windows, so it is a nice environment to visit. The café bar and tables are all wired for telephone and data connections so that anyone visiting the office can use this space to get a bit of work done.

Meeting Rooms

All office environments require meeting spaces. When ASA concepts are applied, the need for meeting space will likely increase. The organization will need a variety of meeting spaces including

- Small meeting rooms (100 ft^2) to accommodate up to 4 people
- Medium-sized meeting rooms (180–225 ft^2) to accommodate 5 10 people
- Large meeting rooms (250–300 ft^2) to accommodate 11 16 people

ASA Components: Task-Oriented Space

Task-oriented space represents the areas where users will perform their typical "desk" tasks. These spaces include a broad range of quiet concentrated space to open library carrel-type space. The following are a few examples of this type of space.

Retreat Space

The retreat space is typically a small workspace (approximately 64 ft²) designed for focused, solo work (Figure 4-3). The users include those who need quiet space for their heads-down desk work. The workstation includes a PC, telephone, and space for one person.

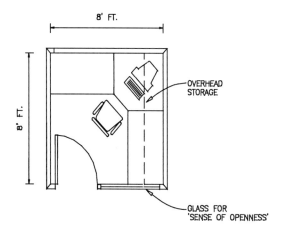

Figure 4-3 Concentrated retreat space.

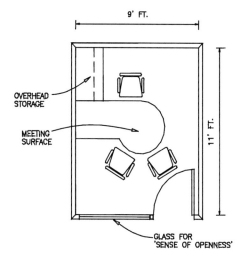

Figure 4-4 Concentrated meeting space.

Concentrated Meeting Space

The concentrated meeting space is designed to accommodate focused work that requires small, ad hoc meetings—which are not practical to book in advance. The space is approximately 100 ft^2 and includes a PC, telephone, work surface for concentrated activities, and a small meeting table (or desk extension) with two guest chairs (Figure 4-4).

Manager/Meeting Office

The manager office/meeting room relies on the concept of using one physical space for two purposes. One part of the office is designed as a typical workspace with a work surface, personal computer, telephone, and chair. The other part of the office is a meeting space with a small-meeting table and three chairs (Figure 4-5, left). When the manager is not using the office, a partition can be pulled across the space to separate the working area from the meeting area, thus allowing a meeting to occur in the space without disturbing the privacy of the vacant work area (Figure 4-5, right).

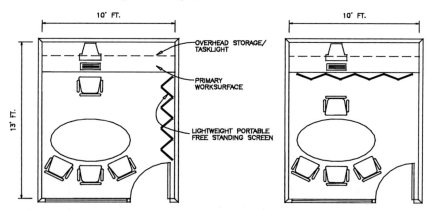

Figure 4-5 Manager's office/meeting room set up for manager (left) and meeting (right).

Phone Booth

A phone booth is an extremely small, approximately 24 ft^2 (4 × 6 ft) space that is used for making and receiving phone calls. This space is particularly useful for calls that require a high degree of concentration or are confidential. The phone booth space includes a telephone and room to plug in a notebook computer (Figure 4-6). The organization may want to include a few slightly larger phone booths to more comfortably accommodate wheelchairs.

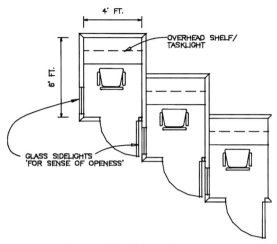

Figure 4-6 Phone booths.

Activity Setting

An activity-setting space is designed and equipped for a specific activity. For example, a drawing review station might be set up with a drafting table for laying out large drawings. This space can be shared by a number of users, as most people will not need to be at this type of specialty space every day of the week. The size of this space will vary based on the equipment required.

Open Office

The open office is a workspace that is open to other workspaces. The open office includes a work surface, personal computer, telephone, and desk chair. The open office space may or may not use partitions.

Carrels

The carrel concept is similar to that used by libraries. The concept is to provide a small space for an employee to plug in his or her notebook computer and to access a telephone. The carrel space is wired to the network and has task lighting built into the carrel. Typically, four carrels are accommodated in approximately 60 ft^2 (Figure 4-7).

The carrel concept is now appearing in many public places such as airport departure lounges, bus stations, and even on trains and ferries. The broad use of this design concept should make it easier for employees to become familiar with the concepts.

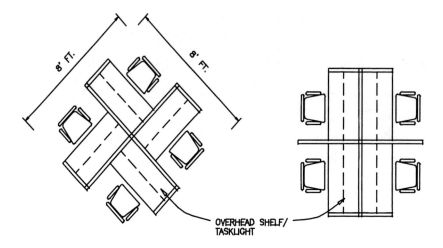

OVERHEAD SHELF/
TASKLIGHT

Figure 4-7   Carrels.

ASA Groupings

The previous section provided examples of ASA components. These components can be grouped together to provide some interesting solutions. This section includes a few examples of how these solutions can be implemented.

Team Space

The team space defines the area dedicated to a particular team of users. The team space usually includes personal storage areas, a common filing area, quiet meeting space, concentrated workspace, open offices, and a common casual area.

Team space is used by work teams. This space must be designed to support communications and interaction among team members. The teaming space usually includes heavy use of open space with furniture that can be easily moved to create activity settings that work for the team. These activity settings can last any length of time and the furniture is easily moved to create new spaces. Liberal use of whiteboards (fixed and mobile) is also a common characteristic.

Figure 4-8 shows a generic example of a team space. In this floor plan, the workstations are not separated by screens; instead the entire team space is open, allowing staff to easily communicate with each other without having to get out of their chairs. The middle of the space is a grouping of movable tables that can be used for team meetings or restructured for any other purpose. The space also includes a phone booth space that can be used for privacy and quiet

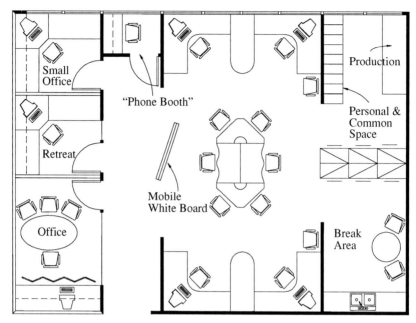

Figure 4-8 Small team space.

when making phone calls as well as two retreat offices for quiet, heads-down work. The space also has a mobile white board for impromptu meetings, allowing the white board to be moved to any spot in the team space.

The team space shown is a very simplistic example of how employees can be structured into a specific area. In most organizations, the teaming space will be larger and therefore the sharing of the manager/meeting, retreat, and phone booth spaces becomes more economical. Figure 4-9 shows a larger team space with an internal meeting table and common files.

The In Focus Systems Inc. team environment discussed earlier in this chapter used Steelcase's personal harbors to create a team space that Steelcase refers to as its "caves and commons" approach. Figure 4-10 shows an example of this type of arrangement. The caves and commons approach is best suited to highly collaborative teams that will work either from the large teaming table in the middle of the space or from the separate personal harbors. Each personal harbor takes up a 45 ft² and has a cylindrical door that provides a high level of visual and acoustical privacy.

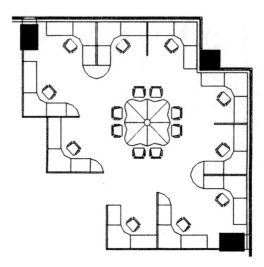

Figure 4-9   Larger team space.

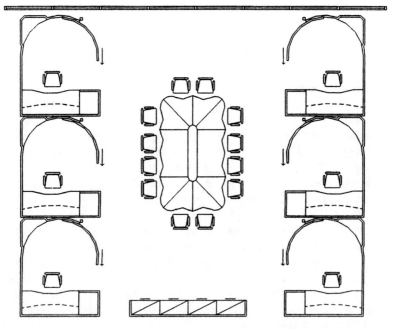

Figure 4-10   Caves and commons approach.

Group Address

Group address defines an area dedicated to a specific group. This will likely include a wide range of space components. The use of the space is determined by the group, though the furniture provided is likely not as portable as that in the team suite.

Free Address

Free address represents space that is available to any user in the department. This space is available only on a first-come, first-served basis, with no guarantee of the type of space the employee will receive. The free address concept is best for those who cannot schedule when they will be in the office.

Engaging Space

An important element of ASA concepts, and of work transformation in general, is sharing of space. Often, a challenge of sharing space is finding a space. The most common ways to secure a space are through making a reservation (hoteling) or on a first-come, first-served basis (moteling).

Hoteling

Hoteling is the concept of being able to call ahead to reserve a specific workspace. The term hoteling is commonly used, as the process is similar to reserving a room at a hotel. Some business procedures need to be established to accommodate the reservations. This can include a computerized reservation system, the use of e-mail scheduling tools, or a paper-based system (sign-up sheet). Many organizations that use hoteling also establish a concierge function to ensure that the workstation is equipped with all the features the user has requested. Hoteling works best for individuals who can accurately forecast when they will be in the regular office.

Moteling

Moteling is the concept of using space on a first-come, first-served basis. The term moteling is used, as the process is similar to pulling in to the next available motel with a vacancy. There are no business procedures necessary to implement moteling. Moteling works best for individuals who cannot accurately forecast when they will be in the regular office.

Identifying Who's Where

A common challenge for those who work within an alternate work environment is determining where specific individuals are located. In the traditional office, this is fairly easy, as each individual has a specifically assigned work-space, often with the persons name on the entrance. However, when ASAs are used, individuals could be anywhere in the office—or even outside of the office.

There are a few options available for solving the problem of locating individual workers. The key is to have the group involved in selecting the option they wish to use. It is critical to get good group participation, as they will be the ones who will have to make the system work. The following are a few strategies that can be considered.

Room Identification System

There are computer systems available that will track who is where and make this information available to anyone on the network. These systems can work by having users log in to the system and register their presence or through an electronic badge that could be used at each workstationIf this approach is to work effectively, then a personal computer needs to be available at the entry point of the office location to assist visitors in finding the individual they are seeking.

Telephone

Each user of the space will have a unique phone number that will follow the person to the workspace they have chosen. One way of finding a particular employee is to have a courtesy phone available at the entry point of the office for use by visitors, who can phone the individual they are looking for. That individual can then come and greet the visitor or provide directions to the current workspace.

Bulletin Board

The most common approach used by organizations is to have a bulletin board at the office entry point to notify visitors and fellow workers of workspace assignments. The bulletin board should include a list of the employee names and the office number(s) in which they will be located that day. Immediately beside the list of names must be a map of the work area that identifies the workspaces by number. For offices that routinely will be receiving visitors, it is helpful if each workspace is identified with a number plate.

Alternative Space Arrangement Design Consideration

The following are some of the common challenges to consider when designing ASAs.

User Support

The key to successfully designing ASA solutions is to gain support from those who will be working in the space. Because ASA concepts represent a significant change from the traditional definitions of space, it is critical to involve the end users in the process of designing the new space. Remember, the space is theirs; it has to work for them. So include them in the process.

The design team also needs to also consider the degree of change associated with ASAs. The users need to recognize the changes and communicate the changes within their group. The design team should facilitate some of the early communications by providing the entire group with information on ASAs and their benefits, and the process the group will be undergoing.

Ergonomics

A safe and productive work area is mandatory for every design. When space is shared by multiple users, the issue of adjustability and ergonomics becomes critical. Shared spaces will require that some work surfaces be easily adjustable by the end user. In addition, all desk chairs and task lighting must be adjustable to accommodate sharing.

Portability

Many designers want to put furniture in a particular place more or less permanently and have it moved only by professionals. When designing ASA solutions, it is important to remember that some furniture needs to be portable, allowing the users to move it to meet their specific requirements.

Technology

The technology used by the group must also be portable. If workstations are being shared, then it is best to have employees with notebook computers. This strategy attaches the technology to the person and not to the physical space, making it easier for the individual to work from any location. This degree of portability means that the workstations must have network connections that are easily connected to the users notebook computer. (Typically, this is done through the use of some type of docking station. See Chapter 5 [pp. 107–108] for details on notebook computers and docking stations.) In making this decision, the organization must also take into consideration that notebook computers are more costly then desktop machines. The extra portability comes at a cost that must be offset by a benefit. In the case of mobile workers who have been using a desktop machine at their assigned workstation and a notebook for the road, the cost of technology will *drop* as these workers will now not need the desktop machines; they can use their notebooks for in the office as well as on the road.

The technology must also support the telephone requirements in a shared-space environment. Users will have an assigned phone number so that the telephone will ring at the workstation in which they are located. This "follow-me" phone strategy must be implemented to make the space acceptable to the users.

People-to-Workspace Ratios

The designer must identify an appropriate ratio of people to workspace that will provide everyone expected to be in the office with an appropriate place to work. The ratio can be targeted to the average number of people expected; a larger-than-average number expected; or a less-than-average number. The less-than-average approach is clearly more aggressive than the others and assumes that people can use spaces other than individual workspaces during high occupancy times. The designer will need to work with management to determine how aggressive the space sharing strategy should be.

The common rules of thumb that I use for people-to-workspace ratios are as follows:

- 2.5–3.0:1 for mobile workers
- 1.7–2.0:1 for teleworkers

Functional Workseat for Everyone

The concept of sharing space means that there will not be an office for every employee in the group. However, the ASA design should plan for providing at least a functional workseat for everyone if everyone happens to be in the office at the same time. A workseat is defined as a chair with a phone and notebook network connection. This can be in the casual seating areas, carrels, phone booths, and so forth.

DESIGNING OFF-PREMISES SOLUTIONS

The design of off-premises ASA solutions involves considering solutions that are outside of the regular workspace. This includes guest offices, telework centers, home offices, and mobile offices. These type of spaces are usually not considered when designing traditional offices but are critical for supporting ASA designs.

Guest Officing Design

The concept of a guest office is that an employee has a workspace in another office facility that is remote from the regular office. The most common implementation of this occurs when an employee is working on a project with another department or organization. The employee may be required to be on site at the other location full-time for an extended period of time. In this scenario, a temporary office will be allocated based on the need of the individual.

The guest office should be designed to contain the basic elements required to perform the job. Some of the design components described for the on-premises options may be most appropriate for the guest office.

The guest office should not be treated as a "permanent" home, as the employee will have a home base elsewhere. The employee's workspace in the regular work area should be either shared by others or allocated to someone else until the employee returns. The design of the regular office should also provide some drop-in space for when the employee returns for meetings and the like.

Telework Center Design

Telework centers (also referred to as satellite offices or neighborhood offices) represent a group of workstations located in a remote facility. These stations are used part-time (two to three days per week) by employees who live in the neighborhood of the telework center. These employees spend the rest of their week working out of the regular office.

The telework center contains a variety of concentrated workstations, as the majority of the work performed will be heads-down desk work. The space in a telework center is typically reserved ahead of time by the teleworkers.

Telework centers are usually either a corporate-owned or shared facility. The corporate facility is used exclusively by one organization; a shared facility is used by several organizations. The shared facility requires more effort to ensure that the broad range of tenant requirements can be accommodated. A decision-making process must also be developed to prevent or resolve any competitive conflict, security, or confidential issues among the participating organizations.

The biggest issue in developing a telework center is determining where it should be located. The goal should be to locate it close to where employees live. Ideally, employees can reach it by alternative transportation modes (on foot, by bicycle, or by public transportation), thereby significantly reducing the time, energy, and expense of commuting.

The best starting point in determining the location of a telework center is to analyze where employees live. This can be done by analyzing the organization's employee database by postal or zip code. In selecting the location(s), the organization should ensure that a reasonable amount of travel will be eliminated. In other words, if the regular office is in the downtown core, then establishing a telework center two miles away from the regular office will provide only a minimal benefit to employees. However, if the telework center is 15 miles (25 kilometers) away from downtown and closer to where a high proportion of potential teleworkers live, then the savings in commute time will be significant.

Once the district has been identified, it is necessary to find a facility. The first step in this process should be to look internally and determine if the organization has any facilities in the district. For example, if the organization is the head office of a grocery chain, perhaps there is a grocery store in the district where a number of head office employees live. If so, maybe a portion of the facility could be converted into a telework center. This may seem odd at first. However, the organization likely already either owns the property or leases it long term. The incremental cost of adding a telework center to the facility will likely be less than buying or leasing a new space.

The concept of ASAs encourages new and creative ways of looking at space. A telework center does not even need to be in a traditional office complex. It could be in a shopping mall, a small strip mall, or landmark building (a common strategy in parts of Australia, where such buildings are called heritage homes).

For example, the British Columbia Buildings Corporation and the BC Systems Corporation established a joint telework center outside of Victoria, British Columbia, in 1992. This telework center was placed into a small commercial strip mall, replacing a carpet store that had occupied the space. The location was on the main transit route and was in easy biking or walking distance for several of the participants. It should be noted that the other retail merchants in this mall were extremely skeptical about the telework center. Their prime concern related to the potential loss of business from losing a retail merchant. The end result, however, was that the remaining merchants enjoyed a slight increase in business, as the teleworkers shopped at their stores during the days they were working at the telework center. More importantly, these same teleworkers rediscovered the shops in their own neighborhood and starting doing the majority of their shopping locally rather than downtown.

The telework center should be primarily designed for heads-down work. Figure 4-12 shows a generic design of a telework center. The example does not include an area for administrative support or a reception area, as these functions typically are not needed in a telework center. Also, the space is organized as traditional cubicles, as it would only be on rare occasions that team members would be working together out of the same telework center.

A study by Cornell University found that telework centers work well for employees and employers. The main problem was "the failure to conceptualize

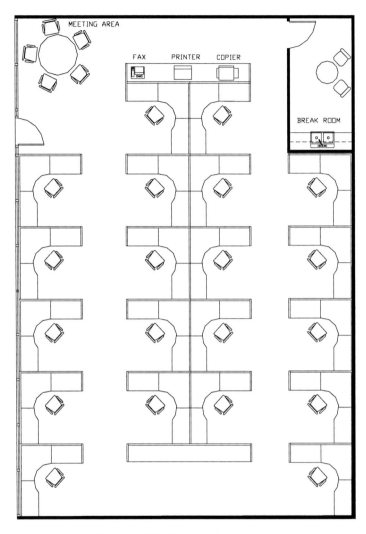

Figure 4-12 Telework center.

telework centers from their inception as a new form of work that has the potential to combine cost savings with productive and effective workers."[12]

The Cornell study also concluded that many telework centers have been primarily viewed as a solution to problems associated with traffic congestion and air pollution or as a way to demonstrate the value of new telecommunications technologies. In themselves, these goals are unlikely to generate enthusiasm or commitment on the part of executives. The key to success with the telework center, like all other forms of alternative officing, is to ensure that their implementation is based on firm business benefits.

An example of a telework center focused on business results is the MCI Rally Center in Boston, MA. MCI opened this first rally center in January 1996 with the goal of supporting its mobile work force while also cutting costs.

The starting point for the center was the automation of over 5000 sales and service employees with portable technology. The redesign of the traditional office environment accommodated these mobile workers by establishing a nonterritorial workspace.

The MCI office in Boston is 24,500 ft^2 (35% less than the previous office) and is designed to accommodate 138 mobile workers and 25 dedicated employees (manager, administrative staff, etc.). The space includes a hearth area, which, like a living room in a home, is the center of the office, and moveable seating for small to large meetings; a café space that has power, data, and voice capabilities at all bar and table locations; a viewing area for standard and broadcast video; a resource center with sales and support literature; and a supply area for mail and office supplies.

A mobile worker's typical day at the rally center starts by stopping at the "home base," where lockers are available for all mobile workers. Each locker contains a rolling file cart that can be used to move the employee's personal items to any workstation. Employees have the choice of working in open team spaces, the quieter heads-down area, any of the common areas, a large range of meeting rooms, or the "cone of silence" rooms, which provide the maximum level of privacy.

Architect Ethan Anthony, Vice President of Hoyle, Doran and Berry Inc., who designed the rally center, explains:

> The key was to design the office so that it would not become obsolete by the changes happening internally at MCI. We've been working with MCI for 10 years. It is such a fast-paced [company] that before our design was even built, something within MCI—like team arrangements—had already changed and the office no longer met the company's needs. We had to come up with a plan that was more adaptable to constant change.[13]

The MCI telework center is an excellent example of totally rethinking the way office space is designed, and it reflects the need to adapt to constant change—something applicable to most organizations. The key to success is to be flexible.

HOME OFFICE DESIGN

Organizations that offer employees AWAs likely have some employees who are teleworking. These employees spend part of their week (typically two to three days) working from home and the remainder of the week working in the regular office. Some organizations also use work-at-home employees, who spend their entire week working from their homes.

Designing a home work space is a challenging task. The key considerations should be the location, size, furniture, layout, and environmental considerations.

Location

The home workspace should be separated both physically and psychologically from the living space of the home. The teleworker should have a designated workspace that is used only for work. It should have a door that can be closed during working hours to keep unwelcome visitors out—and after working hours to keep the teleworker out.

The ideal location for the home office is near the front door. This setup is most appropriate for those individuals who have clients seeing them at home, or who have a regular courier service dropping off and collecting work items. In situations where a separate room is not available, the teleworker should consider establishing some form of temporary boundaries—screens or furniture—that are kept in place during working hours.

The teleworker should also consider locating the work space to minimize visual and auditory distractions. For example, locating the home office so that it faces a busy street may not help productivity. Teleworkers who need to concentrate should keep away from the noisy areas of the house. The workspace should also be designed so that it is not easily accessible by other family members. Dr. Penny Gurstein, an architect and Professor at the University of British Columbia, has extensively studied architectural implications of home-based workers. In her 1990 doctoral thesis on the topic, she recommends that the ideal situation is a workspace with a private outside entrance and is not accessible from inside the house.[14] Gurstein's concept, however, is probably not possible for most teleworkers without extensive renovations.

According to Brad Schepp, who has studied teleworkers, the two least desirable locations are in the teleworker's bedroom or in the family room.[15] The bedroom is the most inappropriate location, as the teleworker would be in the same room for the majority of the day. The family room is usually the primary room in the dwelling for relaxing. Teleworkers who use their family room as their home office may find that, at the end of the day, it is impossible to relax in the room if they are in constant visual contact with their work.

Size

The size of the home office should depend on the type of work performed and the amount of equipment and storage required. If teleworkers expect to have clients visiting them at their homes (something that is discouraged by most organizations), they will need enough space to accommodate guest chairs. Teleworkers who require a lot of storage space for files and supplies will also require additional space.

The minimum space for a telecommuter should be 64 ft^2, with the preferred size being 80–120 ft^2. In some municipalities, the size of the home office may be restricted by land use regulations. Teleworkers need to check with the local municipal government to determine if they require a "home occupation permit" in order to telework from home and to check on any zoning bylaw restrictions. If a permit is required, there will likely be restrictions on how large the home office space can be, the type of activities that can take place in the home office space, and the type of alterations allowable to the exterior of the building.

Furniture

The furniture for the home office should be adequate to hold the equipment to be used, while still leaving enough desktop space for other activities. Ergonomic furniture should be used wherever possible for both comfort and productivity. Teleworkers should ensure that their desk has enough space for the screen, a tray mounted under the desk for a keyboard (for notebook users, it is ergonomically best to have a separate keyboard), and the notebook computer.

Teleworkers should also consider their storage requirements. Many teleworkers find that they need a small filing cabinet to hold files and supplies. Some organizations may even insist that their teleworkers have lockable, fireproof file cabinets to ensure that valuable company files are not lost, stolen, or destroyed by fire.

In recent years, the major furniture manufacturers have recognized the need to provide solutions to the home office marketplace. In addition, most furniture, office supply and home-renovation stores now sell some type of home office furniture. Organizations with full-time teleworkers should seriously consider acquiring proper ergonomic furniture for their home-based employees. Most of the vendors have developed a broad range of home office furnishing that will fit into the decor of most homes.

Layout

The home office should be organized such that the teleworker can move easily about the workspace. A cluttered, disorganized layout will result in lost productivity and raise safety issues. The home office layout should meet the basic safety guidelines of the Occupational Safety and Health Administration (USA) or the local Workers Compensation Board (Canada).

Environmental Considerations

The teleworker must be concerned about the environment of the home office: the lighting; power supply; and heating/cooling.

When one is determining the lighting requirements of the home office, the amount of natural light should be considered. Natural light is a definite bonus to the workspace but can also be a major source of glare on computer screens. It is important to ensure that the combination of natural and artificial light will not cause glare on the computer screen or eyestrain when performing regular desk work (not on the PC).

Consideration must also be given to the power supply in the home office. Home offices that are using personal computers, facsimile machines, photocopiers, and laser printers may find that they have a problem if all of this equipment is on the same circuit as other household appliances. Some telecommuters, finding that their home office does not have enough electrical receptacles, may resort to the use of extension cords and power bars. This may overload the power circuit and could represent a fire hazard. In areas where power spikes are common, the telecommuter will want to consider the use of surge protectors or uninterrupted power supplies (UPS) for their computer equipment.

Heating and cooling is also a significant concern. The telecommuter must be able to keep the home office at a comfortable temperature year round.

MOBILE OFFICE DESIGN

Mobile workers are rarely in the regular office, as they work from multiple locations. They essentially work out of their vehicle and/or their briefcase. Most of these workers will have some type of home base where they go to perform their desk work. This home base may be the employee's home, a telework center, or the regular office.

Many organizations completely ignore the mobile office, judging that the mobile worker has all of the basic technology required and will use whatever facilities are available, wherever they happened to be. This approach is definitely inadequate with the growing productivity demands placed on workers and the health and safety concerns associated with inadequate workplaces. The organization must ensure that the mobile workers have the right portable technology to do their job, even if this technology is outside the typical "office standards" (e.g., use of pen-based technologies, personal digital assistants, cellular phones, PCS phones).

Mobile workers who spend a large portion of their time in their cars can benefit from vehicle accessories that will create a more comfortable and safer work environment in the vehicle. For example, MO-V (Mobile Office Vehicle) Co. has developed the AutoExec™, which it describes as a "workspace" for the front seat of your car.[16] It is a writing surface, storage area ,and supplies organizer. Featuring a non-skid writing surface and a pull-out writing area to provide a larger work surface, it is kept in place with the passenger seat belt. MO-V also produces the WheelMate™, which gives the mobile worker another working surface and can be attached to the steering wheel (presumably for use only when parked!).

Consideration should also be given to the home base for these mobile workers. The home base will be the location at which mobile workers, at some during the day or week, complete basic administrative work. This home base could be the employee's home, the regular office, or a telework center.

Another option for the home base for mobile workers can be a distributed virtual office service. The leader in this area in North America has been Kinko's. When Paul Orfalea created Kinko's, he realized that there was a significant market opportunity for providing solutions to the changing business world. Orfalea wanted organizations to see Kinko's as an extension of the organizations office. Today, Kinko's, which operates 24 hours a day, 7 days a week, offers a wide range of products and services that assist mobile workers, home-based workers, and traditional office workers. These services include all the traditional copy-related services as well as self-service personal computers, videoconferencing, office rental, computer services, and modem connections. In essence, a traveling salesperson could be covering a wide territory and yet have an office to stop in at in any city where Kinko's has a location.[17]

Impact on On-Premises Design

In all cases, remote workers will be coming back into the regular office on some timetable. Teleworkers will be in the regular office on a part-time basis every week, mobile workers may be in once a week if their home base is in the regular office, and work-at-home employees will likely be in the office once or twice per month.

It is important to identify these remote workers and to determine when they will be in the regular office and what they will be doing when they come in. The type of space they require will likely be quite different from the traditional space provided today.

REAL ESTATE CONSIDERATIONS

One of the goals of ASAs is to reduce the organization's overall real estate investment. The concepts of shared offices, mobile working, and teleworking all collectively help to reduce the overall requirement for office space. The challenge that many organizations have is actually realizing these cost savings.

The first problem to overcome is to ensure that the organization has enough employees using the work transformation concepts. If the organization has 1000 employees and only 10 employees are working remotely, then it is highly unlikely that the organization will be able to realize the overall cost savings from space savings. To gain a critical mass, most organizations need to create a scenario where at least 5–10% of the overall population of office workers are able to work remotely and therefore share space. Under these circumstances, enough space can be recaptured and released.

Let us assume that the organization has been able to implement the work transformation concepts with a large number of employees. The net effect has been the reduction in floor space required by several departments. The challenge now is to turn this vacant space into a financial benefit.

The first step is to analyze where the now vacant space resides. It is likely that this space is spread throughout the facility. If the distributed space is too small to sell, lease, or sublet, then the facilities group will have to "restack" the facility to place all of the available space into a contiguous segment.

Many organizations that are renting space feel that they can turn empty space into a financial benefit only when their lease expires. This may be the case in some truly locked-in leases. However, in most cases, the organization can sublet the space. The key to success is to involve a commercial real estate professional who is familiar with the marketplace for office space in the size range the organization has available.

Some larger organizations have built buildings in which they are the sole tenant. In these situations, the implementation of ASAs will reduce the real estate costs only if the organization is able to release other leases in the same city to move employees into the now-available space or if the organization is prepared to open up the office building to accommodate additional tenants. The security issues associated with the latter alternative need to be weighed very carefully.

Mahlon Apgar IV, formerly a partner with McKinsey & Company and now President of Apgar and Company, a corporate real estate counseling firm, has written extensively on the topic of getting better value from the organization's real estate investment. Apgar suggests that

The tradition of central locations, high-rise, often grandiose buildings and private, enclosed office space that shaped the expectations of past generations of managers and reached its zenith in the 1980s is giving way to innovations that are both less costly and more productive: the virtual office; hub and spoke office networks; and the office hotel to name a few.[18]

Apgar suggests that organizations analyze its occupancy costs by first comparing the growth of revenues and other operating costs to the growth in office space and cost per square foot and to develop an occupancy cost-to-revenue benchmark for the future. He also suggests developing a lease-aging profile that shows the future real estate commitments and the potential to change them. Again, flexibility is the key to ensuring that the organization can adjust to future changes.

Apgar has also developed guidelines for gaining the maximum value from the organization's real estate investment. The following are his ten key guidelines as reported in the *Harvard Business Review* in November 1995:[19]

1. Real estate supports corporate strategy by leveraging locations, layouts and leases to reduce costs, increase flexibility, and improve productivity.
2. Managers develop occupancy strategies and objectives by evaluating the company's competitive situation as well as by analyzing internal operations and corporate culture.
3. The company uses objective, complete information to reveal portfolio opportunities, help formulate regional plans, and decide among location, layout and leasing options.
4. Cost–benefit analysis begins with the business decision, not with the real estate decision; managers understand that the company's needs will change during a facility's life.
5. For affordability-driven decisions about occupancy strategy and cost control, affordability is determined by considering a business unit's profit structure and competitive situation—not by conforming to market and industry standards.
6. Managing space demand is the main lever in sustaining affordable costs once the company has reduced its space supply and has begun to use facilities more efficiently.
7. The company uses a zero-base analysis of space needs and costs to challenge standards that are set by industry benchmarks and best-practice examples.
8. Workspace is allocated when and where it is needed, instead of being assigned by entitlement.

9. Employees are involved in planning alternative, more affordable work space; the greater their stake in its benefits, the more willing they will be to accept such changes.

10. Facilities are designed with generic and adaptable featuressuch as modular engineering and systems furnitureto maximize interior flexibility and sale of subleasing potential.

Many of Apgar's guidelines directly support the concepts described in this book. The main points are to ensure that

- The real estate decisions support the business strategy.
- Space demand is effectively managed.
- Space is allocated where and when needed
- Employees are involved in the process
- Flexibility is maximized

Apgar's guidelines are echoed by Robert E. Weissman, chairman and CEO of Dun & Bradstreet. Weissman explains

> In the past, our real estate was configured to support a series of silo businesses—not corporate goals. It also impeded our ability to communicate across businesses. Those internal factors, combined with D&B's status as a large, complex public company, gave us an overhead burden that some of our single-focus competitors don't have a serious competitive disadvantage. We were diverting dollars from customer value to real estate expense. Now were removing the source of those costs and using our real-estate portfolio to push speed-to-market and competitiveness.[20]

James McKellar, Associate Dean, External, at the Schulich School of Business, York University, and Director of the Program in Real Property, describes space as a firm's second most expensive resource after people. The pressure to reduce office space consumption is coming from the flattening of organizational structures, reduction of middle management, changing skills, outsourcing, information technology, and the penchant to cut overhead costs.

McKellar, who previously was Director of the Center for Real Estate at the Massachusetts Institute of Technology, explains that

> Forces of change within the economy are not just shaping tomorrow's world; they are reshaping the real estate industry of today. There is no greater evidence of the impact of change on this industry than the cloud that has been cast over its 20th Century icon—the downtown office building. There is widespread concern that the tide may be turning against a product that only reach its zenith less than ten years ago.

These concerns stem primarily from the economic restructuring on where we work and live.[21]

McKellar feels that

The opulence of the downtown high-rise built in the '80s may be incongruous with the culture of many of today's small, but successful firms. Signature designs by world-famous architects, marble lobbies complete with atriums and waterfalls, generous tenant improvements, large floor plates and grand plazas with sculpture courts are not what attracts firms in the '90s. Tenants today are comfortable with a casual dress code, as likely to place a ping-pong table in a meeting room as table and chairs, and more excited at the prospect of linking into a broadband communication system. These are workers willing to pay extra for air conditioning after 5 P.M. and on weekends, who need somewhere to eat at midnight, invariably need their car to call on customers and have no interest in a five-year lease.[22]

McKellar also feels that the real estate industry needs to rethink office buildings, suggesting that

The greatest threat to downtown lies with current building owners who find themselves with products created for another era, with marketing plans and lease arrangement geared to tenants that no longer exist, and with an attraction to bricks and mortar that no longer matters.[23]

In considering real estate issues, the facilities staff must decide if the organization is going to renovate the current space or move to a new facility. It is critical for the success of work transformation that the facilities group carefully analyze how the organization will implement the ASA concepts to determine the amount of space needed. It is important *not* to fall into the old trap of merely adding up the number of staff by rank and applying the organization's old space standards (the way many organizations have done for years).

Major factors in the decision to move or not will likely be the condition of the current facility and the extent of ASAs that the organization intends to implement. If radical corporate-wide changes are expected, then the facilities group must ensure that the current building can provide the level of flexibility required (in terms of architectural limitations, wiring potential, common building services/facilities, etc.).

The facilities group should also look at the entire real estate portfolio to look for creative ways to use existing space (e.g., the grocery store example on p. 90). If the organization plans to utilize telework centers, it will find that it is much more cost effective to utilize existing facilities than to lease or purchase new space. The real estate issues are usually critical to the success of the work transformation business case. It is critical to address these issues with the same commitment and energy that are used to address the design of the new space.

SUMMARY

The facilities management portion of work transformation is primarily about designing and implementing ASAs. There are a wide range of ASA concepts, from teaming spaces to full-time at-home offices. The most successful work transformation implementation concepts are those that include a range of all of these options.

To successfully implement ASAs, the facility's designers must thoroughly understand the components for both common areas and task-oriented workstations. The best design incorporates a wide range of solutions, allowing staff the choice of what environment will best support the work that they are doing. In some cases, such as with the nonterritorial office, this choice of work location can be made on a day-to-day basis, thus providing the ultimate in flexibility.

The implementation of ASAs also brings challenges. These include determining how to find people when they are constantly changing offices, how the technology will support the degree of flexibility required, and how to involve staff in the design process. These challenges can all be overcome by treating ASAs as a significant change, with the organization putting its best efforts into educating staff on the concepts and obtaining their input.

Alternative space arrangements can also include dealing with off-premises solutions such as telework centers, mobile work, home offices, and guest offices. Each of these brings its own challenges. Again, the facilities group needs to work with the cross-functional team to really understand the requirements and to develop potential solutions.

Finally, no discussion of work transformation would be complete without considering the real estate component. This element is absolutely critical to delivering the actual bottom-line benefits that management will be expecting.

NOTES

1. Johansen, Robert, and Swigart, Rob. *Upsizing the Individual in the Downsized Organization: Managing in the Wake of Reengineering, Globalization and Overwhelming Technological Change.* Reading, MA: Addison-Wesley, 1994, pp. 63–64.
2. Ibid.

3. Gordon, Gil. Speech at Telecommute '94, "The Well-Intentioned (But Slightly Misguided) Confusion of Means and Ends in Large Organizations Today," October 26, 1994, San Francisco, California.

4. The New Workplace, *Business Week*, April 29, 1996, pp. 106–117.

5. Ibid, p. 111.

6. Ibid, p. 112.

7. Ibid, p. 113.

8. Ibid, p. 113.

9. On Site Marketing, Haworth Inc., 1996.

10. Ibid.

11. Becker, Franklin, and Steele, Fritz. *Workplace by Design: Mapping the High-Performance Workscape*. Jossey-Bass, San Francisco, 1995, p. 73.

12. Telework Centers: An Evaluation of the North American and Japanese Experience. Cornell University International Workplace Studies Program, December 1993.

13. Wintroub-Calmsen, Diane. Stop-n-Go Workplace: MCI Dials Up the Office of the Future. *Interiors*, May, 1996, pp. 42–47.

14. Gurstein, Penelope C. Working at Home in the Live-In Office: Computers, Space, and the Social Life of Households. Ann Arbor, MI: UMI Dissertation Services, 1990, p. 176.

15. Schepp, Brad. The Telecommuter's Handbook: How to Work for a Salary Without Ever Leaving the House. New York: Pharos Books, 1990, p. 174.

16. Gordon, Gil. Working on the Road in Style and Comfort. Telecommuting Review, 13 (5), pp. 14–15.

17. Kinko's website: www.kinkos.com/main

18. Apgar, Mahlon IV. Uncovering Your Hidden Occupancy Costs. Harvard Business Review, May–June 1993, pp. 124–136.

19. Apgar, Mahlon IV. Managing Real Estate to Build Value. *Harvard Business Review*, Nov.–Dec 1995, pp. 162–179.

20. Ibid, p. 162.

21. McKellar, James. Suburbs Are Hot, Downtowns Are Not. *Business Quarterly*, Summer 1996, pp. 51–56.

22. Ibid.

23. Ibid.

5

Information Technology

Information technology (IT) is enabling organizations to implement work transformation. Today's technology is not as "mysterious" as it was in the past, and it can be used by most computer-literate individuals. In most cases, the technology needed to support work transformation is readily available and reasonably affordable.

Alternative work arrangements (AWAs) such as variable work hours, modified work weeks, and phased retirement do not require any additional IT. Their only impact on technology may be in terms of the hours of support that are provided. Those AWAs that involve working outside of the regular office will require an investment in IT. Similarly, the implementation of minor changes to space (i.e., teaming space) has little impact on technology. However, other alternative space arrangements (ASAs) such as space sharing, telework centers, and nonterritorial strategies have a significant impact on IT.

This chapter reviews the basic IT strategies required to support work transformation, the technology components commonly used today, and some of the technologies that are quickly emerging.

DEGREE OF CHANGE

There is a broad range of technologies that can be used to support the implementation of work transformation.

Figure 5-1 shows that the starting point for work transformation is the implementation of basic computer technology in terms of personal computers (PCs), local area networks (LANs), wide area networks (WANs), electronic

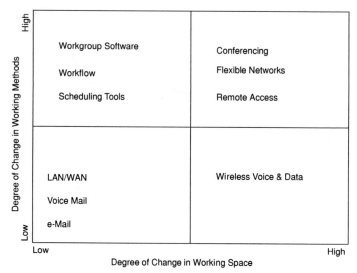

Figure 5-1 Positioning of enabling technologies in terms of change.

mail (e-mail) and voice mail. These enabling technologies are considered a fundamental starting point for work transformation. This is a fairly low-risk position for most organizations in the late 1990's. Organizations that do not have these technologies at minimum will likely find that they are severely restricted in their ability to support the work transformation concepts presented in this book.

The implementation of wireless voice and data solutions is critical to supporting mobile workers. These employees could be working from anywhere, so basic cellular or digital-based communications will be mandatory. The move to wireless *voice* communications for mobile workers is very common today. The move to wireless *data* communications for these same mobile workers is less common but must become a standard technology, offering to fully enable the mobile workers.

To support a greater shift in working methods, the technology group must begin to support workgroup software and scheduling tools. These software tools will support teams which are geographically distributed as well as make it easier to schedule meetings and resources in the work transformation environment. The implementation of these software tools is not a minor undertaking. The risk of failure with these tools is not as much in the area of technical expertise but more in the area of the business practices which use these tools. A good business analyst working with a strong technical person can help to overcome these implementation challenges.

The upper right-hand quadrant of Figure 5-1 represents the greatest change, highest risk, and best potential business return. The tools in this quadrant support the remote worker's interaction with the organization and more specifically with their teams. The use of video-, document-, and audio-conferencing is critical to effective communications among geographically distributed employees. The remote access technology is obviously critical for accessing the regular office to retrieve e-mail, run applications that are available only on the network, and exchange electronic files.

The upper right-hand quadrant also includes increased flexibility in networks. The implementation of nontraditional officing strategies will likely mean the broad-scale use of notebook computers, which will go with the employees and can be used from any physical workspace. This means that each workspace must be "network enabled." In other words, it should be possible for employees to choose a workstation, plug their notebook into the local area network, and arrange to have their personal telephone number ring at that workspace. This essential component of the work transformation program is a simple concept in theory but is more complicated in reality.

The best implementation strategy for work transformation is to operate in all four quadrants. The technology group must follow this lead and provide enabling technologies that will support all four of these quadrants.

INFORMATION TECHNOLOGY STRATEGIES TO SUPPORT WORK TRANSFORMATION

The implementation of work transformation requires the implementation of a series of supporting IT strategies. Prior to the work transformation concept, the technology for a traditional organization was reasonably straightforward. It included high-speed links to distributed or branch offices and perhaps accommodated the occasional after-hours user who would dial-up from their home. Figure 5-2 shows this traditional model.

Work transformation completely changes this old paradigm. The new paradigm has people working from all the traditional locations *plus* telework centers, their home (during prime time), their vehicle, other offices (clients, temporary accommodations, etc.), a hotel room, and so on. The new widespread *work anytime, anywhere* concept, often referred to as the virtual office, is illustrated in Figure 5-3.

The following key strategies should be addressed to successfully support work transformation.

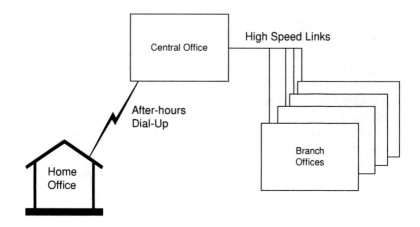

Figure 5-2   Traditional office voice/data communications.

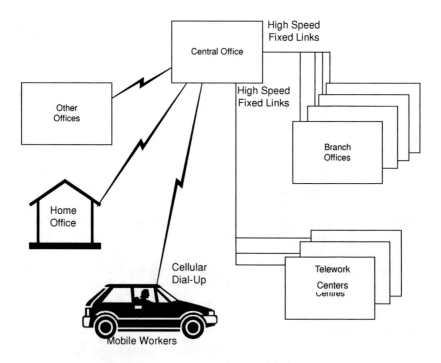

Figure 5-3   Virtual office configurations.

Personal Computers

One of the primary technology decisions in supporting work transformation is the strategy for personal computing. Nearly every white collar worker has a personal computer on his or her desk. For the average employee, these machines have become as standard as a telephone.

There is a wide range of personal computers available on the marketplace. It would be inappropriate to suggest which vendors are the best or what type/size of hardware should be chosen. Organizations should research this directly, keeping mind such basic issues as compatibility, for example, when purchasing notebooks and docking stations.

The issue that most technology managers have to come to grips with is how to provide the right machine to each employee at the right location. The use of traditional desktop models is usually the most cost effective for those employees who work in the office all week and tend to work from the same physical desk location. Employees who are working remotely or in full nonterritorial arrangements in the office are best equipped with notebook computers.

The notebook solution, in essence, attaches the technology to the employee rather than to the physical workspace. This approach allows the employee to work at any physical workspace merely by taking their notebook with them and "plugging" it into the local area network. The notebook is also an excellent solution for teleworkers, as they can take them home for telework days and then bring them back into the office on their regular office days.

Some of the mobile workers may not need the full power of a notebook computer. For some of these users, a personal digital assistant (PDA) might be more appropriate. These devices have only the functions needed by the user and are typically lighter and cheaper than a full notebook computer. Today many of the PDAs available also have capability for e-mail, which is becoming essential for all workers.

Hardware Components for Notebook Users

Remote workers will need a modem. The modem allows users to connect their personal computer to other computers and networks. Modems come in various sizes and types; the best solution is to buy the fastest, smallest, and easiest-to-use modem that the organization can afford. As modem speeds are increasing every year, employees with notebook computers will want to utilize modems which come on PCMCIA cards. These small cards, about the size of a credit card, slip into the notebook and have a jack for the telephone line. The cards are lightweight and will serve the purposes of both teleworkers and mobile workers.

Another component to consider is a network interface card (NIC). The NIC allows the user to "plug" a personal computer into the network at the regular office, telework center, or even possibly at a customer's office. Plugging into the network will allow the user to use shared devices (e.g., printers, plotters, and scanners) and to access or share files with others. Like the modem, the NIC can also be purchased as a PCMCIA card, which makes the modem more portable. This solution is ideal for those with notebook computers.

Some users of notebooks find the keyboards too constraining and the displays too small for some uses (e.g., large spreadsheets). Often, notebooks are adequate for occasional use but can become cumbersome when used for an extended period of several hours. In these cases, the organization should consider the use of more ergonomic external keyboards and external video monitors. Most notebooks have a jack in the back for attaching a full-sized keyboard. This approach is especially useful for those users who have to enter a significant amount of numeric data (most notebooks do not have a separate number pad).

Some users also prefer the use of a full-sized display. If the user is a heavy user of graphics software, CAD (computer-assisted design), or other applications that are image intensive, then an external display is appropriate. The cost of the displays is coming down but is still a significant investment. The organization may want to consider spending more on the notebook computer to upgrade the screen rather than acquiring a separate screen.

Another commonly used hardware component is referred to as a docking station. The docking station allows the user to take a notebook computer and attach it to the network, full-size screen, full-size keyboard and other peripherals by merely sliding the notebook into the docking station. This approach makes it very easy for the user to connect all of these items without having to play with the cables at the back of the notebook. Docking stations are a great invention for the worker in the new workplace. The challenge today is that no standards exist for docking stations, so if the organization wants to use a physical workspace that has a docking station that is not compatible with some employees' notebooks (because it is made by a different manufacturer), then these employees are out of luck.

Software Solutions

There is a broad range of software applications that support work transformation. The most powerful of these applications is that of workgroup, or collaborative computing. This is a category of computing that supports the activities of people working in groups to achieve a defined business purpose. This technology helps people work together more effectively to facilitate information sharing, organize information into actionable knowledge, and productively interact with others.

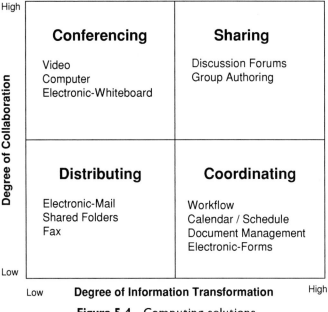

Figure 5-4 Computing solutions.

Figure 5-4 categorizes a few of the basic workgroup computing tools by the degree of collaboration and information transformation required.

These workgroup computing solutions are essential to supporting today's cross-functional teams, geographically dispersed teams, and employees who are working on multiple projects in multiple locations. Physically bringing team members together to support workgroup interaction is often difficult and usually very expensive.

Workgroup computing technology is now being used by organizations to address these challenges. The technology combined with adjustments to business processes can significantly improve the productivity and effectiveness of a work team.

Data Communications

Data communications is the name of the game for those employees who work remotely. Data communications is used to allow users to connect to their network and to share files to perform the same activities they would typically do from their full-time dedicated workspace in the regular office.

There are a tremendous number of data communications options available. The IT department will undoubtedly have an opinion on how the data communications should be provided. However, a word of caution is in order regarding the potential solutions. In the past, most IT departments supported dial-up data communications only on an after-hours, ad hoc basis. The level of service and support that might have been acceptable to these occasional, casual users would probably not be acceptable to those who need the service in "prime time" for critical job functions.

The starting point in establishing the data communications is to develop a remote access strategy. This strategy will apply to teleworkers and mobile workers who will be working from remote locations. There are several remote access options available. The following are a few of the common ones.

Remote Control

The oldest method of remote access is through the use of remote control software. These products allow a user to set up an office computer running the remote control software and then connect to it from home (or another off-site location) using the same software. The remote user can remotely control all the functions of the regular office computer from home. This way the user is able to access all the data and applications on the regular office computer and the network to which it is attached.

There are several drawbacks to this solution. The first and most important is that this software requires a dedicated personal computer (PC) at the central office to run at the same time as the remote user's. Typically this remote control is established by connecting to the PC on the employee's regular office desk. This arrangement certainly negates the potential for space sharing, as the computer at the workstation is being used by the remote worker. Remote control solutions are also prone to security problems and response time concerns.

On the positive side, the remote control solution is relatively inexpensive and represents a reasonable solution in either small organizations or those where only a few (1–10) users are working remotely.

Application Servers

Another group of products available for remote access is referred to as application servers. Application servers distribute program execution and operation among multiple computers in a network. They form part of the "client/server" computing environment commonly referred to as distributed presentation management (DPM). Under a system employing DPM, application execution occurs on the application server, while only compressed screen images are displayed on the "intelligent" client workstations.

Application servers provide Windows-based users the opportunity to access remote data and applications while enjoying better response time than using remote control software. The application server solution is good for small to medium-sized organizations, with 10–20 remote workers.

Remote Access Gateway

The best solution to accessing the network remotely is through the use of a remote access gateway. This solution allows users to connect directly to their local area network (LAN) through a common network gateway. The remote access gateway is typically a more expensive solution than the remote control or application servers but does hold the greatest level of security and speed of the three.

Remote access gateways are becoming more common in organizations as more remote workers are added (best when there are more than 20 users).

As noted previously, modems are the key to data communications. There are basically two choices available in communications protocols. The first choice is to use analog data communications to access the organization's network using traditional modems—typically at lower speeds. The second option is to use higher speed digital methods. The most common digital method is the use of ISDN, which is explained on pp. 126–128. Figure 5-5 shows the typical data communications set up for the home-based teleworker.

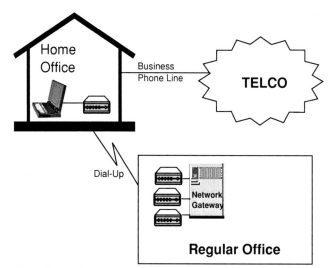

Figure 5-5 Typical data communications for home-based teleworker.

Voice Communications

Whereas data communications enable the remote worker to electronically connect to their regular office location, voice communications are equally critical to the success of any remote work program by allowing the remote worker to talk to other employees, customers, vendors, and so forth.

The key to the voice communications strategy is to make it seamless. In other words, when someone phones the employee at the regular office number, it should automatically ring to whatever location at which the employee is working. This involves the use of a few basic telephone company features such as call forwarding and voice mail.

Call forwarding allows the remote user to call-forward their regular phone to their remote location. The forwarding will be transparent to the caller, who will reach the employee regardless of location. The other component to communications for remote workers is the use of voice mail. Voice mail will automatically provide the caller with the opportunity to leave a message. This is particularly helpful for home-based teleworkers who have only one phone line for both voice and data (talking on the phone and connecting to other computers with their modem).

Next is the issue of extra telephone lines. Virtually all teleworkers will need one business phone line installed in their home. This additional phone line will be for business use only and can accommodate both voice and data traffic. This will work best for teleworkers who do not need to be connected to their network all day long. These teleworkers can dial in for e-mail messages or to exchange files. This can be done a few times a day for relatively short periods of connect time. Those users who need full-time access to the network may need two telephone lines to accommodate both their voice and data requirements, or may wish to consider getting ISDN service, especially if rapid transmission of data is desired (see ISDN, pp. 126–128).

It is critical for organizations to recognize the importance of providing a telephone line separate from the home line. Organizations that ask employees to use the employee's existing personal residential service will find that it is difficult to maintain the desired seamless voice communications strategy.

Consider the example of Meredith, who is a teleworker using her own residential phone line for both personal and business use. She teleworks three days a week from home and receives approximately 10 calls a day from customers and staff. An important issue has come up with a customer and the office is trying to reach Meredith. Unfortunately, it is 4:00 P.M., and her teenage son is home talking on the phone. The caller finally gets through and ends up leaving a message on the family answering machine. This scenario is unacceptable in a business environment. The few dollars it costs to install and operate an additional telephone line in the employee's home is well worth the investment.

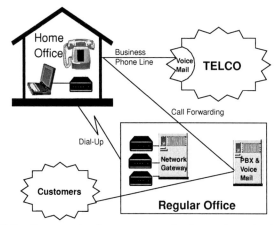

Figure 5-6 Communications strategy for home-based teleworker.

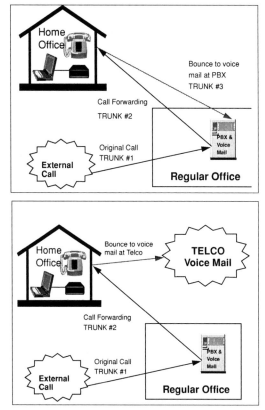

Figure 5-7 Trunk impact if (top) bouncing back to PBX and (bottom) using Telco voice mail.

Figure 5-6 shows the typical voice communications strategy for the home-based teleworker. The employee will likely have two voice mail boxes: one at the office (which is attached to the organization's private branch exchange [PBX, or voice computer]) and one that is offered by the local telephone company. The reason for this is to minimize the number of trunks (physical phone lines) that will be used by a single call. This situation is illustrated in Figure 5-7. The external call to the employee will utilize one trunk to get to the organization's PBX. The PBX will be programmed to know that the employee is not working in the office and will forward the call, thus utilizing a second trunk. If an unanswered call is directed into voice mail at the organization's PBX, then a third trunk is required to accommodate the request for voice mail. In essence, one unanswered external call to a remote worker takes up as many resources as three calls to a worker at the regular office.

The services offered by telecommunications providers vary across different jurisdictions. The suggestions described above represent the basic features that should be available. Organizations should contact their local telecommunication provider to find out what other, more advanced features would better meet their needs. (See also Emerging Technologies, p. 125.)

Security

Security is a primary concern for most organizations that implement work transformation. Many organizations are concerned about hackers getting into their networks and computers when they offer remote access. These security concerns are well founded, and appropriate actions should be taken to reduce the risk.

There are several solutions available to organizations. The first is to institute some type of password security on all remote access facilities. This will require all users to enter a user identification and password to access the facilities, with sessions being terminated after a reasonable number of attempts (usually three to five). This strategy is considered by most to be a bare minimum.

The next step is to use communications software to ensure that the right user is trying to sign on from the right location. Some organizations do this by using a dial-back feature within the communications software. In this scenario, a teleworker dials into the organization, provides identification, and is then disconnected by the regular office computer. This computer then initiates a call to the teleworker's computer using a telephone number recorded within the software. This strategy helps to reduce the chances of someone hacking into the network from a location that the regular office computer is not programmed to accept. However, this strategy is ineffective for mobile workers or those teleworkers who may be dialing in from multiple locations.

Another security precaution is to encrypt the data transmissions. Some remote workers who are dealing with sensitive materials connect to their regular office in encryption mode. This approach means that anyone trying to intercept the transmission would have to be using the exact same encryption algorithm to decipher the messages.

A new strategy that is starting to become popular is the use of hardware and software solutions. One common strategy is to use a "security token." The token is a credit card–sized card that works in conjunction with hardware and/or software access control modules. One such example is the SecurID token from Security Dynamics. The SecurID token automatically generates a unique, unpredictable access code every 60 seconds.

According to Kenneth Weiss founder of Security Dynamics,

> To gain access to a protected resource, a user simply types his or her secret personal identification number (PIN), followed by the current access code displayed on the SecurID token. The technology synchronizes each token with a hardware or software access control module (ACM). Authentication is assured when the ACM recognizes the token's unique code in combination with the user's secret PIN.[1]

The key to selecting a security strategy for the organization is to balance the cost of security with the level of risk that it is prepared to accept. The analysis of cost versus risk might be best handled either by the organization's internal risk management group or an external consultant.

Support

How to support remote workers and employees who work outside of "normal" business hours is an IT challenge that is often overlooked. This is not a trivial issue and should be included in the overall analysis.

Most organizations that have implemented work transformation concepts notice an increase in support requirements during the first few months an employee is working remotely. During this period, the user is learning to be totally self-sufficient and will undoubtedly encounter problems with aspects of their technology which they may have taken for granted in the office. Those who are working remotely now need to concern themselves with the initial troubleshooting of a problem, regular operational-type activities (e.g., backing up, virus protection) and learning to use new hardware and software (e.g., modems, communications programs). Some of these initial challenges can be overcome with proper training—though it is unlikely the organization will be able to train the remote worker for all possible occurrences.

Once remote workers move past the initial challenges, they should be able to operate in the same fashion as if in the regular office. Most organizations notice that the number of support calls from remote workers is approximately the same as those in the traditional office. However, the IT support staff needs to remember that remote workers will likely have different questions from traditional office staff, and the resolution of these questions may be more challenging. The most common area of questions will be related to the data communications. This will include problems related to the physical modem (at either end), communications software, remote access gateway, and telephone lines. The support staff must have the ability to track down these problems and resolve them.

Employees who choose to work variable hours or a modified work week may also find that support is somewhat lacking during "shoulder hours" (times before and after traditional working hours). The IT group needs to remember that supporting these users is important.

Some organizations, particularly those with remote workers who work anytime of the day, find that support at extremely odd hours is lacking. For example, a "night owl" worker who teleworks from 10 P.M. to 6 A.M. will not have someone to call for support. Some organizations support this type of employees by either outsourcing to a support vendor that runs a 24×7 operation (24 hours a day, 7 days a week) or having support funneled to other global corporate offices (in other time zones) that are working during the local down-time.

A key to success is providing the level of support that is commensurate with the benefits being provided. If there is only one person needing support outside regular hours, then it is probably not worth the investment.

Technology to Support Disabled Workers

Depending on the type of remote worker and the job being performed, some special technology may be required. For example, if one aspect of the telework program is to utilize disabled employees who are not able to easily commute to the office every day, then the IT strategy should include specialized equipment to accommodate their specific needs.

The United States Department of Justice has an extensive website on the Americans with Disabilities Act (ADA). The website explains that

> The ADA was signed into law on July 26, 1990. It contains require-
> ments for new construction, for alterations or renovations to buildings
> and facilities, and for improving access to existing facilities of private
> companies providing goods or services to the public.[2]

The ADA website (www.usdoj.gov/crt/ada/adahom1.htm) provides links to information on the Act and organizations that supply resources to the disabled. This can be a valuable asset in linking with other organizations that may have tackled some of the same technology problems.

Call Center Technology

Employees who work at call centers are ideal candidates for a remote work program. A call center is a function that either receives calls from customers (inbound call center) or makes calls to potential customers (outbound call center).

Inbound call centers usually have employees with access to customer-service oriented applications; they are connected to an automated call distribution (ACD) computer. Customer calls come in to a common number; the ACD computer sends the call to the next available agent; the employee then deals with the customer query. A few examples of this type of function include credit card inquires, airline reservations, catalog shopping, banking transactions, information dissemination, insurance claim registration, and renewal of subscription services. In fact, there is a significant move by many organizations to this type of external customer service.

Inbound call centers are ideal candidates for teleworking because the load of incoming calls is usually not directly aligned with the optimal job-shifting strategies that the organization may want to use. For example, a company with peak call periods between 6:00 A.M. to 9:00 A.M. and 5:00 P.M. to 8:00 P.M. will find great difficulty in accommodating the call volume. One option is to have two overlapping shifts, though this, of course, creates a surplus of agents during nonpeak periods. The more cost effective option is to split-shift employees. Unfortunately, most employees do not want to split-shift, as this doubles their commuting time and reduces their personal family time. However, agents working from home will usually be more prepared to split-shift, as the impact of a second commute is eliminated.

Another major benefit of using remote agents in a call center operation involves customers who are in different time zones. Consider an organization on the West Coast that services customers across three time zones. This organization will need to have a shift of people starting extremely early to support the early morning calls. In many cases, this means having employees in the office by 5:00 A.M.—an option that may not be appealing to employees who would have to get up at 3:30 to make it to the office by 5:00 A.M. These employees will have less of a problem starting at 5:00 A.M. if they are able to work from home. These employees have no commute and are probably getting up around this time in order to arrive at the traditional office by 8:00 A.M.

To be successful, the inbound call center with remote agents (teleworkers) must have the right technology in place. This will include providing the teleworker with access to the applications they have in the office. The applications and the data communications strategy need to be established such that the response time at home is *not* significantly different from the response time in the traditional office. Remember, the agent is having to deal with customers—if the agent has to wait 3 times as long for each response from the computer application, the extra delay will certainly have an impact on the level of customer satisfaction.

Teleworkers will also need to be equipped with the same telephone features at home as they have in the traditional office. This will require the acquisition of tools to allow the centralized ACD to distribute calls to the teleworker. Typically, this involves an upgrade at the central site and the use of a remote agent device at the teleworker's remote location. Figure 5-8 illustrates the technology required for both home-based and telework center–based call centers.

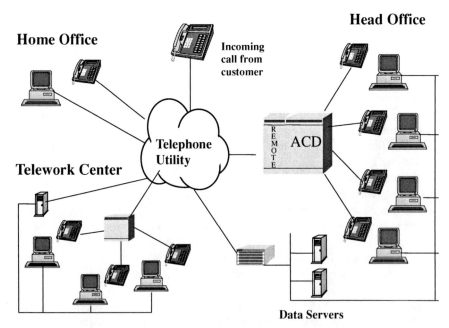

Figure 5-8   Technology to support virtual call centers.

The outbound call center initiates calls to customers and potential customers. Outbound calls typically involve some type of telemarketing or customer follow-up service. These call centers are also challenged with the time of operation. If the outbound call center is interacting with corporate customers, then staffing during normal business hours is fine. If the outbound call center is interacting with the general public (i.e., residential customers), then calls to their homes during normal business hours will be inadequate.

Telework is an appropriate solution for outbound call centers, as employees at these locations typically work during nontraditional hours. Many do not like having to commute to a central facility to make their evening calls. They prefer the opportunity to perform their job function from home. Like their inbound counterparts, they must have timely access to the appropriate technology. If they do not, they will be ineffective in fulfilling the objectives of their calls.

Functions performed at both inbound and outbound call centers are ideal candidates for teleworking. The job is performed via the telephone with access to appropriate computerized applications. If the call center provides appropriate levels of response, support, and technology to teleworkers, the organization will find that the quality of work performed will increase dramatically.

Telework Centers

The technology strategy for a telework center will vary based on whether the facility is designed for exclusive use by one organization or is to be shared with other organizations that may have different technology requirements. The exclusive-use telework center will likely be limited to those large companies with enough employees living in a particular area to justify a stand-alone center. Other organizations will have to look for shared telework centers to meet their requirements.

The following is a list of the basic technology that should exist in a telework center:

- Local area network (LAN) in the telework center
- Ethernet connections at each workstation in the telework center
- Networked laser printer
- Color monitor at each workstation
- Desktop personal computer at some stations
- Plug-in (network, monitor, and power) capability for connecting a notebook computer (provided by the user)
- Stand-alone facsimile machine

Data communications for the single-organization telework center is a simple matter of connecting the center with the organization's network via a high-speed communications link. Data communications in the shared telework center is a much bigger challenge. Each tenant will need to connect to its own network at their central office. Unfortunately the potential tenants may not all use the same type of network, in which case there will be a challenge in finding a solution that will accommodate the broad range of technology being utilized.

There are several ways to address the problem of different network needs. One solution is to provide each workstation with a dial-out facility and a modem (or to consolidate the modems into a common modem bank). This way the tenant could connect to its central network via the same mode as home-based telecommuters. This simple dial-out strategy is utilized in many shared telework centers in the United States (Figure 5-9).

Another option is to connect the telework center to the tenants' networks on a dedicated basis. This approach would allow the tenants to run at higher speeds (typically 56 kbps to T1). The dedicated connections are more reliable, and the higher speeds will help to enhance the productivity of the telework center tenants. The higher-speed lines will also allow tenants to access applications that cannot be effectively run on lower-speed dial-up facilities (e.g., CAD, GIS, imaging applications).

The dedicated communications should be through a WAN provider such as the local telephone company or technology outsourcer. The technology required would include the use of multiprotocol routers that are able to accommodate users running the common data communication protocols (i.e., TCP/IP,

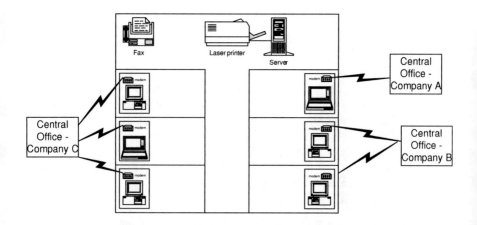

Figure 5-9 Dial-out facility for telework centers.

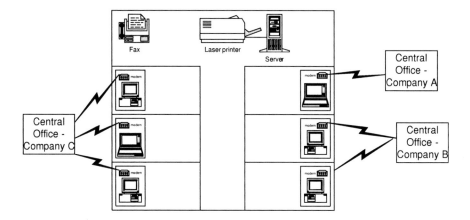

Figure 5-10 Multiprotocol router strategy for telework center.

SNA, and DECNet). This would be combined with appropriate emulation software for users to run on their specific workstations. The LAN in the telework center would connect to the router, which would then connect to the WAN provider. The technical logistics of this type of arrangement can be developed by the potential WAN providers (through a request for information/quotation). Figure 5-10 illustrates the multiprotocol strategy.

Another data communications solution would be to limit the data communications to one type of communications protocol. This solution would be similar to the approach described above, only the tenants would be restricted to specific protocols. This approach would probably work if the restriction was TCP/IP, which is the open systems standard. Many organizations are either working with this protocol today or plan to move to it in the near future. If the specific protocol was to be limited to SNA (IBM proprietary protocol), then the tenants would be restricted to only those that use SNA. This latter example would severely limit the number of tenants that could participate in the center.

The best solution for the telework center is probably a hybrid of the dial-out and multiprotocol router strategy. This approach would allow the telework center to provide high-speed service to larger tenants that would be prepared to pay for the dedicated connection and lower-speed service to those that want a lower-cost solution. Figure 5-11 illustrates the hybrid strategy

The voice communications requirements are much easier to deal with than the data communications requirements. The telework center could have its own PBX, with each workstation having a single-line telephone set with a

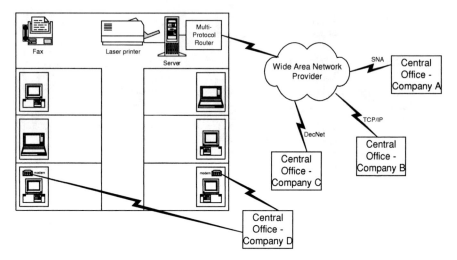

Figure 5-11 Hybrid data communications strategy for telework center.

preassigned number. The tenants of the telework center should utilize an automatic intelligent networking service from the telephone companies. This service provides employees with one phone number, which can be programmed by the employee to go to the central office location, telework center, home, cellular phone, and so on. The employee would forward this virtual phone number to the telework center during the days they are working at the center. When finished at the center, the employee would then change the call forwarding back to the regular central office location. This service typically includes a single voicemail box, regardless of the location of the employee.

Integration of the Telework Center with Home-Based Teleworkers

The telework center could also be integrated with home-based teleworkers in mind. The telework center could have a high-speed broad-bandwidth connection to a WAN that would connect to each tenant's network. Organizations with home-based telecommuters could have these telecommuters dial into the nearest telework center and then connect onto the WAN. This arrangement would eliminate some long-distance charges and would be a low-cost method for improving the speed of communications for home-based telecommuters. Figure 5-12 illustrates this integration.

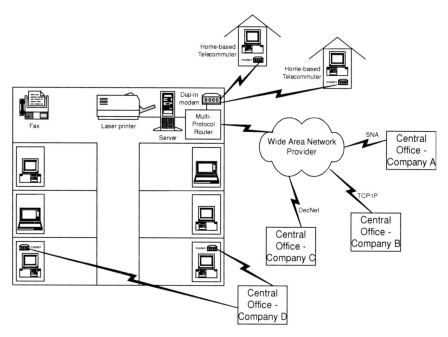

Figure 5-12 Integrating a telework center with home-based teleworkers.

Communications for Mobile Workers

The mobile worker will be working from multiple locations and will require a separate set of technology solutions. Mobile workers will likely be equipped with a cellular or digital telephone or a digital pager to allow them to be reached at any location.

These workers will also be equipped with either a small notebook computer or some sort of PDA, which will have the specific functions that are needed by the employee. For example, the UPS delivery people carry a PDA that allows them to track the parcels they are supposed to deliver and provides an electronic capture of the receiver's signature. These PDAs do not include spreadsheet and word processor capabilities, which are common in personal computers, as the delivery people do not need these functions. In essence, the PDA provides only the functions the user needs, thereby reducing the weight and size of the device (which is critical for mobile workers) and the learning curve to use the technology.

Whatever device the mobile user has, it will undoubtedly be necessary to electronically connect with the regular office. The user will do this with modems which may be either run through the cellular or digital network or connected through the regular telephone system. If the organization equips mobile workers with cellular modems, the technology group should work directly with the local cellular provider to ensure that the data transmission will be successful during all periods of the day. Some mobile users utilizing cellular modems find that it is difficult to connect to the network during peak traffic times (e.g. 7:00 A.M. to 9:00 A.M. and 4:00 P.M. to 7:00 P.M.) due to the volume of voice traffic on the network.

Most mobile workers will have a "home base" of some sort. This will be the office location where they complete their paperwork and perform other "heads-down" activities. Many mobile workers are choosing to set up their home base in their own homes. These individuals set up their home offices in a fashion similar to home-based teleworkers, though they will not spend as much time working from these offices as their telework colleagues. Other solutions for the home base are to have a "drop in" space in the regular office, a branch office, or a telework center.

Changes to the Traditional Office

The traditional office will also require a technology strategy if remote workers are to share space. As described in Chapter 4, the traditional office will undergo a significant transformation to accommodate this new way of working. The IT will have to be flexible enough to support these changes.

The main change to the traditional office will be allowing employees to share workstations. For remote workers, this entails creating an office environment where they can take their notebook computer and plug into the network. For the IT people, this means ensuring that the communications addresses assigned to the personal computer are dynamically allocated, ensuring that any computer can be connected to the network port in any office. These offices may also include a PC docking station, full-sized screen, and full-sized keyboard. In addition, each office should have an easily accessible power receptacle (at desk level) for plugging in the notebook computer and other devices (e.g., phone battery rechargers).

The voice strategy needs to also be adjusted to accommodate remote workers who will be returning to one of several shared workstations. The goal is to have the employee's phone ring at the physical workstation they are currently using. Several solutions are possible based on the features available in the organization's telephone computer PBX. Some PBXs are structured such that employees can be assigned phantom phone numbers, which can then be directed to the physical phone in the office where they are working. Other solutions include using personal communication devices such as Northern Telecom's Companion, which is a cordless phone system that can be used anywhere within the building.

In summary, it is critical that enough time be allocated to develop the appropriate IT strategies and tactical plans to support the work transformation environment. The IT strategies should be tightly linked to both the human resources and facilities management strategies to ensure that a cohesive solution is created.

Information technology groups will find that hardware, software, and integration vendors will be pleased to help with the development of these strategies. The technology group should remember that it is easy to "dive off the deep end" by considering some fancy technology that may not be required. The costs of the technology should be included in the business case. This approach should help to ensure that the organization is investing only in the technology required to attain the business benefits.

EMERGING TECHNOLOGIES

There are numerous emerging technologies that are worthy of careful consideration in developing the technology strategy to support work transformation. A few of these technologies are in use in some portions of the world, whereas others are just starting to gain acceptance. The following primary emerging technologies worth watching.

Internet

It seems unusual to place the Internet in a category called "emerging technologies" when there were already approximately 10 million users in 1997. However, the use of the Internet to support remote workers is just starting to take hold, so I think this placement is appropriate.

The Internet creates a potential opportunity for organizations to connect their remote staff to the organization's primary work location. The remote worker can dial into the Internet and then use a virtual private tunnel (VPT) through the Internet to make a secured connection to the organization's server. This solution is still relatively new, but it does appear to deal with the security issues that have been raised in the past few years.

The Internet and the concept of network-centric computing appears to be the next technological wave. Data communications and the sharing of information is critical to the success of the Internet and work transformation. Watch the developments in this area very closely.

Network Centric Computing

The first wave of computing was characterized as the "glass house" where centralized computers were accessed by dumb terminals. The second wave of computing—where most organizations are today—saw PCs on users' desks with some attempt to interconnect these users. The third and coming wave of computing being pushed by several key technology vendors is the concept of network centric computing (NCC).

Louis Gerstner, Jr., IBM Chairman and CEO, writing about NCC, notes

> We've put a 1985 mainframe on the desk of the clerical workers of the United States and many other parts of the world, and the utilization of that device is, by some estimates, 17% of its capacity. NCC recentralizes and reenergizes the importance of servers—very powerful transaction and database servers that will manage both applications and data in a secure fashion. It doesn't make sense to put increasingly massive storage and application programs on individual desktop computers.[4]

IBM's vision of network-centric computing emphasizes three developments that will mark the potential transition to a universally connected global computing environment:

1. The recentralization of the role of the network server.
2. The de-emphasis of the standalone client as a self-contained device
3. The growing importance of the far-reaching broadband network.

Futurists such as Paul Saffo at the Institute for the Future in Menlo Park, CA, see the NCC strategy as being a key technological role in enhancing our ability to share information. "Ultimately, the Internet is about community. It's about connecting people to other people in information-rich environments."[5]

ISDN

The single biggest technology complaint from remote workers is the slowness of data communications. Most remote workers find today's high-speed analog modems to be slow. As organizations start to make greater use of graphics, image files, video clips, and sound bites, the need for a faster data communications solution becomes even more urgent. An Internet user visiting a fascinating World Wide Web (WWW or web) can experience profound frustration as the user's supposedly high-speed analog modem churns away for 2–5 minutes before the images finish appearing on the screen.

One solution to this challenge is to use Integrated Systems Digital Network, or ISDN, which is available from most telecommunications providers today. ISDN is a significant enhancement over basic phone services (POTS—Plain Old Telephone Service), the familiar dial-tone service your home phone is probably connected to today. This enhancement is similar to the way Microsoft Windows is an enhancement over DOS—it allows users to do more things, quicker, and easier. As a service, ISDN is available using the same telephone wiring currently used in the home or office, usually resulting in low installation costs. And because ISDN and POTS networks are fully integrated, ISDN users can talk to POTS users and vice versa.

The fundamental difference is that ISDN is a digital service, whereas POTS is analog. This means that instead of the signal being continually amplified as it crosses the network, it is cleanly regenerated at each point in the network. As a result, many of the annoying issues with POTS, such as line noise, poor connections, and echo, are eliminated or reduced. If you have ever used a fax and had to re-send a document due to poor quality or an interrupted transmission, then you can appreciate the benefits of a virtually error-free digital connection.

One of the key advantages of an ISDN channel is that it can carry any type of voice, video, or data traffic—and it does this much faster than a POTS connection. In fact, each ISDN channel is more than twice as fast as the fastest phone line. For those who like all the numbers, a typical POTS connection will range from 9.6 kbps (kilobits per second) to a maximum of 33.6 kbps, depending on line quality. In addition, the speed must be negotiated by the devices at each end (the whistling noises at the beginning of a fax or modem call), a process that can take upwards of 30 seconds. An ISDN channel operates at 64 kbps, each and every time. Since there is no negotiation, these connections are made in as little as 2 seconds. With less time spent connecting and with a faster line, more time can be spent working.

Another benefit of ISDN over POTS is that ISDN has two information-carrying channels on each wire, compared to one for POTS. It is similar to having two telephone lines coming into the home, with the advantage of only having to install and pay for one. These channels can be used separately, as two POTS lines would be, or together, which doubles the speed at which information can be transferred.

Douglas Frosst, of Gandalf Technologies in Ottawa, explains that "ISDN allows the user to spend the day teleworking, not telewaiting."[6] Frosst prepared Figure 5-13 to show the connection of the ISDN circuits to the home office and the regular office.

With ISDN, the voice and data traffic is provided over the same cables. The benefit of ISDN is that a user can be connected to another computer running at a speed of 128 kbps, and then when a call comes through, one of the two ISDN channels is disconnected from the computer connection (reducing the connection to 64 kbps) to accommodate the voice call. When the user is finished with

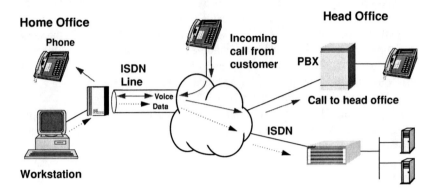

Figure 5-13 IS DN telework implementation. (Courtesy of Gandalf Canada.)

the call, the ISDN device will reestablish the data link to 128 kbps by bringing the second channel back on-line.

Figure 5-14 shows the configuration at the teleworker's home office, where the fax, telephone, and personal computer all have ISDN access. This way the single ISDN service can be used to handle voice, fax, and data traffic.

ISDN is not new technology. ISDN concepts have been around for almost 20 years, but only in the past few years has it been readily available in urban areas. Before considering ISDN, the IT group should investigate the penetration of ISDN service offerings from the local telecommunications service provider. They may find that the ISDN service is not readily available in the residential neighborhoods where potential remote workers reside.

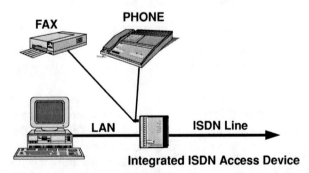

Figure 5-14 Teleworker's home office ISDN components.

A cost analysis is also important when considering ISDN. The cost of the service varies from city to city. In most cases, the cost of ISDN is very close to the cost of two separate standard business lines. If this is the case, then ISDN may be an appropriate solution for users who require two business lines at home (one for voice traffic and one for data).

Though the operating costs for two standard business lines or one ISDN service are more or less the same, the initial setup costs are different. The cost of a typical integrated ISDN access device will be significantly more than the cost of the highest speed analog modem, and remember that the organization will need to have similar devices at both the teleworker's home and the regular office. The regular office device will, of course, be shared by more than one remote worker.

The marketplace for ISDN seems to be slowly expanding. However, many industry experts are advising caution before investing large sums of money in this technology. These experts have been waiting for ISDN to become widely used for years (based on telephone company marketing) and are therefore skeptical and uncertain as to whether this "older" technology will be a stepping stone to something better or the foundation for future higher speed communications. Whatever you believe, it is important to consider the potential of ISDN as a way of providing higher speed and higher bandwidth service to remote workers.

Cable Modems

The cable companies have entered the data transmission arena to compete for the lucrative residential data communications market. Most cable companies have developed cable modems that allow teleworkers to connect to their regular office network via the cable network.

The race is now on to see who will capture the high-speed home telecommunications void—the telephone utilities or the cable companies. Many consumers are now investigating how to use the existing cable system to provide high-speed communications and broadcast-quality video conferencing. The big question today is whether cable communications is ready to support true business traffic? The best way to explain cable modems is to compare them with the other telecommunication options available. As Ed Moura of Hybrid Networks Inc. explains,

> A typical analog telephone modem on POTS (plain old telephone system) can support up to 56 kilobits per second (kbps). The telephone company can provide ISDN service using two phone lines for a combined transmission speed of 128 kpbs. Cable modems range from

500 kpbs to 10 megabits per second (for comparison purposes, a pure fiber optic cable is capable of carrying 2.4 gigabits per second).[7]

The jury is still out on cable modems. They do represent a significant improvement in speed, but it is still uncertain as to how secure they are and how the cable networks will handle the potential data traffic. However, this is another technology the IT group should be watching carefully.

ADSL

A newer technology being marketed by the telephone companies is called asymmetric digital subscriber line, or ADSL, and is 75 times faster than a 28.8-kbps modem. Using ADSL it is possible to download data at 2.2 Mbps and upload at 1 Mbps. This equates to downloading 100 pages of text in approximately 1 second and loading a typical web page in approximately 1/10th of a second.

ADSL is designed to compete with the cable modem. It runs over a regular telephone line, though this line must be within 4 kilometers (2.5 miles) of one of the phone company's switching offices.

ADSL is very new and its eventual success is hard to predict. The good news is that it shows the extent to which the speed of remote access is changing. With continued developments at this pace, it will be possible for even more people to work remotely.

Desktop Video Conferencing

Desktop video conferencing is beginning to establish a foothold in the area of supporting remote workers. Like all new technologies, desktop videoconferencing has had a slow start. However, as prices have dropped and quality has improved, these products seem to be positioned to take off.

Dr. Richard Baker, Chief Scientist for PictureTel in Boston, MA, explained at a recent video conference that 15 years ago the adoption of industry standards for facsimile transmission made the technology ubiquitous. Today, very few businesses can survive without it. Baker believes that the next significant shift will involve "video mail," which will have a similar impact to fax in the 1980s.

The major advancements in the video conferencing area has been the use of ITT standards, which allow users to communicate with each other without having to worry about which product the receiver is using.

Many people were excited about the potential of video conferencing when AT&T introduced its Display Phone several years ago. These same people were in turn very *dis*appointed by the speed and size of the unit (2–4 frames per second). Desktop videoconferencing products run at higher speeds (8–15 frames per second)—this is much more appealing. The integration of video and desktop tools also allows for showing presentations, reviewing documents, jointly creating spreadsheets, etc., through the use of an electronic whiteboard, which is displayed at the same time as the video.

Desktop video conferencing has a role to play in the future of remote work. The information technology strategy should include how video conferencing will be integrated into the remote work arrangements over the next few years.

Imaging

The concept of the paperless office was broadly discussed in the early 1970s as the solution for the late 1980s early 1990s. Well, we are well past the early 1990s, and offices are using and storing paper at record levels. The new technologies have, if anything, *increased* the amount of paper used, as many users choose to print on-line information to keep a "permanent" and more portable record.

There are many reasons as to why the true paperless environment has not been established. One reason is the cost and effectiveness of imaging technologies. Ten years ago, the cost of imaging technology was so high that it could realistically be considered by only very large organizations with "deep pockets" to fund the new technology. Today, the cost of imaging technology has dropped dramatically, and now more companies are starting to reconsider it.

Imaging technology can be a tremendous benefit to remote workers. Employees who are either mobile workers or teleworkers find that they can use imaging technology to have paper documents which are sent to the regular office made available on-line. This allows these remote workers to access all aspects of their job from anywhere, at anytime.

Imaging is not a solution for all organizations. Organizations should, however, consider the potential of imaging as a method of supporting work transformation.

Cellular Digital Packet Data

Cellular Digital Packet Data, or CDPD, is the latest advancement in data transmission over the cellular network. CDPD is the result of a consortium of U.S. cellular carriers that created the uniform standard for sending data over existing cellular telephone channels. The goal of the consortium was to find a cost-effective, reliable, flexible, two-way wireless communications service for mobile workers.

CDPD is designed to exploit the capabilities of the Advanced Cellular Mobile Services (AMPS) infrastructure in place throughout the United States and Canada. CDPD is open and usable by anyone, but it is particularly well suited to mobile workers, as it offers a high-speed, relatively low-cost solution.

One of the characteristics of transmission across cellular telephone channels is that there are moments when the channel is idle (approximately 30% of the actual air time is unused). CDPD technology is able to detect and utilize these otherwise wasted moments by packaging data in small packets and sending it in short bursts during this idle time. The net result is being able to transmit data without affecting the voice systems capability.

CDPD takes advantage of the existing cellular network by using equipment that can access both voice and data. The hardware can be a hand-held AMPS telephone or a small modem, which can attach to a notebook computer. The only adjustment is having to extend the antennae on the modem.

CDPD is an interesting solution because it appears to be reasonably affordable for the carriers, which should result in making it affordable for consumers. When data is sent using the unit, the user is, of course, only paying on a per-packet basis, which should lower the operating costs. This will likely be a great benefit to mobile workers, who typically are just sending and receiving e-mail while on the road.

The use of CDPD will not affect the voice capabilities, so the cellular connection can have two uses. The vendors suggest that CDPD will soon make high-speed wireless data communication at affordable rates a routine occurrence. The cellular advantage is that users will not have to be tethered to a physical telephone line, so the opportunities for new locations to work from are greater.

The CDPD solution is worth considering for those organizations that have usually avoided traditional cellular transmission approaches due to the high cost and questionable reliability. The CDPD seems to have solved both of those problems. If the organization has mobile workers, then CDPD may be an important aspect of the technology strategy.

SUMMARY

There are a broad range of technologies available to support work transformation. The challenge is to pick the technologies that will help the organization meet its specific business needs. For example, picking video conferencing to allow managers to have "face-to-face" interactions with teleworkers is probably not the best investment to make. However, using video conferencing to enable all teleworkers to participate in group sessions or to review drawings or other deliverables with team members could help your organization attain one of the defined business objectives.

The technology required to support remote workers is fairly basic. Notebook computers and modems have been around for a long time. Many organizations start their work transformation program just by using basic technology and then gradually introducing some of the new technologies.

Remember that the best technology is the one that will enable employees to be most effective. Avoid the trap of selecting the latest "gee whiz" technology just so that you can tell your colleagues and associates that you have the latest and greatest.

NOTES

1. Security Dynamics. Securing the Information Age . . . Minute by Minute from the Security Dynamics Web Page at www.securid.com
2. U.S. Department of Justice. Americans with Disabilities Act. ADA Home Page at www.usdoj.gov/crt/adsa/adahom1.htm
3. TCP/IP is the open systems standard communications protocol, SNA is IBM's proprietary communications protocol, and DECNet is Digital's proprietary communications protocol.
4. Watson, Todd. Network Centric Computing. *Software Quarterly, 3* (1), 1996, pp. 21–26.
5. Ibid.
6. Frosst, Douglas. Teleworking, Not Telewaiting. *Telework International, Fall*, 1995, pp. 1–2.
7. Mourra, Ed. Cable Modems Show Promise, but Don't Hold Your Breath. *Telecommuting Review, 13* (3 [March]), 1996, pp. 5–7.

6

Gaining
Management Support

To this point, this book has focused on each of the three critical components of work transformation, as shown in Figure 6-1.

Chapters 6–8 will focus on the process of integrating these components into a work transformation program. This chapter will review the steps required to gain management support, Chapter 7 will describe the implementation, and Chapter 8 will describe how to continue to evolve the work transformation program.

Figure 6-2 shows the high-level processes for the key steps that will be described in these three chapters.

Figure 6-1   Integrating key strategies to support work transformation.

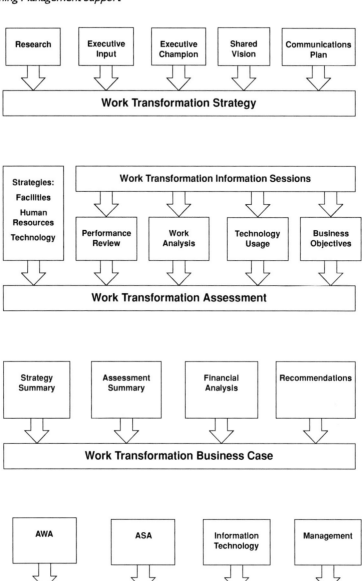

Figure 6-2 Work transformation process.

One of the most significant challenges of implementing work transformation is gaining management support. There are always more potential opportunities than funds available, so it is critical to gain management support at the strategic, tactical, and financial levels. In most cases, this is not a minor undertaking.

This chapter reviews the keys to successfully gaining management support: creating a common strategic vision that can be supported by senior management, assessing the tactical appropriateness of work transformation, and developing a business case to demonstrate the business impact of these initiatives. Figure 6-3 illustrates these key steps.

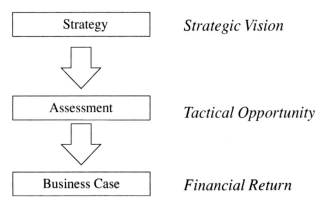

Figure 6-3   Overview of steps for gaining management support.

WORK TRANSFORMATION STRATEGY

Gaining management support entails helping management understand the concepts, with the goal of developing a shared strategic vision of work transformation. This process may be seen as encompassing five key steps:

1. Doing the necessary research
2. Gathering executive input
3. Finding an executive champion
4. Presenting this shared vision for support and approval
5. Communicating the strategy to the rest of the organization.

Figure 6-4 summarizes these steps.

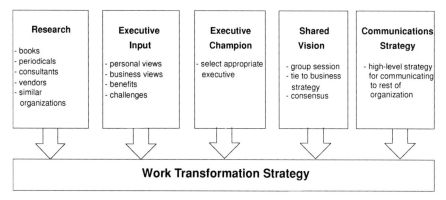

Figure 6-4 Steps for developing management support of work transformation strategy.

Research

The best way to start when considering any new idea is to research. The front-end research will help the organization to better understand the concepts of work transformation, how it could be applied in the organization, and the successes (and failures) that others have experienced.

Research is considered by some business managers as an academic exercise that is best left to universities. The research needed for developing a work transformation plan is hardly in the realm of the leading-edge, original investigation that is typically associated with academic institutions. To research work transformation, the organization should simply gather information on what others have done and the options available, consider the views of consultants who specialize in this area, and evaluate the success that has, or has not, been achieved.

Doing this research need not be difficult. Although work transformation is seen as a relatively new topic, in fact, various aspects have been around for years. The key is to evaluate the literature on available and emerging work transformation components and to determine a conceptual view of what the organization's specific program should look like.

The best way to research these topics is to refer to books and periodicals that contain work transformation information, search the Internet, and gather information from consultants and vendors.

There are several excellent books on the topics of alternative work arrangements (AWAs) and telework. There are also many excellent books on the topic of alternative space arrangements (ASAs) and office space design. Periodicals that specialize in human resources, information technology, or facilities management topics from a management perspective will likely have articles on these topics.

Searching the Internet's World Wide Web (WWW) is another interesting way to find information on work transformation. The best approach is to use the available search engines to find sites that refer to such topics as alternative work arrangements, telework, telecommuting, virtual office, and alternative officing.

Information can also be gathered from consultants who specialize in work transformation and vendors who supply products to these markets. Consultants and vendors can usually be found via the Internet, from references in articles, or through recommendations from those who have already implemented these concepts. Many of the product vendors have research available along with glossy marketing material on the benefits of work transformation. A few of the leaders in this area include the following:

- *Furniture Vendors*
  - Haworth
  - Herman Miller
  - Steelcase
- *Technology Vendors*
  - 3Com
  - Ascend
  - IBM
- *Telecommunications Companies*
  - Bell Canada
  - Pacific Bell
  - MCI

This book contains a bibliography of web-based information (p. 278), which can be used as a starting point. Any research should include an analysis of both the positive and negative aspects of work transformation. When researching AWAs, it is critical to focus primarily on the *business benefits*, with the *employee benefits* being secondary. This statement might seem strange, as it is generally accepted that there are significant employee benefits to be derived. To secure support at both the executive and middle manager level, however, it will be crucial to focus on the business results. Research that is based heavily on employee benefits will be perceived as centered on promoting employee perks; it will not receive the kind of executive attention required for successful work transformation implementation.

Another means of locating references is to talk to those who have already implemented the same or similar concepts. These references will likely be the organization's best route to other research materials, consultants, and product vendors. The real value will be found in talking to other organizations in the same industry. Quite often, knowing that a key competitor or a respected peer has implemented the concepts will increase the desire of senior management to investigate work transformation. It should be noted that some of your competitors who have successfully implemented work transformation may be reluctant to share information, particularly if they feel that they have gained a competitive advantage in the marketplace as a result of their work transformation program.

Remember, the goal is to gather sufficient information that will allow for a full and balanced discussion on the potential for work transformation within the organization. Research findings presented to senior management should be focused and relevant. Many companies attempting to conduct thorough research spend far too much time re-inventing the wheel with background information. In these cases, the vision usually becomes lost and the concept rarely moves forward.

Gathering Executive Input

Getting a work transformation program off the ground can be attempted either at the grass-roots level—with the hope that it will grow—or by presenting the concepts to senior management and taking more of a top-down approach. The first approach has been tried in numerous organizations, as it represents the least line of resistance—in the short run. Most have seen their programs basically go nowhere, as they often do not have the support of senior management. If an organization is to benefit from the expected space savings, these savings will be achieved only if the program is widely used throughout the organization.

Working with executives to develop a shared vision is a good method to ensure the necessary level of support to make this significant change successful. The best way to start is to approach a few of the executives and "bounce" the idea around with them. Get them to buy into doing a short, focused project to investigate the potential of work transformation and to develop a work transformation strategy. Find an executive who will sponsor this initial step. This sponsor will make the business case legitimate and open the door to the rest of the executive team.

The first step in communicating to the executives is to ensure that resources assigned to developing the work transformation strategy have a reasonable understanding of the concepts. At this stage, it is often worthwhile to utilize the services of an experienced consultant, who can bring credibility to the project and shorten the learning curve for the organization.

One-on-one meetings should be held with each executive .It is best to start at the top and work your way down. Remember that executives with line responsibility will be more influential in the process than those who represent the service function.

These meetings should determine the executive's viewpoint and gauge their level of support. An effective approach is to ask for their personal and business views on these concepts. Work transformation is something that virtually everyone has a personal opinion on, but this personal view may not be the same as their business perspective. For example, I interviewed one executive on the topic of implementing a telework program, and she was completely opposed to the concept. Upon further questioning, I discovered that the executive had tried working at home to write a report. The executive chose to work at home because of the time pressures for the assignment and the lack of quiet time available in the regular office. Unfortunately, the executive's home was not conducive to quiet work (she had a nanny and two preschool-aged children at home), and she did not have the personality to successfully distance herself from the home distractions. The result was that *for her, at that time,* telework was a bad thing! However, it was clear that for other employees telework could probably work. It is interesting to note that this executive went on to become one of the key champions of AWAs within her organization.

The one-on-one interviews should also focus on the potential business benefits and drawbacks. What do the executives think would be the positive and negative aspects to the organization? This approach makes the executive think of work transformation concepts in business terms and not in terms of the personal employee benefits. The discussion on business benefits and challenges should include some "gazing into the future" to discuss how the organization would change under work transformation and how these changes could affect the organization's critical success factors.

The discussion of work transformation should also include a review of where these concepts might work within the overall organization and more specifically within the executive's organization. The executive should also be asked to consider the potential of using some of these new ways of working themselves. The goal here is to break through the concept that these ideas are only for the workers and not for the management. The process of thinking about the applicability for themselves also starts to bring them into the discussion personally—this, in some cases, it may help to solidify their support.

The goal of the one-on-one interviews will be to gain support from each executive individually by openly and honestly discussing the issues. The goal is not to "strong arm" the executives into agreement but to lead the discussion to the point where the executive can make an informed business decision.

The discussions are performed within the privacy of the executive's office where they can "think out loud" about the potential ramifications without having to worry about what their peers or the CEO thinks. This approach also gives each executive some time to "digest" the work transformation concepts and to be prepared for a group discussion, which will occur later in the process.

Finding an Executive Champion

Input from the individual discussions should be documented and used to assess the overall interest level of the organization and to help decide on which executive would make the most appropriate champion for work transformation. The one-on-one discussion findings should be summarized and reviewed with the eventual executive champion.

Many executives believe that the champion of a work transformation program should be the vice president of human resources, facilities management, or information technology. I totally disagree! If the VP of human resources is appointed, people will likely feel that this initiative is being driven by human resources and is "just another soft, people-oriented initiative, which has limited business return." If the VP of facilities management is appointed, people will likely feel that this initiative is being driven by facilities management and is "just another way of reducing the size of my office and making the building less functional—there is certainly no business value in this approach." If the VP of information technology is appointed, people will likely feel that this initiative is being driven by information technology and is "just another piece of new technology which we probably don't really need."

The problem is that the service departments bring their own "baggage" with them. The key to success is to show that all three service areas (human resources, facilities management, and information technology) are working together to deliver a successful business solution. Although the head of any of these areas might be more than capable of being the executive champion the best champion will likely come from one of the "delivery" business units. For example, if the VP of operations is the executive champion, the organization will be more inclined to consider the initiative as having bottom-line business value and will be more prepared to give support.

Once a potential executive champion has been identified, that person must understand what being a champion entails. In projects such as this, which require significant change, the champion will be under tremendous pressure to revert back to the comfort zone of "how we used to do it." The champion's role is to maintain the organization's enthusiasm for the concepts during the most difficult periods.

Shared Vision

The primary goal of the work transformation strategy is to develop a shared vision of the work transformation concepts. The executive team should meet to realize the work transformation vision. The best way to start is by briefing the executive team on the findings to date (from the research and one-on-one interviews), with particular focus on the key issues and opportunities that have surfaced so far.

The potential business benefits of work transformation should be directly linked to the overall corporate strategy and key corporate business objectives. For example, the work transformation program could be designed to improve customer service, support teaming strategies, reduce unit costs, and enhance employee satisfaction. The vision should embody these expected benefits, and it must show how the work transformation strategy connects to the overall corporate strategy.

The work transformation vision is still evolving at this point, and will be reviewed and tuned even as the work transformation is being implemented. The goal is to build a strategy around the common vision and to continue to form and share the vision throughout the organization.

The final step of the work transformation strategy process is to gain executive support to move on to the assessment of appropriateness. This is, of course, not a trivial effort. However, if the basic research has been performed, all the executives have been involved in the process, and an executive champion has been found, then moving forward should be much easier.

The key to moving forward will be ensuring that all of the executives share the vision—that they understand the business opportunities work transformation could potentially deliver and how these business opportunities support the overall corporate strategic plan. It is also critical that the executives see the strategic value in going forward. This will not happen if the work transformation is focused on soft benefits or strictly on employee benefits. Executive support is generally directly tied to the hard benefits, which must either impact the bottom line or be considered strategically important.

Communications Plan

Once the vision is established, it is time to develop a high-level communications plan. This plan will focus on informing the rest of the organization about work transformation and the vision for how it can be used to support the overall corporate strategic plan.

The communications plan will have to address the three generic groups common to most organizations. These are senior management (executives), middle management, and the rest of the employees. In most cases, employees will enthusiastically support AWAs, as they can directly benefit, and will accept ASAs, as long as they can see the benefits they can personally receive. Excitement about ASAs will be much diminished if employees see them merely as management's way of reducing the amount of space they are "entitled to."

Even after the visioning process, senior management will likely still be somewhat skeptical of the concepts. It is important to continue the discussions with them, focusing on the longer-term benefits and opportunities.

The most challenging group is the one in the middle. Middle managers are generally extremely skeptical about a concept that involves managing people they cannot see, or extending the work hours for staff in modified work weeks—which they believe requires them to put in longer hours themselves—or managing people who work from multiple locations in the central office. To be frank, middle managers are running scared! Over recent years, they have been targeted as the group that has been squeezed out of the organization, and it is understandable that they will often look at work transformation as merely another way of reducing their power.

The ultimate success of the work transformation program will be based on the organization's ability to create a shared vision at the executive level and then to take this vision and turn it into a business case that can be supported by the middle managers. It must also be possible to convert this shared vision into a workable, usable program that employees will support.

Consensus

The work transformation strategy phase should include a common vision for work transformation, a high-level communications plan, and plan for performing the work transformation assessment. Having reached a consensus on the strategy, the executives and should be supportive of moving forward with the concept.

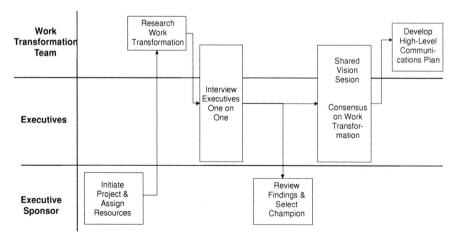

Figure 6-5 Work transformation strategy phase: work process.

At this point, they probably have not fully committed to work transformation—instead, they have committed to continuing the analysis to determine the tactical and financial viability of these concepts within the organization.

An important decision to be made by the executives at this point is the extent to which they want to study work transformation. In some larger organizations, it may be better to perform the work transformation assessment in a single division or department, or in a few departments; it may not be practical to study it across the entire organization. The executive team should provide input as to which group(s) should be involved, ensuring that the results can be reasonably extrapolated across the organization.

The work transformation strategy phase is now completed. Figure 6-5 summarizes the work processes required to complete this phase.

ASSESSMENT OF APPROPRIATENESS OF WORK TRANSFORMATION

Once the work transformation strategy has been agreed upon, it is time to proceed with an assessment of appropriateness. Senior management are likely still to be somewhat skeptical of the concepts but are at least prepared to invest some time and money to see whether these new concepts can be justified.

The assessment process will help the organization determine the appropriateness of work transformation concepts. Assessment is preceded by the formation of a work transformation team and the development of primary human resources, facilities management, and information technology strategies to support work transformation. The end result of the actual assessment will be the analysis of data gathered from staff and recommendations on how to proceed.

Forming the Work Transformation Team

The strategy phase deliverables will probably have been created by a small, dedicated team (1 or 2 people), with some informal input from others. The assessment phase will likely require more resources, though the size of the team will vary based on the size of the organization being studied. The team should be made up of representatives from across the organization, including

- Human resources
- Labor relations (if unions and/or associations are involved)
- Facilities management
- Information technology
- Workplace health and safety
- Corporate communications

The individuals on the team should be empowered to utilize other departmental resources, as required, throughout the project. These individuals will need access to a wide range of expertise. The following is a basic list of the key issues by function:

- *Human Resources*
  - Policies and procedures
  - Workplace diversity
  - Legal or governmental programs
- *Labor Relations* (if unions and/or associations are involved)
  - Union agreements
  - Access to union executives/representatives for input
- *Facilities Management*
  - Real estate portfolio (details of leases and holdings)
  - Furniture investment/strategies
- *Information Technology*
  - Voice and data communications
  - Applications in use
  - Overall computing architecture/strategy
- *Workplace Health and Safety*
  - Ergonomic standards
  - Workplace health and safety initiatives
  - Americans with Disabilities Act (ADA)
- *Corporate Communications*
  - Internal communications
  - External communications

In addition to these resources, some value may be placed in having one or more consultants on the team to bring expertise in the topic and knowledge of how other organizations have implemented these concepts. The use of a consultant can either be as a full project team member or as a leveraged resource that is available for training the team and reviewing deliverables.

The project team should also have an assigned project manager. The project manager will be responsible for developing a project plan, managing the plan, and generally keeping the project within scope and budget. The project manager is also the leader of the business case creation. Remember that a formal project without a leader is a project in trouble.

Key Strategies

The assessment of appropriateness should be based on the three key strategies shown in Figure 6-6.

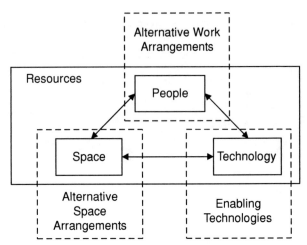

Figure 6-6   Key strategies for work transformation assessment.

Human Resources Strategy (People)

A strategy is required for integrating AWAs into the organization's overall human resources strategy. This focus should be on making AWAs an integral part of the organization's overall strategy, clearly showing how work transformation supports the core business objectives.

The human resources strategy should include a framework for establishing how employees can participate in the work transformation program, the role of their managers in this process, and the methods for measuring success. This strategy will also include linkages to other key strategies such as diversity in the workplace, balancing work and family, and employee equity.

Finally, the human resources strategy should include an overall communications plan outlining how the organization will internally communicate the move to the new work transformation environment. This should include a high-level definition of the key messages, key stakeholders, and basic strategy for how the message will be communicated.

If the organization is unionized, a labor relations strategy should be prepared to explain how the union will participate in the development of the work transformation program. This should include plans for including the union executives, local representatives, and rank-and-file membership. Most successful implementations in a union environment emphasize the importance of involving the union as early as possible in the process.

Facilities Management Strategy (Space)

A facilities management strategy should include the plans for the implementation of the ASAs. This includes a high-level strategy outlining the approach to designing these nontraditional spaces and methods for involving employees in the design and implementation processes.

The facilities management strategy should also address the key real estate issues of owned versus leased space, how financial savings will be realized, and how the space strategy integrates into the human resources and information technology strategies.

Information Technology Strategy

An information technology strategy needs to be prepared which outlines the approach to supporting remote workers, how nontraditional offices will be equipped in terms of voice and data communications, and desktop computing strategies (use of notebooks, portable technology, etc.). The information technology strategy needs to be presented in clear business language, not the "techno-jargon" that unfortunately is common in many such documents.

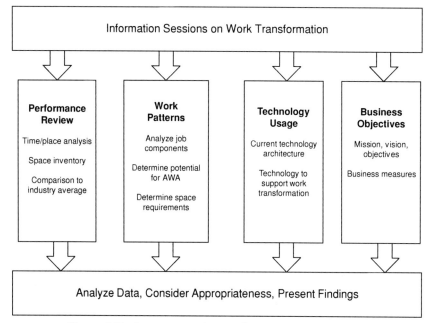

Figure 6-7 Steps to work transformation assessment.

In addition to the hardware, software, and general infrastructure items, the strategy should also include a high-level view of how the technology will support work transformation.

The assessment process, shown in Figure 6-7, includes providing information sessions, gathering data, analyzing the appropriateness, and presenting the findings to the organization—all within the context of the key strategies. The purpose of the assessment is to determine the appropriateness of work transformation solutions. No two situations are exactly the same, so it is important not to conduct the assessment process with a preconceived decision. At the end of this process, senior management will decide whether or not to proceed with a work transformation business case.

INFORMATION SESSIONS

The first component of the assessment process is the introduction of work transformation concepts through an information session. This session includes a review of the basic concepts; the benefits and challenges associated with work transformation; and the processes required to assess, justify, and implement the concepts.

The goal of the information session should be to disseminate information on work transformation and to solicit questions from the audience. Virtually every audience will have an abundance of questions regarding this topic, as nearly everyone has an opinion about how and where work is performed. There should be opportunities to solicit feedback from the audience on the potential for work transformation within the groups represented.

The information session must remain focused on the business benefits of work transformation. It is easy to fall into the trap of overemphasis on employee benefits when talking about AWAs. The goal of work transformation is to deliver business value to the organization through more effective use of work space and working arrangements.

Many organizations like to use external consultants to present the information sessions. The right consultant can bring his or her experience from other organizations to the presentation to help reduce some of the anxiety for those hearing about work transformation for the first time. The experience from other organizations should cover the business benefits achieved as well as the impact on staff. The latter is of prime importance and concern to the audience attending the information session.

If internal resources are used for the information sessions, it is necessary to ensure that the presenters tour other facilities and talk to the staff that work there. They must have enough confidence and knowledge to be able to realistically speak of the successes and failures.

DATA GATHERING

Once the organization is familiar with the work transformation concepts, it is time to start collecting data to study the appropriateness of these concepts. This data could be collected organization-wide or from some component of the organization.

Staff should be informed in the information session about the assessment process. They should be asked for their honest and sincere responses to the surveys and questionnaires, and they should be assured that all survey questionnaires are private and confidential and will be used only by the team for the purposes of this assessment. To ensure confidentiality, the questionnaires should be anonymous, although the respondents' work area, group, or team must be identified to allow the analysts to group the responses.

It is highly recommended that an external consultant be involved in gathering, entering, and performing the preliminary analysis of the data. This approach will assure staff that the information is truly confidential and will result in more realistic responses. Once the consultant has collected the data, a detailed analysis can be done. It should be done in conjunction with the rest of the work transformation assessment team.

The following sections outline the key data gathering components.

Performance Review

The performance review involves an assessment of the current space inventory, a space utilization analysis, and a comparison to similar organizations.

The space inventory is designed to collect information about the organization's space and furniture. Some organizations might have all of this information on a CAD (computer assisted drafting) system or an asset database. For those that do not have an automated system or that need to confirm the numbers, a manual process is required. The most effective and thorough way to collect this information manually is to physically walk around the space and record the dimensions of space and furniture, and perform an inventory of the latter.

Probably the most interesting component of data gathering is determining the utilization of the workspace. The goal here is to determine what percentage of the day each workspace in the group is vacant and what percentage of the week employees are out of the office. This should include all offices, cubicles, and meeting rooms. The workspace utilization observations should be made 2–3 times per day (at different times each day). The observations should be made over a 10–15-working-day period to ensure that all natural work cycles are captured.

The resources collecting this data will need to move throughout the office and observe the status of each workspace. They will record whether a workspace is in use and, if so, by how many people. The data collection should be done by administrative resources that know the group they are observing. The form should be very simple—recording the workstation location and whether it is in use or vacant, and number of people who are using the space at the time of observation.

Data collected should also include the current rules/guidelines under which space is allocated, the amount of space per person (in terms of square feet or square meters per person), the common areas, and the amenities. This information should be compared against industry benchmarks for analytical comparison. This type of benchmark data can be collected from some consultants, real estate professionals, and designers, and by contacting facilities managers in other, related companies.

Work Patterns

The work pattern data is designed to gather data on all aspects of the employee's job, workspace, and technology used. Most organizations use a questionnaire to gather data from all staff. The key topics covered in the questionnaire should include the following:

- *General Information*
  - Current use of AWAs
  - Time out of the office per week
  - Type of office user
  - Best and worst features (e.g., air quality, noise, privacy, access to others) of current workspace
- *Work Activities* (time spent)
  - Doing quiet work
  - Working on personal computer
  - Using the telephone
  - Using centralized office equipment
  - Attending ad hoc meetings
  - Attending scheduled meetings
- *Alternative Work Arrangements*
  - Telework, work at home, etc.
  - Mobile workers

- *Space-Related Issues*
  - Office environment
  - Team dynamics
  - Storing personal/work materials
  - Locating people in the office
  - Communicating with others
  - Learning from others
  - Impact on performance
  - Impact on managerial duties
- *Alternative Space Arrangement Potential*
  - Team space
  - Space sharing
  - Casual areas, quiet spaces, etc.
- *Information Technology Usage*
  - Workstation, hardware, software
  - Applications used
  - Access required
  - Voice communications

Figure 6-8 shows a sample of the format of the work pattern questionnaire.

The ideal scenario is to gather the data from all staff. In some very large organizations, this might be difficult. For these organizations, selective sampling might be a better approach. The challenge with sampling is to ensure that all constituent groups are represented and that they are represented in the proper relative percentage of the total group. For example, if 10% of an organization's staff is mobile salespersons, then it is important to make sure that this group represents 10% of the total sampling.

Technology Usage

Understanding the information technology being used by the group is critical to assessing the opportunities for work transformation. Groups that are novices with respect to information technology may limit the degree of change that can be implemented.

To complete the analysis, information on the following topics should be gathered:

- *Hardware/Software Used*
  - Basic configuration
  - Enhanced configuration
  - Power user configuration

KLR Consulting Inc.
Work Pattern Questionnaire

Group: _____   To Be Completed by: _____

General Information

Are you currently using any of the following alternative work arrangements:

Part-Time ❑	Compressed Work Week ❑	Telework ❑
Job Sharing ❑	Flexible Hours of Work ❑	

Work Activities

This section describes the work activities you perform as a regular part of your job. Please record the amount of time each week you spend on each activity.

Time At Work in the Office	Almost No Time	Little Time	Some Time	Much of the Time	Most of the Time
Doing quiet work	❑	❑	❑	❑	❑
Working on your PC	❑	❑	❑	❑	❑
Using the telephone	❑	❑	❑	❑	❑
Using centralized equipment	❑	❑	❑	❑	❑
Attending ad hoc meetings	❑	❑	❑	❑	❑

Would you be interested in teleworking if it was appropriate for you and your job? Yes ❑ No ❑
If yes: - how many days per week? _____ days/week
        - I would prefer to telework from (check one) ❑ A Telework Centre   ❑ Home

Alternative Space Arrangements

If I was out of the office two or more days per week on a regular basis I would be willing to use:

	Strongly Disagree	Disagree	Neutral	Agree	Strongly Agree
A smaller workspace	❑	❑	❑	❑	❑
Shared open office	❑	❑	❑	❑	❑
Shared manager office / meeting space	❑	❑	❑	❑	❑
Lockers & moveable pedestals	❑	❑	❑	❑	❑

General Comments

_____

_____

_____

Figure 6-8 Sample sections of work pattern questionnaire. (Courtesy of KLR Consulting Inc.)

- *Applications*
  - Name/function
  - Nature of use
  - Technology platform
- *Networks*
  - Servers
  - Printers
  - Protocol/dial-in access
  - Internet
- *Voice Communications*
  - Manufacturer/model of system
  - Features

Business Objectives

Part of the data collection for determining the appropriateness of work transformation is the documentation of key business objectives for the organization. These business objectives and measures will be used to ensure that the proposed solutions will support and enhance the group's ability to reach these objectives.

The input to the business objectives will have been gathered in the work transformation strategy phase. These objectives and related data should now be confirmed/enhanced/expanded through the use of a facilitated workshop. This workshop should include the management team of the group being considered for work transformation or by the senior management team if the entire organization is being studied. The workshop should be facilitated by a business analyst and a support person who will take notes to record the highlights of the meeting.

The key areas of discussion should include the following:

- *Mission/Vision*
  - Review the shared vision developed during the strategy phase
  - Review the current corporate mission/vision
  - Discuss how the corporate vision can be integrated into work transformation
- *Organizational Objectives/Business Measures*
  - Discuss corporate objectives and measures (these should already exist)
  - Document key performance measures that support the objectives and mission (e.g., turnover, absenteeism, transaction volume, cycle time, customer satisfaction)
- *Organization Chart*
  - Review current organization chart
  - Discuss any planned structural and/or head-count changes
  - Discuss span of control, management style, etc.

- *Potential Business Benefits of Work Transformation*
  - Discuss how work transformation could impact business measures
  - Discuss how to measure and evaluate success of work transformation in terms of achieving business benefits

Analyze Data

After the data have been collected, the next step is to perform the analysis. This process will include a statistical analysis of quantitative data and a summary of qualitative data. The goal of the assessment analysis is to determine the potential for implementing work transformation concepts within the group studied.

Space Usage Analysis

The space usage analysis includes reviewing the space inventory and workspace utilization data. The space inventory data should be consolidated to reflect the total amount of floor space allocated to the group and the distribution of this space into

- Open-plan workspace
- Closed-office workspace
- Small meeting rooms (2–5 people)
- Medium-sized meeting rooms (6–15 people)
- Large meeting rooms (16–30 people)
- Shared space (coffee, supplies, photocopier, etc.)
- Circulation space

The existing furniture inventory should be tallied and reviewed. Potential new furniture to support ASAs should be identified at a very high level. The design has not been completed at this stage, so any estimate is merely a guess. The biggest decision to be made at this point relates to the extent to which existing furniture will be reused. Organizations that are making radical changes usually change all of the furniture; those that are taking more of a stepping-stone approach tend to reuse some of the furniture and augment it with some new furniture.

The workspace utilization survey should be analyzed to identify the space usage patterns and location patterns of the space users. The following basic determinations should be derived from this data:

- Percentage of occurrences where the space was in use by one person
- Percentage of occurrences where the space was in use by multiple persons
- Average number of persons using the space (when multiple persons were observed)
- Percentage of occurrences where the space is vacant

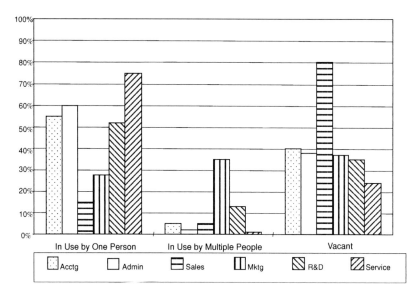

Figure 6-9   Workspace utilization graph compiled from direct observation data.

It is very important how this data is categorized. Some thought needs to go into categorizing it by division, department, team, or possibly by function. The analysts need to experiment with different ways of organizing the data and to perform appropriate sensitivity analysis. Different ways of grouping the data should also help to highlight areas where work transformation concepts can be of greatest assistance.

Figure 6-9 shows an example of a workspace utilization graph for a given organization. The graph shows that the customer service staff (a call center) spend most of their time at their desks, the sales group is out of the office most of the time, and the marketing group often has more than one person in a workspace—probably due to a high level of collaborative work.

Work Pattern Analysis

The data from the work pattern questionnaire should be entered into a spreadsheet or some type of statistical analysis package to show the trends associated with the questions asked. The analysis should include a frequency distribution, median, mode, and average response. The following are the key areas to analyze.

Use of Alternative Work Arrangements

Determine the number of employees who are already using AWAs and the number of people who are already working outside of the regular office. This information should be compared to the data gathered in the workspace utilization survey to find any additional use of AWAs.

Figure 6-10 shows an example of how the existing use of AWAs might be illustrated. In this example, the bulk of the staff is currently working regular hours and days.

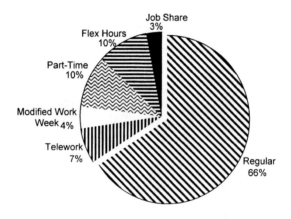

Figure 6-10 Current working arrangements graph compiled from questionnaires.

The analysis should also consider the potential for greater use of AWAs, with particular emphasis on telework and mobile work (as these arrangements have the greatest impact on space usage). Figure 6-11 shows the graphed responses to a question regarding the percentage of work that could be performed remotely. Staff who responded with 0–1 days/week will need to be accommodated for full-time work in the office, those who responded with 2–3 days per week are potential teleworkers, while those who responded with 4–5 days/week are either potential mobile workers or work-at-home employees.

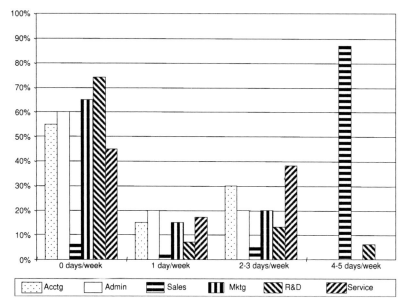

Figure 6-11 Graphed responses indicating percentage of work that could be performed remotely, compiled from questionnaires.

Type of Office User

Determine the type of user the employee is in the office, in terms of one of the following primary classifications:

- *Sitters*[1]
  - In the office 5 days a week
  - Tend to spend most of their time at their assigned workstation
- *Walkers*
  - In the office 5 days a week
  - Tend to spend a large percentage of their office time outside of their assigned workstation
- *Teleworkers*
  - Work from home or a telework center 2–3 days per week
  - Share space on the days they are in the office
  - Have notebook computers and access to a telephone when in the regular office
- *Occasional*
  - Drop in occasionally (anywhere from a few hours to a few days)
  - Regular "home base" is not in this facility
  - Usually have their own technology but need access to a phone

- *Mobile*
  - Work anywhere
  - Typically "road warriors" who are in the office anywhere from a few hours/week to a day/week
  - Usually equipped with cellular phones and notebook computers

Analysis of Work Activities

Produce a histogram showing the distribution of work across the primary activities identified in the questionnaire and the details for each activity. Particular emphasis should be placed on trends regarding the effectiveness of the current space in meeting the users' requirements for each activity. This trend analysis should help to identify the approximate mix of space types necessary in the new alternate work environment.

Figure 6-12 shows an example of how to graph work activities. The call center operation in the customer service group shows a high degree of phone and PC usage; the research and development group has the most informal meetings; while the sales group is usually in the office for scheduled meetings. These data show that (1) the sales people are usually in the office for meetings, so they probably do not need a full workstation, (2) the call center could probably be performed by teleworkers, as they are on the phone most of the time, and (3) the R&D group is probably best suited to a teaming space, given the amount of collaboration that probably occurs during their ad hoc meetings.

Space Issues

The next step is to construct a histogram showing the responses to key space issues such as office environment, team dynamics, storage, communicating/learning from others, impact on performance, etc. The qualitative data on the top three best and three worst features of the current office should also be summarized. Analyze the data by looking for trends in what is and is not working. This will help to identify the mix of space types.

Figure 6-13 is an example of such a graph. It shows the degree of staff interest in some of the shared spaces: café type space is of interest to all respondents, while the soft seating is of more interest to the sales and marketing groups (which is consistent with the amount of time they spend in meetings, as shown in Figure 6-12).

Information Technology Usage

Produce a histogram showing the use of technology, applications, and networks. Key issues here are the extent to which remote access is required and the extent to which portable technology is in use.

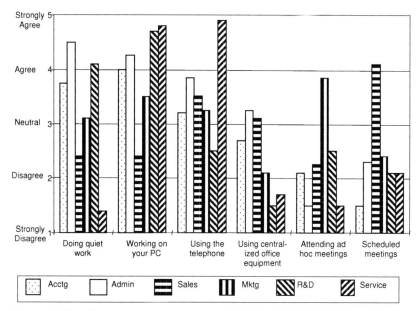

Figure 6-12 Work activities performed while in the office, compiled from questionnaires.

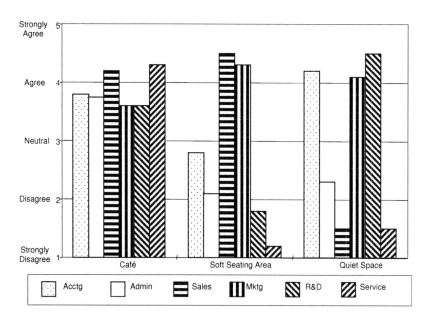

Figure 6-13 Degree of agreement with the statement "I would use the following shared space," compiled from questionnaires.

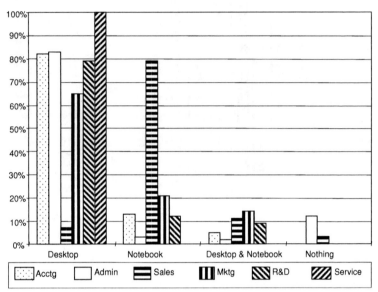

Figure 6-14   Types of personal computer in use by department, compiled from questionnaires.

Figure 6-14 shows the distribution of personal computers by department. The mobile sales force is, of course, primarily supplied by notebook computers while the traditional "in office" groups primarily use desktop computers. This graph shows the areas where the technology will need to change to optimally utilize telework and space sharing. For example, applying teleworking to the customer service group would likely require replacing some of the desktop computers with notebook computers to provide the additional portability required.

Readiness Analysis

An important aspect of the appropriateness assessment is determining how prepared the group is to implement work transformation. This will include analyzing the group in terms of information technology, facilities management, human resources, and business objectives. This data will come from the work patterns questionnaire, the information technology (IT) questionnaire, and the business objectives data-gathering session.

Information Technology

The analysis must include an assessment of the IT infrastructure in terms of the current situation and plans for the immediate future. This should include any comments or concerns about the ability of the technology to support shared office environments (hardware, software, network, and voice communications) and remote access for teleworkers and mobile workers (if appropriate).

Facilities Management

Several facilities management issues need to be addressed: an estimate of potential floor space reductions, the potential to recycle existing furniture, and the ability to construct an ASA design within existing building(s).

Human Resources

Several key human resources issues need to be addressed: the level of union support, the potential adoption of AWAs (and the impact this could have on the ASA solutions), and the ability of management to adjust to work transformation concepts.

Change Adoption

This analysis assesses the readiness of the organization to adopt change. The key issues to be covered are availability of a work transformation champion and sponsor, the attitude of the organization towards change, and the sense of urgency and motivation. This is not easily quantifiable and will require some subjective analysis of the ability of the organization to absorb change.

Business Objectives

One of the most important elements in considering work transformation is whether it will assist the organization in attaining its business objectives. This analysis should identify the business objectives that should be addressed and some of the solutions worth considering.

The key to success in assessing readiness is to remember the degree of change associated with alternative officing. A recent *Business Week* editorial covered this issue directly, suggesting that

> These changes will affect managers, who will have to adjust from measuring productivity by "face time" to managing by outputs. This will be particularly challenging for those managers who favor those who appear to be busy at their desks over those achieving much more on the road, or off huddling at a coffee bar to meet a project deadline.[2]

This challenge is supported by James Hackett, Chief Executive Officer of Steelcase Inc., who suggests that

> It used to be that power was a worker's relative distance to the CEO's office. Now it's one's proximity to knowledge. It will take time for

managers to empower employees to seek that knowledge, whether it's at a customer's office, at a brainstorming session or even in cyber-space.[3]

Positioning Strategy

The positioning strategy should include a high-level view of how the work transformation concepts can be implemented. The implementation strategy must determine where on the change continuum the organization should be positioned.

Work transformation consists of both alternate work arrangements and alternative space arrangements. Determining the extent to which the organization is prepared to implement work transformation requires a determination of how aggressively it wants to both AWAs and ASAs. Figure 6-15 shows the change continuum for both of these work transformation components. The three generic positions on the continuum are identified as *passive change*, *stepping stone*, and *embrace change*.

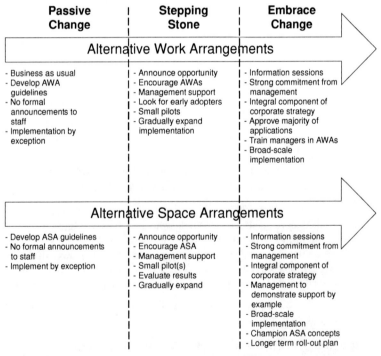

Figure 6-15   Work transformation positioning strategy.

The passive change model involves doing some research and building the basic tools required to support work transformation. The model includes the same ad hoc implementations of AWAs and ASAs, although these efforts are likely to be informal and possibly somewhat "under the table."

The embrace change model shows a full and complete support of the concept from senior management and a complete integration of work transformation into the overall business strategy. This model embraces work transformation and includes aggressive plans to implement the concepts across the organization. The embrace change model is most effective for organizations that have already researched work transformation and are confident that the anticipated business benefits will materialize.

The stepping stone model lets an organization experiment with these new concepts, allowing it to prove the concept through small pilots and then gradually roll out the concept across the organization. The stepping stone model has proven to be the most successful approach for those organizations that are at the early stages of adopting work transformation.

In choosing an implementation strategy, it is necessary to consider the relative position of the organization and to select an implementation model that will best meet the organization's situation, requirements, and culture. It is also important to point out that different models for AWAs and ASAs can be implemented. For example, the organization may be at the point of embracing change for AWAs while being at only the stepping stone stage for ASAs.

Assessment Presentation

The assessment analysis should be documented in a brief report and presentation. The goal is not to show the responses to every question, but rather to focus on the areas that have the most significant impact on the decision-making process.

Assessment should determine the appropriateness of work transformation for each group. The findings should be presented in an honest and realistic manner, and should recommend whether or not the organization should proceed with a business case. The recommendation must be supported by the analysis. An appropriate action plan to move forward should also be provided.

The presentation should be made to the senior management team. It should be focused on helping them make an informed business decision on the consequences of work transformation. If senior management believes that the assessment has shown an opportunity for work transformation to succeed, then approval should be given to perform a business case. Figure 6-16 shows the work processes required to perform the work transformation assessment.

This is the most complicated portion of gaining management support but also the most critical. The effort required to gather and analyze the organization's

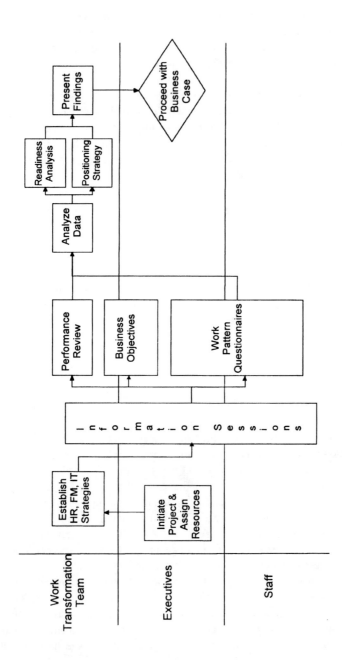

Figure 6-16 Work transformation assessment phase: work process.

data pays off by taking work transformation from a theory that other organizations may have considered and used, and moving it much closer to reality by clearly presenting it within the context of the organization being studied.

BUSINESS CASE

The business case is where all the theory, assumptions, and strategies for work transformation need to be brought together to determine the expected costs, benefits, and ultimate business value.

The business case is a step towards the actual implementation of work transformation. This may seem like a lengthy and complicated process, but it is a necessary one. Organizations that choose to "dive into" work transformation without doing this level of business analysis usually fail—and fail because senior management believes that this new way of working has not met expectations.

The goal of the business case is to establish the expectations. The business case outlines the expected benefits and the methods for determining success. Senior management can then compare the final results with the original expectations that have been documented in this business case. Without such a document, any evaluation can be based only on speculation, interpretation, and perception of the real benefits—a strategy that usually leads to failure.

The business case is a consolidation of the information gathered to date. It includes a brief summary of the research, the shared vision, the key strategies, a high-level summary of the assessment findings, the readiness analysis, and the positioning strategy. In addition, it includes the financial analysis, measures for success, and recommendations. Figure 6-17 shows the key elements of the work transformation business case.

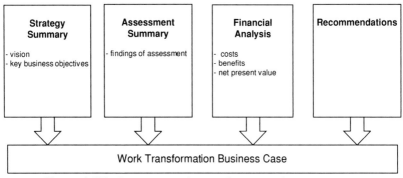

Figure 6-17 Steps to work transformation business case.

Financial Analysis

The work transformation financial analysis is a key component of the overall business case. Most executives are interested in hearing about the concepts, strategies, and plans but will most likely decide on the fate of the business case based on the financial analysis.

The financial analysis should be structured around a standard cash flow analysis spreadsheet. This analysis includes documenting all of the costs associated with the initiative along with the benefits. The costs and benefits are combined to produce a net cash flow. The financial analysis should also include a net present value (NPV) calculation.

The first step in producing the financial analysis is to gather the basic costs associated with the initiative. The costs include the effort (internal and external) to develop strategies, plans, guidelines, and policies to implement the initiative. Other common costs to consider include the following:

- *Human Resources*
  - Training
- *Facilities Management*
  - Facilities for teleworker's home office (i.e., desk, chair, lockable cabinet)
  - Furniture upgrades and/or additions to support nontraditional office design
  - Outfitting costs for new office design
- *Information Technology*
  - Notebook computers and docking stations
  - Remote access facilities
  - Modems and access devices (e.g., ISDN, ADSL)
  - Network enhancements to support nontraditional offices
  - Telephones for remote workers
  - Airtime, long distance, etc.

This list is certainly not mandatory nor exhaustive, but it will provide a starting point for the implementation of work transformation. Some of the costs will be one-time costs, while others will be ongoing operational costs. These two types of costs will be handled differently in the financial analysis, so they should be separated.

Careful consideration should also be given when determining which costs to assign to the business case, and which to designate as business-as-usual costs. The analysis must avoid "double counting" the costs. For example, consider the organization that is replacing its personal computers every three years (a standard practice today). The PC is deemed to be a necessary element to perform virtually all office jobs today. If the organization intends to buy notebook computers for 50 remote workers, then perhaps the yearly upgrade program could be used to provide these machines without incurring additional costs. In other words, the organization is going to pay for the upgrades anyway; so merely reallocate who receives upgrades to ensure that remote workers get the notebook computers and those who will remain as traditional office workers will receive the technology currently in use by the proposed remote workers (assuming this technology is newer than the traditional office worker's current machine). The only incremental cost will be if desktop computers are being replaced by notebook computers (which are more expensive). In this case, the incremental cost is the difference between the price of a notebook and the price of a desktop.

This all cost analysis may sound complicated, but in the long run it will have a tremendous impact on the business case and will avoid placing the organization into a position where it will be upgrading PCs at a rate that is faster and more expensive than necessary.

Once the costs are quantified, the next step is to determine the anticipated benefits. This is more difficult than determining the costs. There will be a broad range of potential benefits to be considered. The following are a few of the common quantifiable benefits and the formulas that can be used to calculate the amount of the benefit.

Productivity Improvements

Productivity improvements are probably the most common benefit of work transformation and certainly one of the most controversial. The challenge with productivity benefits is measuring productivity gains.

The best approach is to take experiences from others who have already implemented these concepts. For example, the implementation of telework shows productivity improvements of 5–15% on telework days. The formula for this calculation is

> Productivity improvement = Number of employees affected
> × Percentage improvement in productivity
> × Average annual salary

Absenteeism Savings

Many of the AWAs will result in a reduction in the level of absenteeism. Research suggests that providing employees with a broader range of work alternatives will reduce the level of absenteeism—usually in the range of 30–60%. This is based on statistics that show that a large percentage of the time employees are absent not because they are sick but because they have to care for a child or an elderly person or they are not well enough to commute to work—although they might be capable of working from home.

The formula for this calculation is

Absenteeism savings = Number of employees affected
  × Average number of days absent per year
  × Reduction in absenteeism × Average daily salary

Space Savings

The most significant intangible saving will be in reducing the total amount of space required. The savings here will depend on the extent to which remote work (telework and mobile workers) is implemented and the extent to which space sharing and the use of nontraditional office strategies are used.

The formula for space saving for those who share space is

Space savings = [Number of remote workers × (Number of
  workstations ÷ Number of remote workers)
  × Average office size in ft^2 × Average cost per ft^2]
  + (Number of ft^2 saved for regular employees through
  nontraditional of fice strategies × Average cost per ft^2)

Office Furniture Salvage

The reduction of office space required will likely result in a surplus of office furniture. Organizations may choose to provide some of this furniture to those employees who will be teleworking, sell the surplus furniture, donate it to charity as a tax-deductible contribution, or some combination of these strategies. If the surplus furniture is sold or a tax deduction is claimed, the money raised should be included as a one-time benefit.

Office Space Avoidance

Many organizations implement work transformation concepts to avoid the need to acquire additional space. This cost avoidance should be included in the business case. Some of the common elements of this benefit include savings in real estate costs (if purchased), tenant improvements, data/telephone wiring, office furniture, moving and engineering/consulting costs associated with setting up the new space. Also included should be the annual operating costs for the new space.

These examples represent a few of the common benefits to be included. There are other benefits for which it is impossible to provide a generic formula. But they should still be counted, as they may be at least as important as the generic ones listed above. For example, consider an organization that has decided to implement teleworking and some minor reengineering to increase the hours of coverage for customer service. These customer service benefits should be quantified and included in the business case.

Once the costs and the benefits have been identified, it is time to consolidate the information into a cash flow analysis spreadsheet. It is important to distinguish the one-time costs and benefits from those that will be ongoing and to identify which benefits are tangible and which are intangible.

To do the cash flow analysis, the analyst must understand some of the basic definitions. One-time costs or benefits are those that are incurred or received once in the life of the analysis. For example, furniture that is purchased to support the ASAs strategy it is considered a one-time cost.

Some of the costs and benefits will be ongoing in nature. For example, the cost of providing phone lines to teleworkers' homes will have an ongoing operational costs. These costs will be incurred in each year of the period being analyzed.

The difference between tangible and intangible benefits is not as clearly defined. Tangible benefits are those that will have a direct impact on the actual cash flow of the company. Intangible benefits, while important, will not have a direct quantifiable benefit. For example, the saving in real estate costs is a tangible benefit, as the savings can be taken off of the bottom line. The improvement in employee productivity may or may not be considered tangible. It will be intangible if the improvement in productivity is not associated with any direct cost saving or revenue generation. In some cases, the improvement in productivity will not result in reducing the number of staff or avoiding the hiring of additional staff in the future. Figure 6-18 shows a typical financial analysis spreadsheet where the costs and benefits have been categorized and entered.

The financial analysis in Figure 6-18 assumes that the value of money is the same in year 1 as it is in year 5. This, of course, is not realistic. Adding a time value to the costs and benefits can be performed by calculating the discounted cash flow and producing an NPV report.

Net present value is the value of all of the investments and benefits taken in today's dollars. Initiatives that have a positive NPV are deemed to be financially viable because the benefits outweigh the investment when future investments and benefits are discounted to represent the value of today's dollars. For example, consider the following two projects that both require a $60,000 investment today. Project A produces benefits of $20,000 a year for 3 years. Project B produces benefits of $25,000 per year for 3 years. Some people might, mistakenly think that Project A is a break-even project ($60,000 spent and $60,000 returned) and that Project B would show a profit of

Cost	Year 1	Year 2	Year 3	Year 4	Year 5	Total
One-Time Cost						
Project Resources	$35,000					$35,000
Information Technology	$25,000					$25,000
Facilities Management	$15,000					$15,000
Human Resources	$5,000					$5,000
Ongoing Costs:						
Information Technology	$10,000	$10,000	$10,000	$10,000	$10,000	$50,000
Facilities Management	$1,000	$1,000	$1,000	$1,000	$1,000	$5,000
Total Investment	$91,000	$11,000	$11,000	$11,000	$11,000	$135,000
Tangible Benefits:						
One-Time Benefits						
Furniture Salvage	$15,000					$15,000
Ongoing Benefits						
Space Savings	$25,000	$25,000	$25,000	$25,000	$25,000	$125,000
Customer Service	$10,000	$10,000	$10,000	$10,000	$10,000	$50,000
Total Tangible Benefits	$50,000	$35,000	$35,000	$35,000	$35,000	$190,000
Net Cash Flow with Tangibles	($41,000)	$24,000	$24,000	$24,000	$24,000	$55,000
Intangible Benefits:						
One-Time Benefits						$0
Ongoing Benefits						
Productivity Improvements	$14,000	$14,000	$14,000	$14,000	$14,000	$70,000
Absenteeism Reduction	$3,000	$3,000	$3,000	$3,000	$3,000	$15,000
Total Intangible Benefits	$17,000	$17,000	$17,000	$17,000	$17,000	$85,000
Net Cash Flow with Intangibles	($24,000)	$41,000	$41,000	$41,000	$41,000	$140,000

Figure 6-18 Basic financial analysis.

Cost	Year 1	Year 2	Year 3	Year 4	Year 5	Total
One-Time Cost						
Project Resources	$35,000					$35,000
Information Technology	$25,000					$25,000
Facilities Management	$15,000					$15,000
Human Resources	$5,000					$5,000
Ongoing Costs:						
Information Technology	$10,000	$10,000	$10,000	$10,000	$10,000	$50,000
Facilities Management	$1,000	$1,000	$1,000	$1,000	$1,000	$5,000
Total Investment	$91,000	$11,000	$11,000	$11,000	$11,000	$135,000
Tangible Benefits:						
One-Time Benefits						
Furniture Salvage	$15,000					$15,000
Ongoing Benefits						
Space Savings	$25,000	$25,000	$25,000	$25,000	$25,000	$125,000
Customer Service	$10,000	$10,000	$10,000	$10,000	$10,000	$50,000
Total Tangible Benefits	$50,000	$35,000	$35,000	$35,000	$35,000	$190,000
Net Cash Flow with Tangibles	($41,000)	$24,000	$24,000	$24,000	$24,000	$55,000
Discounted Cash Flow with Tangibles	($41,000)	$22,222	$20,576	$19,052	$17,641	$38,491
Intangible Benefits:						
One-Time Benefits						$0
Ongoing Benefits						
Productivity Improvements	$14,000	$14,000	$14,000	$14,000	$14,000	$70,000
Absenteeism Reduction	$3,000	$3,000	$3,000	$3,000	$3,000	$15,000
Total Intangible Benefits	$17,000	$17,000	$17,000	$17,000	$17,000	$85,000
Net Cash Flow with Intangibles	($24,000)	$41,000	$41,000	$41,000	$41,000	$140,000
Discounted Cash Flow with Intangibles	($24,000)	$37,963	$35,151	$32,547	$30,136	$111,797
Discount Rate:	8%					

Figure 6-19 Net present value financial analysis.

$15,000. However, when the value of money is discounted over time by 10%, "A" has an NPV of ($5,000) (a loss) and "B" is $8,000. This is because a dollar earned in year three is worth less than the dollar earned today. Using NPV concepts, Project A would be rejected and B accepted. Figure 6-19 illustrates the NPV financial analysis.

The net present value is calculated using the following formula:

$$\text{Discounted cash flow} = \text{Net cash flow} \times (1 + R)^{-(Y-1)}$$

where

R = Discount rate (cost of capital)

Y = Year

For example, the net cash flow after tangible benefits in year 3 is $24,000. The discounted cash flow is $20,576, using a discount rate of 8%. The calculation for this figure is as follows:

$$\$24,000 \times \$24,00 \times 1.08^{-2} = \$20,576$$

In this example, the net present value of the project is $38,491 with the tangible benefits and $111,797 with the intangibles. This shows that the project will have a positive cash flow in that the benefits will outweigh the costs over the five-year period analyzed. If the financial analysis were for only one year, the costs would be greater than the benefits, so it is critical to analyze these types of projects over the long term (5–10), thus allowing enough time for the benefits to offset the costs.

Measures for Success

The business case will include the identification of both tangible and intangible benefits. These benefits are critical to analyzing the financial viability of the project. Organizations must, however, remember to track progress towards attaining these benefits. If they are not able to meet the expected benefits, they may find that the net present value calculation is no longer positive and that the project may not be financially viable (where viable is defined as benefits being greater than costs).

In order to track progress towards reaching the anticipated benefits, the organization should define specific measures of success and methods for tracking progress. In some areas, the tracking methods are fairly simple and straightforward—in other areas they will be more complex.

The following are a few of the common success measures and ideas on how to track progress.

Productivity Improvement

Measuring productivity will be easy for jobs that have specific measures are easy to track. For example, there will likely be specific data available on the number of pages a transcriptionist transcribes per day. His or her productivity could be easily tracked after work transformation is implemented to determine the change. However, examples such as this are few—for most jobs there are not specific, easily quantifiable measures for tracking productivity.

For most jobs, the only way to measure productivity is to break the job into tasks and to determine which tasks can be quantified. The tasks that can be quantified can be measured. For example, an engineer may be responsible for calculating the load on transmission towers in a power utility. The engineer will repeat this task numerous times in a month. Tracking the difference in productivity is accomplished by first gathering baseline data on how long this task takes in the normal work environment and then tracking this same task under the new methods of working. The assumption can then be made that the improvement tracked in a few tasks can be extrapolated across the entire job. It is not foolproof nor scientific, but it is one of the best methods currently available.

Another variation would be to calculate the percentage change on specific tasks, as above, and then to determine the percentage of the overall job that is consumed by these tasks. This will allow the worker to conclude that he or she is at least a certain percentage more (in)efficient. For example, if the engineer above was 20% more productive in calculating tower loads and if this task makes up 40% of the job, then it is reasonable to assume that the engineer is at least 8% more efficient.

Another method of calculating productivity improvements is to have employees estimate the relative percentage improvement based on their own experiences. This approach has been used in many studies and typically shows that the employee will usually report a productivity increase that is likely higher than that realistically achieved. For a more realistic assessment, it is worthwhile for the employee's manager to also estimate the improvement in productivity. The manager will usually understate the improvement. The average of the manager's and the employee's estimated improvement can then be used. This method is even less scientific than the one above, but it will at least provide some indication of the direction and order of magnitude of the improvement.

Reduced Absenteeism

Changes in absenteeism are usually easy to measure. The challenge for most organizations is compiling satisfactory historical information. In order to gauge the degree of change, the analyst will need to know what the level of absenteeism has been prior to the start of work transformation. Once this information is available, it is fairly easy to have employees track the days they are absent and compare these figures to the historical ones.

Space Savings

Space savings will be realized only when the space is released. This can be tracked by the real estate group to determine the final dollar value of the sub-lease, contract, or cancellation.

Improved Employee Morale

Tracking employee morale is difficult. The best way to track morale is through the use of a questionnaire that contains a series of employee morale-related questions. The key to tracking any changes will be to have historical data to form a baseline. The historical data will be even more valuable if it represents the level of employee morale across the entire organization.

Some organizations have existing "employee satisfaction" surveys that can be used for measuring the change in morale after work transformation. If the organization does not have this type of analysis in place, then a few employee morale–related questions should be added to the work transformation questionnaire and follow-up questions should be used as part of the review process described in Chapter 8 (pp. 220–225).

Improved Customer Service

Tracking customer service improvements is also challenging. The best way is to ask customers either through a survey or by random telephone calls. Again, it is best if some overall historical customer service data is available for comparison.

Another way to track changes in customer service may be to track the repeat business from customers, referrals or increases in volumes of existing sales from the same customer. All of these could be construed as strong indicators to an improvement in customer service.

Business Case Format

The end result of this process of gaining management support is to prepare a formal business case and to present the business case to the executives for approval.

Many organizations have their own formal method of preparing a business case. If the organization does not have a standard business case format, the following generic outline could be used.

Executive Summary

The executive summary is a one- or two-page summary of the highlights of the business case. This should include the scope, basic strategy, expected benefits, net present value, and the recommendation.

Objectives

This section explains the purpose of the business case and what is hoped to be accomplished. The objectives should include a very brief background on the approach that was taken to the business case and the ultimate goal (to gain approval to proceed).

Opportunity Description

The opportunity description defines the scope of the project. It describes the definitions of new forms of work and how these concepts could be applied.

Summary of Research

A *very brief* summary of the research that has been performed should be included. This should be no more than a few pages and should focus on other organizations that are in the same industry sector and have achieved success with these concepts.

Vision for Work Transformation

A description of the vision for work transformation as prepared in the visioning process should be incorporated.

Work Transformation Assessment

This is a *very brief* summary of the assessment data focusing on the key findings that have led to the development of this business case.

Business Benefits

A business case by definition must have specific business benefits. These should be identified with a brief explanation as to why it should be possible to attain the anticipated benefits.

Employee Benefits

Implementing new forms of work is a win–win situation for both the organization and the employee. This section should contain a brief explanation of the high-level employee benefits that are anticipated.

Supporting Strategies

This section should document the basic human resources, facilities management, and information technology strategies that are needed to implement work transformation.

Implementation Strategy

The proposed implementation strategy should be stated. If a pilot is proposed, the size and demographics of the proposed pilot should be included.

Readiness Analysis

This is an honest analysis of the readiness of the organization to handle new work forms.

Positioning Strategy

The proposed strategy should document the speed and level of aggressiveness at which work transformation should be implemented.

Financial Analysis

The financial analysis component is presented here. The text portion should include written explanations of how the expected business benefits have been calculated. The spreadsheets should be attached (and cross-referenced) as an appendix.

Success Measures

Include specific examples of how the organization will measure the benefits identified. This section should explain the monitoring mechanisms, how they will be analyzed, and the timing.

Recommendations

The final section—except for any appendices—will be the recommendations of the business case. These are the actions the executives will have to approve, including an agreement to proceed with the implementation of work transformation.

Figure 6-20 shows the process for creating the business case. This is the final step in securing management support for work transformation. The key element of the business case is to make the financial analysis as accurate as possible so that senior management can feel comfortable with the basis upon which they are making their decision.

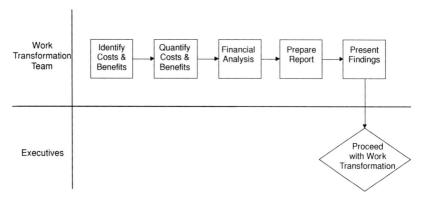

Figure 6-20   Work transformation business case phase: work process.

Examples of Successful Business Cases

Quantifying the benefits for a business case is a difficult process. Many organizations have already implemented these concepts; by reviewing their results, it is easier to determine how likely your organization is to achieve similar benefits.

There are numerous examples of achieving business benefits from work transformation. The following are a few examples of benefits that have been widely reported in the popular press and were included in the Smart Valley Telecommuting Project in the Silicone Valley of California.[4]

The Smart Valley Inc. project showed an overall productivity improvement of 18–23%. This project included companies such as: 3Com, Cisco Systems, Deloitte & Touche, Gray Cary Ware Freidenrich, Hewlett-Packard, Pacific Bell, Regis McKenna, and Silicon Graphics.

Amex Life Insurance

Naudia Wise Ibanez, Senior Employment Relations Professional at Amex Life Insurance, reports the overall productivity increase of 20% for a group of underwriters in San Rafael, CA, who have been teleworking from home 1–2 days per week for the past 5 years. Employee retention is also good, with no turnover among teleworkers in 3 years—this is highly unusually in the life insurance field.

American Express

American Express Travel Related Services (TRS) made the transition to the virtual office concept for its field sales force. The company spent time in the field with the sales agents to find out why the number of calls made per day and the number of new establishments signed up was declining. This also gave the staff a chance to participate directly in the change process.

A complete review of its facilities prompted TRS to changed a lot of things. It had 50 satellite offices around the United States which were used by the sales agents. TRS quickly discovered that the work being performed by the sales agents at the satellite offices could be accomplished at home. In 1994, the company began its change to teleworking and mobile working.

TRS provided a support package for representatives including a Power-Book computer, software, printer, fax machine, copier, two phone lines, car phone, reimbursement for all normal business expenses, and a one-time home-office setup allowance of $1,000. TRS made clear to representatives that 75–80% of the work week was to be spent with customers and prospects, and that less than 15% of the time was to be spent at home. TRS found that the number of calls per day increased by 40%, customer satisfaction ratings went up by 28%, and representative satisfaction rating went up by 25%.

IBM

IBM's Mobility Strategy program involved a rapid conversion of most of its U.S. marketing and services work force to "mobile" status. IBM reported 40–60% reduction in real estate costs per U.S. site, for a savings of $35 million in 1995. Productivity has risen per site by as much as 15%. For the first time ever, productivity, customer satisfaction, and employee satisfaction all increased.

The IBM project applies to more than 20,000 employees. They work from home, customer locations, airports, and remote sites. Andrea Cheatham, IBM's Mobility Strategy representative, puts it this way:

> The bottom-line is that we basically legitimize [remote work] and give people the flexibility to balance when they need to work, when they need to be with their customer and when they need to be with their family. It all gets done now versus having the stress of trying to get it done within a specific time period.[5]

SUMMARY

Gaining management support is critical to the success of the work transformation program. To do this, the organization must do some basic research to understand the work transformation concept and then share this knowledge with the organization's senior decision makers.

To attain executive support, it is necessary to help the executives see the work transformation vision and to have them think of this vision in terms of what business value it will bring to the organization. This visioning process is essential to the longer term success of work transformation—without it the organization will loose site of the reasons why they are changing how and where employees work.

The next step in gaining management support is to assess the appropriateness of work transformation. This includes educating the organization on the concepts and collecting data regarding use of space, work patterns of employees, potential for alternative work and space arrangements, business objectives, and supporting technologies. The assessment provides executives with some hard data about the organization and the potential for work transformation. The assessment does not include any financial analysis—at this stage it is more important to have the executives continue to focus in on the concept, to see the longer term opportunities, and to re-enforce the vision.

The final step is to consolidate the vision and assessment information into a business case. This document includes a complete financial analysis based on the positioning strategy proposed in the assessment process. The business case also includes a net present value analysis which presents the financial viability of the concept.

The executives will now have all of the information needed to make an informed business decision on the fate of work transformation. The efforts to secure management support are critical to the longer-term success of the concepts.

NOTES

1. "Sitters" and "walkers" are terms that were originally coined by Michael Brill of BOSTI Group in Buffalo. They are extremely descriptive terms and have become part of the new office lexicon in many organizations.
2. Let the Walls Come Tumbling Down. *Business Week* editorial, April 29, 1996, p. 138.
3. Ibid, p. 138.
4. Silicon Valley Telecommuting Report, 1995, as found at www.svi.org
5. Ibid.

7

Implementation

We have seen work transformation evolve from a high-level concept, to a strategy that supports the corporate business objectives, to an assessment where corporate information in analyzed in terms of the opportunity, to the application of these concepts to a business case that defines the expected investment and benefits.

This chapter brings work transformation from this theoretical framework to its successful implementation. Implementing work transformation is usually a challenging experience. Unfortunately, because the concepts appear to be fairly simple, some organizations make the mistake of not treating this implementation as a formal project.

The key to successful implementation is, once again, the work transformation pyramid, as shown in Figure 7-1. To be successful, an organization must

Figure 7-1 Integrating key strategies.

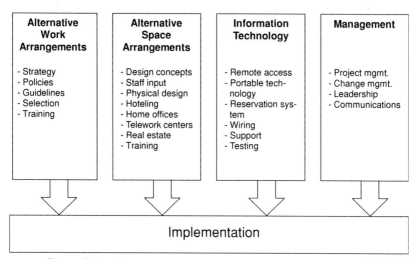

Figure 7-2 Steps to work transformation implementation.

continue to integrate the alternative work arrangement (AWA) concepts (human resources) with the alternative space arrangement (ASA) concepts (facilities management) through the use of enabling information technologies (ITs) to deliver on the business objectives.

The steps to implementing work transformation are shown in Figure 7-2. These include the design of the AWA, ASA, and IT components as well as the key management functions of project management, change management, leadership, and communications. The chapter concludes with an explanation of the resources required for implementation and suggestions on how to gradually introduce work transformation through a pilot strategy.

IMPLEMENTATION OF ALTERNATIVE WORK ARRANGEMENTS

The first step in implementing work transformation is addressing the implementation of AWAs. This implementation involves updating the AWA implementation strategy, developing appropriate policies and guidelines, selecting the right resources, and training.

Strategy

The AWA implementation strategy should have been identified in the work transformation assessment phase, as described in Chapter 6. During the assess-

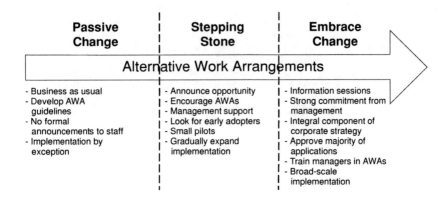

Passive Change	Stepping Stone	Embrace Change
Alternative Work Arrangements		
- Business as usual - Develop AWA guidelines - No formal announcements to staff - Implementation by exception	- Announce opportunity - Encourage AWAs - Management support - Look for early adopters - Small pilots - Gradually expand implementation	- Information sessions - Strong commitment from management - Integral component of corporate strategy - Approve majority of applications - Train managers in AWAs - Broad-scale implementation

Figure 7-3 AWA positioning strategy.

ment phase, a positioning strategy for AWAs was established based on the concept of making a passive change, taking a stepping-stone approach to change, or embracing the change and going for a more radical implementation. Figure 7-3 shows the continuum of options for AWA implementation.

During the implementation stage, it is crucial to identify what particular AWAs will be implemented. Will the organization start with a fairly complete range of work options, or will they be limited? Most organizations are comfortable with the AWAs that represent the least change—usually these include variable work hours, regular part-time, job sharing, and phased retirement. AWAs that involve a greater degree of change—and therefore a greater risk—include modified work weeks, telework, and work at home are more challenging.

If the organization chooses to exclude any of the common AWAs, it should be prepared to defend the rationale for this decision. The defense for including certain AWAs while excluding others should be based on sound business decision making and not just senior management's "lack of comfort."

The decision of what is *in* and what is *out* is critical to the success of the implementation. The implications of the various different options should be considered along with a risk assessment. If the risk is deemed to be too large for the expected return, then the organization should either not implement the AWA or consider implementing it on a "small-scale experimental" basis.

Policies/Guidelines

Policies and guidelines should be developed to help drive the successful implementation of AWAs. The extent to which policies are required will depend on the organization. Those organizations that are heavily driven by policies may want to have strict policy statements in place to clearly define the boundaries of AWAs. Organizations that are not as tightly bound by policies may want to develop a series of guidelines that will provide staff and management with an overview of the concepts and a framework in which these concepts should be applied.

My experience has shown that the best strategy is to have a few key policy statements that clearly define the AWAs, with several guidelines that provide a basic road map of how these arrangements should be implemented. Organizations need to remember that AWAs are about flexibility and adaptability, so it is important not make the guidelines too rigid.

As discussed in Chapter 3, the following are the basic principles for AWA programs that should be integrated into the policies and guidelines for the organization:

- *AWA Fundamentals*
  - Not necessarily appropriate for all employees
  - Not a universal employee benefit
  - Not a condition of employment
  - Participation strictly voluntary
- *AWA Eligibility*
  - Employee must not be on any type of performance improvement process.
  - The employee and his or her manager must complete the appropriate self-evaluation questionnaires and, where appropriate, produce a business case.
  - The arrangement must have the complete support of the manager and the team.
- *Operational Issues*
  - Formal agreements should be signed by the employee and his or her manager.
  - The employee and his or her manager must agree on an appropriate schedule.
  - The manager may revise the schedule to meet operational needs.
  - The employee may request changes to the schedule but must obtain his or her manager's approval prior to making any changes.
  - Those who are job sharing, working regular part-time, or teleworking must be prepared to utilize shared or smaller office facilities when they are working at their regular work location.
  - Appropriate security and safety precautions must be taken by remote workers.

- Cancellation
  - The AWA agreements for variable work hours, modified work week, or telework can be canceled by either the manager or the employee on two weeks' advance written notice.
  - The AWA agreements for job sharing, regular part-time, and phased retirement represent an entirely new employment agreement. Cancellation of these agreements by either the manager or the employee will require two weeks' advance written notice of the intention to cancel.

Selection

The selection of those who will utilize AWAs should be based on the self-evaluation process described in Chapter 3. By this process, the employee completes a self-evaluation questionnaire (SEQ) for the AWA selected to help determine the suitability of the AWA to the employee's own particular situation.

Alternative work arrangements that are deemed appropriate by the employee should then be reviewed by the employee's immediate manager. The decision-making process for some of the AWAs will be more complicated than others. For example, for those employees selecting part-time, job sharing, or phased retirement, their decision will directly impact their wages and the business activities they perform. Employees who select telework or work-at-home arrangements will have several additional issues to consider. Figure 7-4 reviews the decision-making process for remote workers.

Training

The introduction of AWAs brings many new concepts to staff and management. To be successful, the organization must share information about these concepts with all staff—even those who may not want to personally participate in AWAs.

The following are a few of the key training programs to support alternative work arrangements:

Alternative Work Arrangement Information Session

This session introduces the concept of work transformation to all employees and managers. In so doing, it provides a description of AWAs, explains the expected business and personal benefits, and outlines the process to follow to analyze the appropriateness for each person's job. The relationship between AWAs and ASAs should also be explained such that employees realize that some of the AWAs (job sharing, part-time, telework, work at home) are directly related to ASAs (particularly in terms of space sharing for those who are not in the office every day).

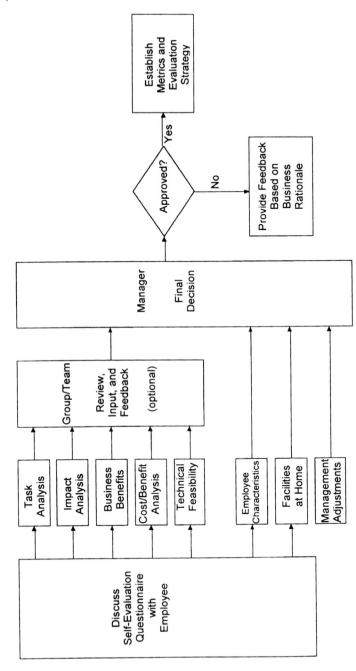

Figure 7-4 Decision-making process for a proposal to work remotely.

The information sessions should include a 30–45 minute formal presentation followed by a 30–45 minute question-and-answer session. Employees and their managers should be encouraged to actively participate in the session. Employees should also be encouraged to access information about AWAs after the information session (these materials should be made available in the corporate library and in each department or, even better, via the organization's Intranet site. The initial information sessions may be best provided by an external consultant; however, once the organization becomes more comfortable with these arrangements, the sessions can be presented by internal HR staff.

Manager's Guide to Successfully Managing Alternative Work Arrangements

This session should provide managers with a greater understanding of AWA concepts, policies, and guidelines, and how to apply them in their departments. Emphasis should be placed on the communication and management style adjustments necessary to successfully manage a mixture of employees, only some of whom may be using AWAs.

Managers must be trained to deal with AWA requests in an open and constructive way and not to make decisions based on their personal perception of the arrangements. The training session must instruct managers that AWAs are to be approved, rejected, or canceled based only on sound business decision-making rationale, not on the manager's "gut feel." As with the information session, this training should initially be provided by an external consultant and then by internal HR staff.

Remote Work Implementation

Training on how to be successful at remote work should be provided for those who will be teleworking or on a work-at-home arrangement. The training should cover setting up the home office, organizing the employee's work, technology tips, dealing with the psychological aspects of working remotely, staying in touch with the rest of the team, and so on.

The remote work-training session should also include specific hands-on training demonstrating the technology to be used, how to operate it from home, support expectations, and how remote workers can diagnose their own technology problems. Technology staff who are providing the training should be prepared to show a live remote connection as part of the training session so that participants can view, first hand, what they should expect when working remotely. This training session should be presented as a joint effort between the HR and IT departments.

IMPLEMENTATION OF ALTERNATIVE SPACE ARRANGEMENTS

The second key component of implementing work transformation is the implementation of ASAs. The ASA implementation involves updating the ASA strategy, developing design concepts, getting staff input, physically designing the space, accommodating those who share space or work remotely, and addressing the basic real estate issues.

Strategy

The ASA implementation strategy should have been identified in the work transformation assessment phase described in Chapter 6. During the assessment phase, a positioning strategy for ASAs was established based on the concept of either making a passive change, taking a stepping-stone approach, or fully embracing the change. Figure 7-5 shows the continuum of options for ASA implementation.

As when implementing AWAs, it is critical that the organization determine which ASA concepts should be considered. Will the organization be open to a wide range of any possible ASAs, or will it be more conservative regarding the implementation of these new concepts? Although it may be difficult to ascertain an organization's exact position in advance, it is important to have at least an understanding of what is deemed to be appropriate, what is considered "leading edge," and what is likely to be dismissed as "in outer space."

For example, it probably is not worth considering the potential for a "meditation room" when the organization thinks that teaming spaces are leading edge.

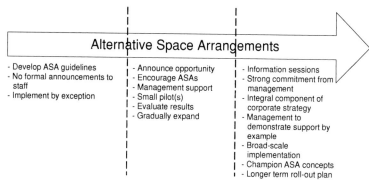

Figure 7-5 ASA positioning strategy.

Design Concepts

It is very important to develop some basic design themes and concepts when preparing to implement new space strategies. The organization should consider the following issues:

- Should cubicles continue to be used? If so, under what conditions?
- Will there continue to be enclosed offices? If so, under what conditions?
- Will casual meeting spaces be considered?
- Will space sharing occur? Will hoteling be used?
- Is team work important to the organization? If so, will teaming spaces be used?
- To what extent will team boundaries be established? Will there be boundaries for departments?

The organization should also develop a set of common design themes and concepts. The following is a set of common design concepts that could be used. The new office environment could:

- Be very open, communicative, and team-oriented.
- Create a feeling of community—versus the current sense of each person having his or her own individual "cell" within the building.
- Be a comfortable place in which to work.
- Be made up largely of team spaces.
- Be free of cubicles.
- Have a few offices for functions that require constant privacy—and locate these on the interior space as opposed to along the exterior wall ("window" offices).
- Have many areas for staff to interact formally (in meeting rooms), informally (in open meeting areas), and casually (in soft seating areas, hallways, etc.).

Once the design concepts are drafted, it is a good idea to have your architect or interior designer develop some prototype drawings of how the space could be structured. These drawings should show different types of team spaces, casual meeting areas, the openness of the design, quiet rooms, galleys for common supplies and equipment, and so on (see, e.g., Figure 4-8, p. 83). The prototype drawings can be used to help solicit staff input and to show staff what some of the concepts could look like.

Staff Input

Staff input is critical to the success of ASAs. If the staff feel that the new design concepts are being rammed down their throats, they will not be at all receptive to the new environment and will likely rebel against it. This, of course, is a recipe for disaster for a change of this magnitude.

The first step in gaining staff input is to bring them up to date on the concepts of ASAs and how they are being implemented in other organizations. All staff should be invited to an information session that should discuss the concepts, why other organizations are trying them, and the process that the organization is about to go through.

The information session should include lots of pictures of what these concepts look like. The pictures should include a wide range of solutions, from minor changes to the traditional office to radical implementations. The more radical solutions will help to stretch the employees' minds about what is possible. The pictures can come from furniture manufacturers, which tend to show their products in showroom-type conditions, and from actual offices where the concepts are used every day. Today there are several organizations that have implemented these concepts, so it is not that difficult to get some real-life examples.

The information sessions should be 40–60 minutes of formal presentation, with another 30–45 minutes available for questions and answers. The presenter should be fully versed in ASA concepts and be knowledgeable about how it has been implemented in other organizations. The goal of information sessions is to educate all staff, open their minds to new ways of thinking about space, and, it is hoped, reduce the anxiety that is associated with a change of this magnitude.

Once information sessions are completed, meetings should be held with individual divisions, departments, and teams to discuss how they operate and to determine which of the ASA components might be of most interest. A key point to remember is that the concept of ASAs is to provide the type of space that best meets the needs of the business activities being performed. The space cannot be designed without first understanding how the business activities are performed—the input from staff must therefore focus on their business processes.

The type of space alternatives to be considered should follow from the discussion of the business processes. At this point, the prototypical layouts developed earlier will help to illustrate the concepts and to assist employees in more accurately describing how they would like their space to function.

Many organizations have their staff organized in teams. It is very important to determine whether the teams truly *function* as a team or whether they are a group of individual workers who form a convenient administrative unit on an organization chart. The type of space(s) proposed will differ greatly based on the degree of collaboration of the team.

This discussion of teaming strategies is an interesting one. Many of the organizations I have worked with have teams that exist more on the organization chart than in reality. However, most of the senior management of these organizations wish that their staff would work more as a team. Team members may, in fact, work individually because of the physical design of their space. They come into the office and "hive" away at their cubicle, occasionally yelling over the partition to other team members, but rarely getting up to interact with each other and usually not feeling like they are really members of a team.

These dynamics are far more common than one might suspect. We have seen tremendous changes in the way teams function and in the cohesiveness and social connectivity between team members when the old cubicles are removed and more open team spaces are implemented. The lesson to be learned here is that not all teams are truly teams. The challenge is to find out who should be a team and which groups have members who truly do their work independent of each other.

Physical Design

The design concepts and staff input lead to the development of the physical design. The interior designers will now be able to translate these ideas and requirements into a drawing. Remember that any office design is an iterative process requiring multiple attempts to deliver the best solution within the budget available. When ASA concepts are overlaid onto the process, the number of iterations will likely increase—so be prepared to exert a bit more effort.

The interior designers may or may not be familiar with ASA concepts. It is critical to determine their level of knowledge early on in the process to ensure that everyone is on the same page—in other words, to ensure that everyone has broken out of the old traditional office paradigm and into the new.

Designing with ASAs brings many new challenges to the designer than a traditional layout. In a traditional layout, the designer can usually come up with a generic footprint for a workstation (based on rank) and then line the stations up on a grid and "plunk" them onto the plan. Now, with ASAs, they must worry about different type of workstations based on business need, not rank; communal areas; space that will be shared by several people; storage for those who share; and information technology issues to support working from multiple locations in the office. The job of doing the design has now gotten a lot harder, and the designer is going to need support from the work transformation team to make this work.

Once the space has been drafted on the floor plan, it is time to market the concepts to staff. Staff will likely have been reasonably open minded through the information sessions and while providing input about implementation, but when it comes to seeing the first real version of the plan, many of them will quickly revert back to their comfort zone (traditional office layout) and will feel very uncomfortable with the layout. It is therefore critical that the designers not only present the plan but that they also market it—put it in the context of the ASA strategy that has been developed to date, relating it to the information sessions and to other ASA sites that they may have visited. The designers must help staff to envision this new space, reduce their anxiety level, and help them become excited about the opportunity that is being placed in front of them.

Sometimes time pressures force designers into looking for the easiest way to please most people—which is usually to revert back to the old traditional styles. Designers should avoid this approach and continue to push staff for strong compelling business reasons as to why they should have the old approach. The answer of "because I feel better in a cubicle," or "I want to have an enclosed office with a the window for the view" are not compelling business-driven arguments for changing back to the traditional layout. There will be situations where the traditional office environment is the best solution—these will become obvious when the business rationale for these arrangements are discussed.

Hoteling

One of the more challenging components of ASAs is the concept of hoteling. Recall that hoteling is the concept of multiple employees sharing a group of common workstations. Hoteling is most commonly used by mobile workers and teleworkers.

The assessment data will have identified the areas where hoteling is possible. Mobile workers are the primary candidates and they usually are found grouped together in specific divisions or departments. Teleworkers represent a different challenge, as they are likely spread across all parts of the organization; establishing hoteling arrangements for them may be more difficult.

An important part of hoteling is how the space is designed. Today many of the hoteling areas are traditional cubicles which can be booked through a reservation system. I have found that many of the employees who work in this type of space are not that excited about their workstations. They usually describe how they are on the road all week and then when they come into office they like to be in an environment where they can interact with other staff rather then be "holed" away in a cubicle. These employees tend to do their "heads down" work remotely, making their time at the office more for interacting with others than doing desk work.

A better solution that we have tried recently is to make the hoteling areas for mobile workers more like team spaces. Using these concepts, staff have the option of sitting at a workstation that is open to others, thereby encouraging and supporting more open communication. These spaces are also usually augmented by soft seating areas and casual meeting spaces that can be used for interactions. The best solutions will also include a few traditional cubicles, quiet spaces, small meeting rooms, and offices that can be booked based on the requirements of the remote worker on the days they are in the office. In essence, a small community of space options is available to the remote workers and the office-based staff they work with.

Storage is a major issue for those who use hoteling. The workstations will likely not contain any permanent storage, so as not to encourage people to always come back to the same workstation each time they are in the office (this will severely impact the compression ratio of people to workstations). As a result, the designer must include some type of personal storage or lockers. These usually contain room for files, books, etc., and include a moveable pedestal that can easily be moved to the chosen workstation (and fit under the desktop). The idea is that when remote workers come to the office, they will go to their locker, retrieve the information they will need during their time in the office, load it into their mobile pedestal, and then roll the pedestal to the assigned desk.

For many people, the concept of having a storage locker brings back bad memories of small high school or factory lockers. It is important to show staff examples of professional lockers and how they can be an effective way of storing their personal items. Most workers are very supportive of the concepts once they wipe away their old vision of a locker.

When determining the number of shared workstations, it will be important to consider the people-to-workspace ratios. As discussed in Chapter 4, this calculation is critical to success. I use the following rules of thumb for people-to-workspace ratios:

- 2.5–3.0:1 for mobile workers
- 1.7–2.0:1 for teleworkers

Finally, the design of hoteled space should provide for a functional workseat for every employee. As discussed in Chapter 4, the ASA design should plan for providing a functional workseat for every remote worker if everyone happens to be in the office at the same time. A workseat is defined as a chair with a phone and network connections. This can be in the casual seating areas, quiet rooms, carrels, phone booths, or meeting rooms.

Teleworkers/Work at Home

In a traditional space plan, the planning begins and ends in the main office. However, with work transformation the organization may now have some employees who are teleworking from home or are full-time work-at-home employees. In these cases, some consideration should be given to the extent to which the organization will become involved in the home office.

In the past, many organizations simply ignored the home office, leaving the responsibility for the home office to the employee. However, today many organizations are beginning to realize that if an employee works from home 3–5 days per week, he or she should have an ergonomic environment in which to work, to support work performance and to reduce the chance of a workplace injury. This concern over the home office will increase in the near future as more and more employees work from home and as more workers' compensation jurisdictions and government labor laws start to force employers to take greater responsibilities for health and safety issues at these "extended office facilities."

As a result, organizations should consider supplying ergonomic furniture to employees who work from home. This does not mean handing down old, decrepit office furniture but rather providing employees with furniture that will meet the ergonomic standards in place at the regular office. This furniture should include, at minimum, a desk that can be set to the right height, a keyboard tray (for using a full-sized keyboard attached to the employee's notebook computer), proper task lighting, and an ergonomic chair.

When selecting furniture for the home, designers should not be looking at traditional office furniture but rather at designs that will more easily fit into the home in terms of scale and interior design. Most of the mainstream furniture manufacturers have recognized the differences in this market and have developed home office lines. Home furnishing manufacturers have also expanded their typical "study desk" to include a complete line of ergonomic home office furnishings.

Telework Centers

Some organizations may want to utilize telework center(s) as part of the work transformation implementation. A telework center is a remote facility that is used by employees who live closer to the telework center than to the main office. The employees use this facility 2–3 days per week and return to the main office for the remaining days.

If the organization is considering telework centers, the first step is to determine where to locate the facilities. The best starting point is to do an analysis of where employees live by analyzing the zip codes or postal codes of the employees' home addresses. This analysis will show the distribution of employees in the surrounding communities and will provide insight into which locations would have the greatest potential in terms of use.

Sizing the telework center is another key step. The organization must determine the number of employees who will utilize the facility, and size it accordingly. This is not as easy as it sounds. The best way to tackle this analysis is to use assessment data (see Chapter 6) to determine approximately how many people could telework and how many would prefer to telework from a telework center versus from their own home. The sizing of the center should use the same people-to-workspace ratios described above.

The next decision to be made is whether the facility will be shared with other organizations or used exclusively by one organization. Most larger organizations prefer to have their own facility versus sharing. In this case, the organization will either have to use one of their existing facilities or find a new one. At this point, it is important to be creative in thinking about where the facility could be located—do not discount any existing facilities until carefully thinking through the potential. Remember that there are tremendous savings if existing facilities can be reused.

If the organization needs to acquire a new facility, be creative in the type of location. It could be in a retail mall, a strip mall, or even a heritage building (a building of historical significance.) It does not have to be in the typical central business district. Remember that the concept is to attract employees who live in the neighborhood to this facility. These employees will likely appreciate being able to walk, bicycle, or drive a short distance to the telework center.

Once the site is selected, the interior designers can design the space. The design will likely be fairly traditional, as most people will be working from the center only 2–3 days per week and will be there to perform their heads down work. The telework center is not a regular office facility, so it will likely not include the typical reception area, administrative staff, office manager, and so forth.

If the telework center is to be shared by multiple organizations, then there are at least two routes the organization can follow. First, the organization can scout the marketplace for existing shared telework centers that can accommodate the organization. This is the easiest solution, as the facility is likely already up and running. The second choice is for the organization to take a lead role in establishing the shared telework center. This is, of course, more challenging because the organization will have to find other organizations that want to participate and will have to set up the technology and design the interiors to accommodate the requirements of multiple organizations.

Real Estate

Obviously, the implementation of ASAs will require some consideration of whether the organization should renovate the existing facility or move to a new space. This is an extremely complicated decision that needs careful consideration.

Renovating existing space might be highly desirable from a short-term cost containment point of view but could also be very disruptive to the organization and could be extremely difficult if the building does not architecturally support the ASA concepts that the organization wants to implement. Another consideration involves the amount of space that the organization will require. The implementation of work transformation will, in most cases, result in a reduction in the amount of space required. The organization must determine if it will be possible and/or practical to release part of the existing space to other tenants. Some organizations that are in large, single-tenant buildings may find this arrangement to be difficult and costly to accomplish.

Moving into a new facility has its own inherent challenges—the selection of the right location, site, and floor plan are critical—and reward. The move to a new location creates, in many cases, a strong sense of corporate renewal which directly supports the change to ASAs.

Whatever real estate decisions are needed, the key is to involve the organization's internal real estate group and/or a representative from a commercial real estate company to assist in the process.

Guidelines

The new space will require a paradigm shift for many employees. One way to alleviate some of the anxiety is to create a basic set of guidelines for use. These guidelines should help employees understand how the hoteling arrangements will work, describe the various types of spaces that are available to staff (quiet spaces, phone booths, meeting rooms, etc.), and emphasize the need for a "clean desk" policy for those who share space.

The guidelines must be written in a way that communicates the new community feeling of the space—how employees should feel comfortable about working from any part of the facility including the more casual soft seating areas, café spaces, and so on. The guidelines should be developed with input from staff at all levels and should be seen as an outline to success in the new space, not as a rule book that has been dumped on staff by management.

Developing these guidelines is a challenging task—the use of a skilled technical writer and a public relations professional is a good investment for this deliverable.

Training

The work transformation implementation training should be held just prior to the implementation of work transformation within a workgroup. The key topics should include the following:

- Review of the definitions of work transformation
- Review of the expected business benefits (from the business case)

- Overview of the functions of the new office environment
- Cultural/psychosocial aspects of nontraditional space
- Office sharing etiquette (how to successfully share space with others)
- Technology training (how to get your phone to ring where you are, reserving workspace, connecting to the network, etc.)
- Understanding that it is okay to use the casual seating areas, coffee room, etc.
- Management's commitment to work transformation
- Letting others know where you are
- How changes in the office environment will affect work processes, communication, etc.

IMPLEMENTATION OF INFORMATION TECHNOLOGY

The AWA and ASA implementation plans will basically determine the level of IT support required. The IT implementation typically involves providing connectivity for teleworkers, ensuring that mobile workers have the right portable technology, implementing a hoteling system for space sharing, developing a wiring infrastructure that will support the proposed flexible work environment, providing technical support to employees, establishing the technology for a telework center, and testing.

Teleworkers/Work at Home

The IT group will have to develop methods of connecting teleworkers and work-at-home employees to the central office. This will involve establishing some type of remote data communications solution, as described in Chapter 5. The solution should be rigorous enough to easily handle the expected volume of traffic, recognizing that the number of remote workers will likely increase over time.

The biggest issue with remote access is the speed of the data connection. The IT group must carefully analyze the needs of these remote workers and recommend solutions that will meet these requirements. For example, employees who will only be accessing their e-mail and doing some basic file transfers can likely survive with a typical low-end analog modem, whereas employees who must be connected to the server all day to access a business application will likely need a higher-speed solution as provided by ISDN, ADSL, or a cable modem (all of which are described in Chapter 5).

In addition to the data communications issues, the IT group will also have to arrange the appropriate voice communications services. This could be as simple as having a separate phone line for voice traffic installed at the employee's home or as complex as installing a remote ACD (automated call distribution) device for call center employees who work from home. The voice solutions will also require considerations for voice mail, call forwarding, and conference calling. The various telecommunications providers can help to determine the package of features that will best meet the organization's needs.

The IT group will also need to arrange for any additional hardware or software that will be required for these remote employees. This could include notebook computers, printers, modems, utility software, and communications software.

Mobile Workers

Mobile workers work from multiple locations using portable technology to support their business requirements. For mobile work to be successful, it is very important that these employees have the right equipment to meet their needs. Organizations that do not properly equip their mobile workers find that these employees must come into the office more often to perform activities that could be done remotely if the right technology were present.

One of the keys to work transformation is having employees share space—if the mobile workers have to come into the office to access technology, then the ratio of people to workspaces will have to be reduced, thus reducing the overall savings. Furthermore, the more often the mobile worker has to come back to the office, the more time is lost that could be spent with customers.

The first step is to determine the requirements and to match the technology to these requirements. Some mobile workers will need only basic technology while on the road and will perform their record keeping and updating from home. In this case, communications technology for these employees should be set up like that for teleworkers. Others will need full capability on the road, which may require fully loaded notebook computers, wireless modems, and small mobile printers. It is rare that a one-size-fits-all solution works, even though this is the strategy that many organizations choose to employ.

All mobile workers will likely need a cellular or digital phone for voice communication. This phone should be equipped with voice mail, call forwarding, and in some cases caller identification. There are numerous packages available from both cellular and digital vendors that should be analyzed and considered.

Reservations Systems

The implementation of hoteling as a strategy for space sharing will require some form of reservations system. There is a broad range of reservation systems available; the key is to select the one that will best meet the organization's requirements.

The simplest reservations system is a manual board whereby employees can identify who has booked what workstation. This system requires some wall space and a resource person who can update the board when a remote worker calls in for a space. This type of arrangement works for a small number of people who are hoteling (up to 15 shared workstations).

The next step up is to implement a computer scheduling system such as is used by employees to schedule their time. This system can be placed on the local area network (LAN), with each shared workstation set up as an individual resource. Remote workers can access the schedules of the available workstations and make a reservation. This system works adequately for small groups of remote workers (10–25 shared workstations) but can be time consuming if a remote worker has to search through the workstation resources to find an available slot.

A more complicated—and preferred system—is an automated reservations system. This systems allows remote workers to book workstations by showing the user which stations are available on the days requested. Most of these systems are also connected to the corporate phone system such that the employee's phone will automatically be routed to the workstation chosen on the days the employee is in the office. This type of solution works well with larger groups of remote workers. The complication is that the system must be integrated into the organization's LAN and phone system (PBX). This solution is best when there are more than 25 shared workstations.

Wiring

Wiring in the traditional office was easy: simply provide voice and data communications at each workstation. With work transformation, the IT group must now consider the potential of providing voice and data communications not only at every workstation but also to all of the functional workseats (in casual meeting areas, phone booths, quiet rooms, café spaces, etc.).

This will involve more wiring than before and more creative ways of bringing the wiring to the employee. All of the shared facilities should have the electrical and communications receptacles at desk level so that it is easy for remote workers to plug their notebooks into the network. Some of the team tables and casual meeting areas will require special wiring monuments (boxes to hold power and communication cables and outlets) to bring power, voice and data to the table top. Most furniture vendors have these type of devices built into their alternative officing furniture solutions.

Voice communications in the office is a challenge in situations where employees could be working from multiple locations. Some organizations are now moving to wireless phone systems within the office to support these type of employees. In these situations, a base station(s) is established in the office and employees carry their cordless telephones with them. There are also some newer telephones available that allow mobile workers to utilize the same physical telephone for use outside the office (on the digital network) or inside the office running off the base station (without incurring air time charges in the office).

Support

Often overlooked in work transformation is the need to provide technology support to remote workers and provide this support outside of normal office hours. The implementation of telework, work-at-home and mobile work will require technology support of users who are not in the building. This may require training support staff in how to diagnose the type of problems that will be encountered by remote workers and potentially installing some type of remote control software that would allow the support person to see what is on the screen of the remote worker.

The issue of support outside of normal office hours will have to be considered if variable work hours and modified work weeks are implemented. This will create situations in which staff will be working before and after regular office hours. Most companies expand their support hours to accommodate these workers, assuming that there is enough volume of activity to support the longer hours of support.

Telework Centers

Corporate telework centers should be wired the same as any other branch or satellite office. Telework centers that are shared by multiple organizations are much more challenging from a technology point of view. The IT group should be prepared to spend significant effort considering the options of providing telecommunications services from shared telework centers. The various options available are discussed in Chapter 5.

Testing

The final step in implementing the technology that enables work transformation is testing the technology to ensure that it works. This may seem obvious, but unfortunately many technology projects get implemented with only minimal testing.

The testing should involve staff who will have to use the technology to ensure that the final product meets the specified requirements. The support staff should also be involved in the testing so that they have first-hand experience with the type of problems that could be expected and how to overcome them.

The testing should not be left until just before implementation. It should be planned and executed in a way that allows enough time to correct any deficiencies and to allow time for retesting.

MANAGEMENT

The implementation of work transformation needs to be treated as a formal project with the appropriate level of project management. Because the implementation represents a significant level of change for the organization, an appropriate change management and communications plan must be developed. Finally, the implementation will require an ongoing leadership role by the work transformation executive champion—to keep everyone focused on the end benefits and not to lose faith in the concept before it is implemented.

Project Management
The initial implementation of work transformation in an organization should be treated as a formal project. Successful projects are well managed, so the use of some basic project management concepts will be essential.

The work transformation implementation will be under much pressure to deliver the expected results. The project must be defined with a beginning and end, scope, expected outputs, and a way of measuring success.

The best strategy for the work transformation project manager is to take a proactive approach to the project. This involves following the six basic project management functions, as defined in the practical project management methodology (P^2M^2): leading; defining; planning; organizing; controlling; and closing.[1]

Figure 7-6 shows the project manager as a juggler—leading the team through these basic project management functions. This is not an easy job. If the project manager fails to deliver on any of these functions, the chances of project success are greatly reduced.

The project management function is critical to the success of the work transformation implementation. Often an individual is assigned the responsibilities of a work transformation project and managing a project for the first time. This person will find it helpful to request some coaching assistance from other, experienced in-house project managers, attend a project management course, and review a book on the topic. The following paragraphs provide a brief high-level explanation of the P^2M^2 components and how they apply to this type of project.

The project manager must first ensure that the project is clearly defined. This will include finalizing the scope (what is included and excluded in the

Leading

Figure 7-6 Project manager juggling basic project management functions. (Reprinted with permission from Kliem, Ralph L., Ludin, Irwin S., and Robertson, Ken L. *Project Management Methodology: A Practical Guide for the Next Millennium.* New York: Marcel Dekker, 1997, p. 33.)

project) and the specific goals and objectives of the project. This information should already be spelled out in the work transformation business case, but it is critical that the assigned project manager review the scope anyway with the executive sponsor to ensure that "everyone is on the same page" in terms of expectations.

The project manager must also prepare a plan for the project. This will include a list of the tasks to be performed, who will do them, and their duration. The project plan will evolve throughout the project and will be the project manager's road map of the current status of the project and remaining efforts. The planning process is particularly critical for a work transformation project, as the activities will be performed by different groups within the organization—many of which may never have collaborated on a project before.

The project manager will also have to establish some organizational structure for the project. This will include the reporting structure for deliverables (outputs produced by team members); who will review these outputs; any quality management practices; and a method for effectively communicating to the team, sponsor, and the organization as a whole. Since work transformation is generally regarded as a new concept, it will be worthwhile to include time for the entire team to review the key deliverables and to provide input on how to improve the process.

Another major function is controlling. This involves gathering data from team members as to the status of their tasks in terms of what has been completed and how much time it will take to complete. Once the data is gathered, the project manager can report the progress of the project through various mechanisms including status reports, project schedules, and budget updates.

The final project management function is closure. As the project completes a major milestone or phase, the project manager should recognize the end of the phase with a celebration to thank the team for its efforts. The closure point should also represent the opportunity for the project manager and his or her team to reflect on the project to date and to honestly evaluate the success and challenges of the project and to learn from these for subsequent phases and/or projects.

Managing a cross-functional project is a major challenge even for experienced project managers. The effort required for this activity should not be underestimated.

Change Management

The implementation of work transformation will represent a significant change for staff, management, and the overall organization. The key to success is to institute a change management program that will support the transition to this new way of working.

Figure 7-7 represents the acceptance and penetration of change over time. Most organizations are still at the early adopter stage, where a few pioneers are starting to experiment with some of the work transformation concepts while

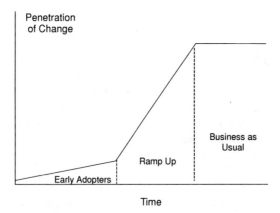

Figure 7-7 Acceptance of major change.

most of the organization is still functioning with the traditional concepts. The figure shows a slow acceptance level of change as the early adopters move through the change process, followed by an accelerated ramp-up period where the change becomes more accepted, and finally a leveling off where the change represents a new definition of "business as usual."

The pattern of penetration of acceptance to change has numerous real-life parallels. Take, for example, the video cassette recorder (VCR). In the early days, very few people had VCRs—they were expensive, clumsy to operate, and required a significant change in our definition of how and where we could watch our favorite television shows or movies. However, once the concept of VCRs became more established and standards were introduced, the ramp-up period began. Today, almost every home has a VCR. We no longer have to go to the movie theater to see a movie—we can go to the corner store to rent a tape. We no longer have to be at our television sets at a specific date and time to see a show—we can merely tape it and watch it later at our convenience. Clearly, today the use of a VCR is considered business as usual.

One of the biggest challenges regarding change is that most people are resistant to change. This is particularly true when organizations force change on staff without involving them in the process. Work transformation represents a huge change to many employees. The thought of not working from the central office every day, sharing space, loosing one's cubicle, having casual seating areas in the office, and so forth is difficult for many employees to envision.

To be successful, the organization must work with employees and help them to understand the changes proposed, the reasons why the organization is transforming the way they work, and how they will benefit from the new environment. Anxiety-management is crucial to success.

One way of ensuring greater success with a change is to implement a change management process. In the past 15 years, I have worked with several change management models. The one that I utilize the most was developed by Linda Ackerman Anderson, principal of Being First, Inc., in Durango, CO.

Ackerman Anderson has an extensive background in change management or what she refers to as "facilitating large systems change."[2] She defines facilitating large systems change as

> The conscious design of the process of changing an organization's strategy, structure, processes, systems or culture, so that the process of change fosters employee commitment and participation, models the desired culture, delivers the intended business outcomes and ensures continuous improvement.[3]

It is clear by Ackerman Anderson's definition that this is not a minor undertaking. To facilitate change, her firm has developed a change process

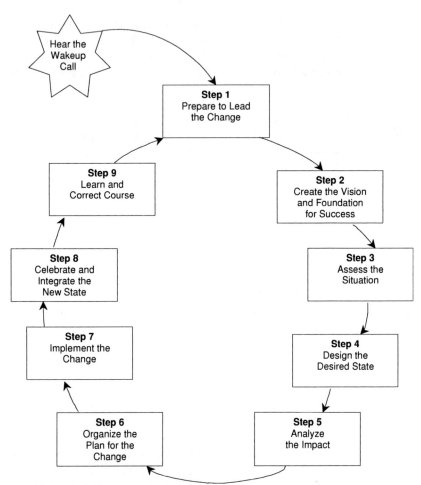

Figure 7-8 The change process model. (©1985, 1993 Being First, Inc., Durango, CO. Reprinted with permission.)

model (shown in Figure 7-8) for dealing with change. This nine-phase model is certainly applicable to the changes associated with work transformation.

Not surprisingly, Ackerman Anderson's change process closely matches the work transformation implementation process discussed in this book. Phases 1 and 2 in the model match the work transformation vision process described in Chapter 6. The first phase positions leadership to prepare to lead the change by understanding the area of opportunity; to build a clear strategy and case for the change; and to develop approaches, processes, and structures for facilitating the change.

The second phase is to create the vision and foundation for success throughout the organization. Building the vision for change is extremely important. Ackerman Anderson explains that

> The vision will provide the entire organization with a sense of relevance and meaning for the change—to provide a sense that we are all in this together. Everyone is an important part of creating a successful outcome and a strong future for this organization.[4]

This phase must also include building the foundation for success in terms of promoting the behavioral changes required to support the change and initiating appropriate rewards that motivate support for the change.

The third phase in the model parallels the work transformation assessment described in Chapter 6. This phase allows the organization to review its current work methods and environment, the organization's ability to absorb change, and the state of the infrastructure (human resources, facilities management, and information technology) to support the change. This phase establishes where the organization is moving from, which helps define the requirements for the desired state. This information also helps in estimating the time and effort required to implement the change by understanding the degree of change that will be required.

The fourth and fifth phases are covered by the work transformation business case (Chapter 6) and by the first steps in the work transformation implementation. The fourth phase establishes the desired state of the new environment. This phase involves designing the nature of the new work transformation programs. During the design, the work transformation concepts flow into a set of strategies that will support the implementation. Unfortunately, many organizations start at this point but then ignore the first three phases. An organization attempting this approach should stop, go back, and establish and accept the need, create the vision and foundation for success, and ensure that there is a thorough understanding of the current situation. Failure to perform these critical front-end tasks will likely result in an incomplete and inadequate work transformation program.

Phase 5 is the analysis of the impact on the organization and its culture and people. How will the organization react? Is the IT infrastructure adequate to support work transformation? What are some of the potential reactions from staff, management, and customers? The assessment of impact should also include strategies for minimizing the impact of the change. This must be integrated into the business case to ensure that all components of the work transformation process have been included.

Phases 6 to 8 in Ackerman Anderson's model represent the work transformation implementation process described in this chapter. At this stage, the change management activities should be integrated into the implementation project plan. The plan should include a "pacing strategy"—outlining what is realistic for the organization.

Phase 7 represents the actual implementation of the work transformation program, which takes the organization through a period of time when the new state of working is formalized. Phase 8 involves integrating the new work transformation environment into the culture of the organization. This will be accomplished as the change is accepted. It is also critical to remember that getting this far has taken a lot of energy and effort from many people—these people should be recognized, and the entire organization should celebrate the move to the new environment.

The final phase is to monitor and course-correct—this parallels the maintaining momentum phase described in Chapter 8. Remember that change never ends. Change must be constantly evaluated, tuned, and repositioned as appropriate. This final phase will be ongoing until the work transformation program is formalized and is no longer a change but rather just a natural way of working.

Ackerman Anderson's change model and the process for work transformation outlined in this book recognize that some form of change management is critical to the success of a change as significant as work transformation. Whatever change process is chosen is not as critical as following some formal process to effectively manage the transformation.

LEADERSHIP

The need for executive leadership is critical to the success of work transformation. This book has suggested the need for an executive champion who will fill this leadership role. The challenge for this person will be to provide the level of leadership necessary to make a change as significant as work transformation as success.

Ronald Heifetz, Director of the Leadership Education Project at Harvard University's John F. Kennedy School of Government in Cambridge, MA, and Donald Laurier, Managing Director of the Laurier International Limited, a management consulting firm in Boston, MA, have been studying leadership for some time.

Heifetz and Laurier suggest that companies today are facing adaptive challenges. This adaptive work is required when "our deeply held beliefs are challenged, when the values that made us successful become less relevant, and when legitimate yet competing perspectives emerge."[5]

Heifetz and Laurier believe that getting people to do adaptive work is the mark of leadership in a competitive world. Executives have to break a long-standing behavior pattern of providing leadership in the form of solutions and specific directives. They need to recognize that the true adaptive solutions are found across organizational boundaries and with employees at all levels. This, of course, is certainly the case with work transformation, where the key to success is integrating technology, facilities, and human resource strategies and where involvement of all staff is critical. Those executives who initiate work transformation as a traditional top-down directive will probably find that the organization is not able to gain the full business value from this transformation.

Heifetz and Laurier suggest that "business leaders have to be able to view patterns as if they were on a balcony. It does them no good to be swept up in the field of action."[6] In other words, to make work transformation happen, executives must take a step away from the operational and hierarchical issues and look at the bigger picture. The "balcony" provides executives with the perspective of the overall organization and allows them to see the corporate context of work transformation. They can then use this perspective to mobilize staff towards the adaptive changes necessary to make it a success.

Another challenge for the executive champion will be managing the distress level of employees going through the work transformation change. Employees who will be working in new environments, in new ways, with new behaviors are sometimes distressed about the efforts and sacrifices required of them. Employees will likely be uncomfortable about losing their office space, changing their hours of work, and not coming to the office every day. They will look to the executives for direction. The easy way out is to provide an edict; however, this is rarely successful. Instead, executives must "disorient" their staff away from their current definition of how and where work is performed to allow them to develop the new definitions which are required to make work transformation successful.

The executive champion must create a balance between having people feel the need to change and having them feel overwhelmed by change. Heifetz and Laurier suggest that "a leader has to have the emotional capacity to tolerate uncertainty, frustration and pain. They have to be able to raise tough questions without getting too anxious themselves." When changing the definitions of how and where work is performed, it is often easy to "let up" on the pressure to change and allow the organization to fall back to a less stressful equilibrium. This will, of course, work against the transformation. What the leader needs to do is know when to slightly release the stress and when to turn up the pressure. This balancing act is critical to maintaining the organization's focus on work transformation.

The work of Heifetz and Laurier describes leadership as a learning strategy. To be successful, a leader must engage people in confronting the challenge at hand, to adjust their values and beliefs and perspectives, and, most importantly, to learn new habits. The work transformation concept is relatively easy to comprehend, but making this actual change is a dramatic process for any organization. The principles described above should be carefully considered by those who will lead their organizations into this new definition of how and where work is performed.

COMMUNICATIONS

An important part of the implementation of work transformation is the development and implementation of an appropriate communications plan. Successful change management also depends on communication. To obtain optimal awareness, understanding, and support of employees, managers, union representatives, customers (internal and external), and shareholders, the work transformation team must communicate effectively.

The following is an outline of a communications plan:

Purpose

This is the primary reason for creating the communications plan. The purpose is usually to create awareness, understanding, and support for the work transformation program.

Objectives

These are the *communication* objectives, not the *program's* objectives. They should be specific and describe what is to be achieved or what action the stakeholders should take. Objectives could be to inform, encourage participation, increase use, promote, solicit support, gain acceptance, listen, get input, and educate. They could be stated as follows:

- To gain awareness and understanding of work transformation among employees and customers
- To gain support for work transformation among participating employees, their managers, and coworkers
- To inform customers of the customer service improvements associated with work transformation
- To encourage participation by employees and managers in the work transformation program

Key Messages

The key messages should be the 3–5 succinct statements that will be used repeatedly in the communication. They are the messages that you most want the stakeholders to know and remember. Generally, they state the benefits of the work transformation program.

The following are a few of the key messages that could be included:

- Progressive employer dedicated to balancing work and family
- Participating employees have ... [reduced transportation costs, balanced work and family, and reduced stress]
- Employer has benefited from ... [increased job performance, enhanced ability to retain and attract valued employees, and reduced office accommodation costs]
- Customers have realized improvements in . . . (hours of customer service, quicker turnaround time]

Audiences/Stakeholders

The groups of people that have a vested interest in the work transformation program, would benefit from knowing of it, or whose support/understanding is required. Try to subdivide large groups (e.g., "employees" or "customers") into smaller subsets to better target the communication. For example, customers could be subdivided into large, medium, and small companies or by logical grouping of what they buy from your organization.

Actions

A point form list of actions (tasks) including who is responsible for them and the targeted completion date for each. The actions are listed by audience and describe how the communication will be done and, to some extent, what will be communicated. This becomes the action plan for monitoring progress and making changes. The communications action plan should be integrated into the overall project plan (outlining specifically who is going to do what and when, and the action items for each stakeholder group).

Communication Tools

Communication tools to be used to implement the strategy include e-mail, live presentations, brochures, newsletters, static displays, and the corporate Intranet site.

Resources

Identify the resources (human and financial) required to implement the plan. The financial information should be integrated into the overall project budget.

Vulnerabilities/Potential Issues

This should be a list of issues that could hamper the success of the project. Be honest and try to anticipate things that could blind-side your team. It is prudent to include preemptive actions to avoid these potential issues.

Evaluation

The communications strategy for the project should be evaluated in terms of the measures of success identified for the work transformation program. This evaluation should be done at key milestones throughout the project and again at the end of the project. Any corrective actions that result from the interim evaluations should be added to the action plan.

The communications plan should be developed in a session with the team members that is facilitated by the corporate communications person (or the person on the project who is filling this role). The most important aspect of the communications plan is to continually review it, tune it as required, and evaluate it to ensure that your key messages are getting across. The evaluation should be done by soliciting feedback from a sampling of the stakeholder groups.

RESOURCES

The implementation of work transformation will require a cross-functional team with representatives from human resources, facilities management, information technology, and the participating business areas. External resources such as management consultants and product (furniture and technology) vendors can, through their experience, help the team avoid some of the common pitfalls experienced by others.

The type and number of resources required will depend on the extent of the implementation. Those who choose only to implement a portion of the possible work transformation options may not need as diverse a team as those who will be working with the full range of options.

The following are the key resources that should be involved in the project and the skills they will bring to the team.

Project Manager

One individual on the team should be assigned as the project manager. This person will be responsible for organizing the project, developing the project plan, and managing the project to completion.

Human Resources

The human resources representative(s) will be responsible for establishing the AWA guidelines and policies. This function is critical to the success of the project, as it will help to guide the people aspects of the implementation. Human resources will also integrate the work transformation training into the organization's overall management training program (if one exists).

Labor Relations

Organizations with unionized workers should involve the labor relations group. This group will work with the union representatives to ensure that work transformation can function within the context of the existing collective bargaining agreement or through the development of a memorandum of understanding.

Labor Union

The team should include a representative(s) from the union(s) involved. These representatives could be the union executive, an individual appointed by the union to investigate work transformation, or a shop steward from the area affected. The union representative must be empowered by the union to make decisions and accurately reflect the union's executive and members' views on the concepts.

Corporate Change Management

Some organizations have a separate change management function. In this case, a representative from the corporate change management group should be involved in the project. If a separate change management function is not available, then another team member should take on this role (typically this will come from the human resources group).

Corporate Communications

Some organizations have a separate corporate communications function that is responsible for developing and implementing communication strategies and plans to both internal and external audiences. Any organization that wants to use the implementation of work transformation as a way of receiving positive press coverage must ensure that a skilled communications person is part of the team.

Facilities Management

The implementation of alternative space arrangements will obviously require representation, input, and support from the facilities management group. The facilities management representative(s) will be responsible for working with architects, interior designers, furniture vendors, and contractors to design the building, develop space plans, and coordinate the physical implementation. The leasing or real estate portion of the facilities management group should also be involved if the pilot is to include the use of telework centers, subletting of existing space, or acquisition of a new facility.

Information Technology

Information technology creates the opportunity to implement work transformation. The team must, therefore, include representative(s) who can participate in developing the strategies and plans for supporting this new way of working along with the expertise in designing and implementing the necessary technological solutions. The information technology representative(s) will likely need access to key IT resources in the areas of voice communications, data communications, remote access, and help desk support.

Business Unit Representative(s)

Representatives from the areas affected by the work transformation implementation should be part of the project team to ensure that the team is able to remain focused on the benefits the business unit(s) expects to derive.

External Consultants

For many organizations, the implementation of work transformation is a venture into unknown territory. Some organizations choose to rely on their internal resources to research the concepts and to learn by "trial and error." Another approach is to utilize one or more management consultants who have already been through the process with several other organizations. The consultant can be an expert resource on the project and should be responsible for ensuring that the team is able to avoid the common pitfalls that he or she may have seen before. This should reduce the overall risk of the project and reduce the time required to complete it.

Vendors

Facilities and information technology vendors can be a useful addition to the project team. The use of the vendor who supplied the furniture to the traditional office facility will speed up the process of determining how this furniture can be reused to support the ASA concepts. As well, technology vendors who have expertise in remote access products can be of tremendous assistance to the team. In most cases, the vendors will work with the team on a part-time or as-required basis.

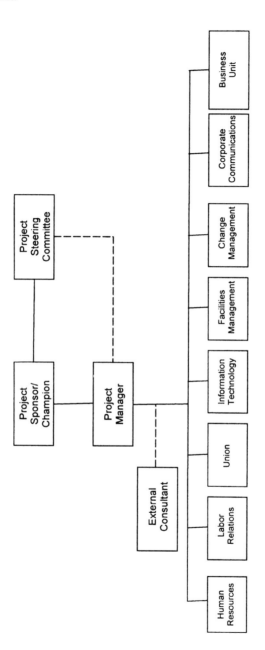

Figure 7-9 Work transformation project organization chart.

Project Sponsor/Champion

The project sponsor should be an executive who is responsible for selecting the project manager, securing funding for the project, facilitating the acquisition of needed resources, approving key deliverables, and providing overall guidance to the project manager and the team. The project sponsor should also be widely recognized as the champion of work transformation within the organization. This role is critical to the success of the project, so the champion must be fully conversant in the concepts and be an evangelist for the cause.

Project Steering Committee

The project steering committee should be a group of executives from across the organization that may be immediately or eventually affected by the project. These executives will provide guidance and direction to the project team, particularly in the areas of change management, potential business impact, and overall corporate communications. The project sponsor should chair the project steering committee and should be a member of the committee providing regular status updates and input.

The organization chart illustrated in Figure 7-9 is obviously designed for either large organizations or those organizations that want to widely implement the concepts across the organization. Note that these project functions do not necessarily require full-time resources. In many cases, the resources can work on the project part-time.

The key to the project's success will be to ensure that the basic functions described above are covered in some way, regardless of the size of the organization.

PILOTING

Implementing work transformation will be most successful when the organization recognizes the degree of organizational, personal, and cultural change associated with this new concept. The implementation will not be a minor undertaking. The costs of a large-scale implementation could be high, and the expected benefits may not materialize.

A common starting point for any project that requires significant change is to have a pilot. The pilot represents a low-cost, low-risk method of ensuring that the expected business benefits can be achieved. Success in achieving the benefits in the pilot will help the organization in making the longer-term decision on the potential benefits of broader scale implementation.

Pilots can also be used as a method of gradually introducing new concepts to organizations—not every organization nor every individual can deal with significant change. The pilot represents a way of getting around this challenge. The pilot also creates a learning model for the organization. Peter Senge, author of *The Fifth Discipline: The Art and Practice of the Learning Organization*, has taught us to create environments where everyone in the organization can learn and apply this learning to the overall benefit of the organization. The pilot concept shows the organization how these new work transformation ideas can be applied. It helps to alleviate some of the anxiety that employees and managers may have towards the concepts while creating a "laboratory" environment that allows for changing the parameters of the "experiment" to see how the changes can be improved.

The pilot should be of a size and length that is representative of the magnitude of change being implemented. The typical pilot period is 4–9 months. Anything shorter than 4 months may produce erroneous results, as most participants take 6–8 weeks to adjust to the new environment, then start to excel for another 6–8 weeks, and only then reach a steady state. The measurement of the pilot should be based on the steady-state condition.

The first step in selecting pilot participants is to understand what is being piloted. If the organization is piloting only AWAs, then there is an opportunity to use a cross-section of resources from across the organization. In this scenario, the pilot will be primarily interested in selecting individuals rather than groups. If the organization is piloting only ASAs, then it will want to limit the pilot to a division, department, or team. In this scenario, the pilot includes selecting groups rather than individuals. If piloting both AWAs and ASAs, then it will be necessary to draw from groups within the organization that can reasonably utilize both new work arrangements and new space arrangements.

Selecting Participants for Alternative Work Arrangement Pilots

Quite often, organizations suggest that the implementation of AWAs should be applied only to a specific job function. For example, a company may decide that all technical writers could telework from home. These jobs would obviously be prime candidates for telework, but what would the pilot show? Probably that telework is successful for technical writers. Moreover, the pilot would be perceived by many in the organization as being appropriate only for technical writers. This would obviously not be the best strategy.

Other organizations suggest that the pilot should be for a specific department. Again, the results of the pilot tend to be interpreted as applying only to the single department and not necessarily transferable to others. Some organizations believe that the best way to pilot work transformation concepts is to implement them within the human resources, information technology, or facilities management departments. In my opinion, there could not be a worse choice! If the only participants in the pilot are selected from one of these key areas, it will be perceived by the organization that the concepts developed by these groups are self-serving. This is not the optimal way to start a pilot.

A better way to structure an AWA pilot is to ensure that the participants represent a reasonable cross-section of jobs, departments, and functions of the organization. This means having participation from junior administrative resources to executives in the pilot. A cross-section of departments is also useful. This cross-section should include representatives from what is considered the key business units (those business units that are most directly responsible for the organization's success). The pilot should also include a range of functions from internal support areas, to customer service, to key business delivery functions.

Another component in establishing a successful pilot is the selection of appropriate participants. This will include a cross-section of jobs, departments, and functions, and a reasonable cross-section of individuals. Some pilots are filled with "superstar" employees—those employees who will likely excel at virtually anything they do. Loading the pilot with this type of employee may seem like a plausible strategy to ensure a successful result. The actual results are usually the opposite. The pilot itself is a success, and the employees are perhaps more likely to show how the concepts can be implemented successfully. However, the organization should not perceive the pilot to be a success, as it does not represent the "average" worker.

The solution is to ensure that the pilot includes an appropriate cross-section of employees, from average performers to superstars. The only proviso that I would suggest is that employees who are underachieving, experiencing performance difficulties, or under some type of performance review program should not be included in some aspects of the pilot. For example, these employees may not be appropriate for working without direct supervision.

If the cross-section of employees, jobs, departments, and functions is appropriate, then the pilot will be deemed to be realistic and the results will be more widely accepted within the organization.

The pilot size should be significant enough to make an impact. It should include at least 15 to 20 people, although the size will vary based on the size of the organization.

Selecting Alternative Space Arrangement Pilot Participants

Selecting participants for ASA pilots involves selecting groups that can best model the use of these new space concepts for the rest of the organization. The selected groups could include those who will share space, use team spaces, or use areas designed for collaboration.

A key role of the ASA pilot group will be not only to prove that the ASA concepts are appropriate but also to provide the rest of the organization with a demonstration site. The ability to show others what the new space looks like and how it functions will go a long ways towards reducing the anxiety levels of staff who will be moving into these new types of spaces in the near future.

The pilot should include at minimum 15 to 20 people, although it would be better to have multiple, space-oriented pilots with 40 to 70 employees involved. The actual size of the pilot will depend on the size of the organization and the extent of the changes being piloted.

Many of the same rules apply to selecting groups for involvement in the ASA pilot as those outlined in the AWA pilot above. It is important that the chosen groups are perceived as being representative of the organization so that it is not a stretch to visualize how the concepts could be extrapolated to other parts of the organization.

SUMMARY

Implementing work transformation can be an exciting and challenging project. The starting point is to develop the necessary AWA, ASA, and IT components to enable the intended solutions.

The AWA implementation must include basic policies and guidelines to provide a framework for how AWAs will be applied within the organization. The selection process should be guided by self-evaluation questionnaires, which will help employees and their managers determine which AWAs are most appropriate. The implementation should include training for all staff to introduce them to the new concepts, for managers to help them manage employees using AWAs, and for staff who will be working remotely (teleworkers, work-at-home employees, and mobile workers).

The ASA implementation must address the basic facilities management issues. This will include establishing a basic set of design concepts, meeting with staff to educate them on ASA concepts, and gathering information on how they function and which ASA concepts could be applied. The next step is the physical design, which is an iterative process of experimenting with different ASA concepts and reviewing these with staff. If the implementation includes hoteling, then appropriate steps need to be taken to accommodate staff storage and to provide "community-based" facilities that can be shared by the remote workers.

The ASA implementation also goes beyond the central office to consider the furniture needs for teleworkers and work-at-home employees. This will include solutions that are scaled to the home environment while still meeting the basic health and safety requirements of the organization. If telework centers are to be included, it must be determined where these centers should be located and what size they should be. The interior design of the telework centers will likely be somewhat traditional, although it will exclude the typical administrative functions and facilities found in the central office.

The real estate group will become involved in the ASA implementation in assessing whether to renovate the existing facility or move to a new one. It will also have to address the most cost-effective method of securing telework center facilities if this is part of the work transformation program.

The extent of IT implementation will depend directly on the extent of AWA and ASA concepts being applied. The IT implementation will likely have to address technology needs for teleworkers, work-at-home employees, and mobile workers. This will include understanding the requirements of these groups and finding appropriate solutions. The technology group will also have to address the hardware and software required for a reservations system if hoteling is to be used for space sharing. Wiring of the new facilities will also be a key issue, especially in the shared common areas. Finally, it will be critical that all technology solutions are thoroughly tested by the end users prior to implementation.

The implementation of work transformation is not a minor undertaking. There are several key management roles that must be addressed. Project management and change management are critical to success. The organization must recognize the need to formally manage the work transformation implementation. It is crucial not to scrimp here—the implementation will be addressing a broad range of objectives and a cross-functional team that will need direction. The approach described in this book follows a proven change management model. Organizations should ensure that they establish some structured approach to change management.

Successful work transformation must be guided by leadership at the top. Executives must learn to help by letting employees adapt to this new way of working. These approaches will not only help work transformation but will also assist the organization in other business initiatives. The final management component is a good communications plan. This plan will help all staff stay informed of the implementation, which should help to reduce some of the anxiety associated with this degree of change.

The project team created to implement work transformation should include representatives from the three key service groups (human resources, facilities management, and information technology) along with support from the business areas, unions, change management, corporate communications, and possibly external consultants. It should be a truly cross-functional team to address the broad range of issues described above.

A key decision in the implementation phase is to determine the extent to which work transformation will be applied. Many organizations improve their chances for success by breaking the implementation into smaller more manageable pieces. These smaller stepping stones can be in the form of a pilot or a series of pilots. The pilot participants should be carefully selected to represent an appropriate cross-section of the organization.

NOTES

1. Kliem, Ralph L. Ludin, Irwin S. and Robertson, Ken. *Project Management Methodology: A Practical Guide for the Next Millennium*. New York: Marcel Dekker, 1997.
2. Ackerman Anderson, Linda, Anderson, Dean, and Marquardt, Martin. *The Future of Change Management*, 1998.
3. Ibid.
4. Ibid.
5. Heifetz, Ronald A., and Laurie, Donald L. The Work of Leadership. *Harvard Business Review*, January–February, 1997 pp. 124–134.
6. Ibid, p. 125.
7. Ibid, p. 128.

8

Maintaining Momentum

The previous two chapters have described how to gain management support for work transformation and how to implement a work transformation program. This, however, is not the end of the process. It may, in fact, be only the completion of the first of many iterations of changes that will eventually lead to dramatic changes in the organization's workplace.

Unfortunately, many organizations stop after the first implementation of work transformation. They believe with the change now "completed," it is time to move on to other business issues. The reality is that most organizations that stop at this point fail in trying to expand their work transformation programs and often revert back to traditional ways of working. The key elements of maintaining momentum are to

- Review the current program
- Tune the program accordingly
- Identify the issues that have caused failures in other organizations to ensure that steps are taken to avoid these classic problems
- Reinforce the business case
- Update the basic work transformation strategies
- Expand the work transformation program

REVIEW

To maintain momentum, it is necessary to review the steps that have been taken towards work transformation, with the goal of learning from these experiences.

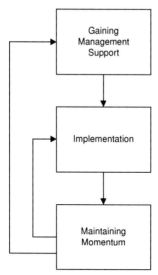

Figure 8-1 Iterative process to achieve work transformation.

This needs to be done whether the work transformation has been just a pilot, the organization has pursued an "embrace change" approach of implementing all of the concepts at once, or it is performing subsequent implementations as part of the iterative process shown in Figure 8-1.

The review should be performed 4–9 months after implementation, based on the size of the implementation and the magnitude of the changes being implemented. Any review at earlier than 4 months may produce erroneous results, as most employees take 6–8 weeks to adjust to the new environment, then potentially overachieve for another 6–8 weeks before reaching a steady state. All measurements should be based on the steady-state condition. The key is to find the steady state. For most changes, improvements/challenges will rise to a peak, then be followed by a correction down to a "normal" level. This new normal level is the steady state. Typically, it is reached when the following three situations have occurred.

1. Euphoria/shock of the change has worn off
2. "Improvements" have peaked, dropped a little, and then levelled off
3. "Challenges" have peaked, lessened in magnitude and impact, then become accepted as part of the new way of working.

As will be shown, however, the approach to reviewing each type of implementation is slightly different.

Pilot Review

The purpose of the pilot is to test the work transformation concepts and to document the extent to which the expected business benefits have been delivered.

The pilot review plan should include methods for gathering data, analyzing it, and reporting on the results. The data-gathering methods typically include questionnaires and focus groups. All of the data-gathering methods must be designed to gather data on the specific areas being measured. The questionnaires should be administered prior to the start of the pilot to record baseline data, possibly at the halfway point of the pilot (for pilots longer than 6 months), and definitely at the end of the pilot period. All questionnaires should include progressive questions to ensure that trends can be tracked.

Figure 8-2 shows an example of the work transformation assessment questionnaire. Note that the first three questions under team dynamics appear on the original work pattern questionnaire (baseline data), while the following four questions are the progressive questions. The follow-up questionnaire, therefore, allows the organization to gauge both the change in response to the original questions while also providing the opportunity to gain more specific knowledge of why work transformation has affected the responses to the original questions.

The questionnaires should be simple, checkbox-style documents that can be completed quickly and easily. The checkbox style also allows for easy tabulation of results and associated trend analysis. The end of the questionnaires should also include an area for additional comments on any relevant information that was not adequately addressed in the checkbox-style questions.

The questionnaires will gather structured information regarding the pilot. The focus groups are less structured and will deliver anecdotal "stories" from those directly involved in the pilot and those affected by it.

The focus groups will often create opportunities for deriving more abstract information about the pilot. The focus groups should be led by an external consultant. Internal support resources (i.e., from human resources, information technology, or facilities management) should typically not be part of the focus groups. Including the support individuals tends to either subdue the conversation, as the participants are uncomfortable opening up with someone who is part of the organization, or turn the meeting into a complaint session where the participants "dump" on the support groups. The primary purpose of the session is to gather factual, realistic information, not to provide a forum for political posturing.

The review should not be restricted to just employees who are directly participating in the pilot. The changes involved in this type of pilot will be broader than just the employees who participate. Data should be gathered from all participants, along with input from their managers, coworkers, and possibly customers (internal and external).

KLR Consulting Inc.
Assessment Questionnaire

Group:_____   To Be Completed by: _____

Team Dynamics
This section describes how your team interacts in the new work environment.

Team Dynamics	Strongly Disagree	Disagree	Neutral	Agree	Strongly Agree
The office provides good places for a team to work together.	❑	❑	❑	❑	❑
The office design is conducive to team-building.	❑	❑	❑	❑	❑
My team communicates effectively within the office	❑	❑	❑	❑	❑
Teaming spaces have enhanced team communication	❑	❑	❑	❑	❑
Sharing common areas and storage has brought the team closer together	❑	❑	❑	❑	❑
My team is more cohesive since work transformation	❑	❑	❑	❑	❑
Casual meeting spaces are effective areas for team interaction	❑	❑	❑	❑	❑

Alternative Space Arrangements
Now that I'm out of the office two or more days per week on a regular basis I use:

For Remote Workers Only:	Strongly Disagree	Disagree	Neutral	Agree	Strongly Agree
A smaller workspace	❑	❑	❑	❑	❑
Shared open office	❑	❑	❑	❑	❑
Shared manager office / meeting space	❑	❑	❑	❑	❑
Lockers & moveable pedestals	❑	❑	❑	❑	❑
I am more productive when I'm in the office now	❑	❑	❑	❑	❑
My new work environment supports better interaction with my colleagues	❑	❑	❑	❑	❑

General Comments

_____
_____
_____

Figure 8-2 Sample pieces of Work Transformation Assessment Questionnaire. (Courtesy of KLR Consulting Inc.)

Full Implementation Review

The full implementation strategy will be used by organizations that want to fully embrace the work transformation concepts and are prepared to implement the concepts through one major implementation. This strategy represents a higher risk than the stepping stone approach (using pilots to start), but it can be very effective for organizations that are using work transformation to reinforce other dramatic business, culture, and behavioral changes.

The full implementation review should be performed using focus groups and questionnaires to determine the success of the implementation. The questionnaires should focus on the key business objectives that were expected to be achieved by the implementation. The baseline data for a full implementation will likely come from the assessment data gathered during the work transformation assessment phase. The review questionnaires should ask progressive questions (building on the assessment questionnaire) to allow for a reasonable trend analysis to be performed.

The ideal scenario is for all employee to complete the review questionnaire. In very large organizations, this may be difficult and/or costly, so a sampling of employees may be more appropriate. If a sampling strategy is used, then the organization must ensure that the sample is truly representative of the organization.

Focus groups should also be held to solicit feedback. These groups should be structured in the same fashion as described for pilots. They will, of course, represent only a sampling of the overall organization, as it would not be feasible to include all employees.

Review of Subsequent Implementations

If an organization is taking a stepping stone approach to implementing work transformation, then numerous implementations will be performed over time. In this scenario, it is critical that the organization review each implementation to ensure the lessons learned are captured and applied to subsequent implementations.

In this scenario, each of the implementations will probably include expansion of existing work transformation concepts and some changes. The changes put forward at each implementation should be reviewed in detail. The expansion of existing work transformation concepts probably does not need to be reviewed, or at most at a cursory level.

The review of these incremental changes can be done through short, focused questionnaires to those affected and through focus groups. Remember that the amount of effort involved in the review should be directly related to the degree of the incremental change and the risk associated with these changes.

For each type of review, it is critical to ensure the review results are understood and accepted by the organization. The reviews must be seen as being honest, realistic, and objective. Many organizations turn to outside consultants to perform this task. The consultant can be used to construct questionnaires, gather data, analyze trends, and report back on the overall success of the implementation without singling out any specific participant. The consultant will reassure the participants that the raw data will be used exclusively by the consultant for the analysis and will not be returned to the organization. This type of "arms-length" relationship should help the participants feel more comfortable in providing honest responses during the data-collection process.

As the ultimate goal of the review is to learn from the changes that have been implemented, it should determine whether the changes have worked and to what extent the business objectives have been met. If these goals have not been achieved, then it is critical to understand why not. The data gathered from participating staff is part of the puzzle of determining success. The resources performing the review should compare these results to results from other, similar organizations to gain greater insight into the actual success.

The ultimate deliverable of these reviews is to learn from the experiences and to tune the work transformation program to better achieve the expected business benefits. The lessons learned through this review will be used to update the key work transformation components and to provide a framework for the next iteration.

CLASSIC CHALLENGES

The reviews will likely identify several areas of difficulty with the implementation of work transformation. The following are a few of the classic challenges that other organizations have experienced. These challenges are presented here to help organizations recognize them and learn from the experiences of others.

Pilots

Many organizations have been able to bring work transformation programs successfully to the end of the pilot stage but then have failed in trying to expand the programs to the entire organization. Often this failure is due to flaws in the pilot strategy.

Some pilots use the strategy of including only a small, specialized group that is not perceived by the rest of the organization as being representative. In these cases, the concepts are often expanded within the specialized group but usually do not extend to other parts of the organization. This pitfall can be avoided by ensuring that key decision makers consider the pilot participants to represent a reasonable cross-section of the organization.

Another problem with the pilot may be a lack of communication. If a thorough communications plan does not exist, the work transformation concept itself and the success of the pilot may go unnoticed. It is critical that the communications plan be broad enough to reach all staff and management. To prevent this problem, the communications plan described in Chapter 7 should be followed.

The most common problem with pilots is the perception of informality. Many pilots that are "informal" in nature are not widely accepted by the organization as a whole. A prevailing belief is that if the pilot is not formalized, then it cannot be that important to senior management—and therefore middle managers may not pay close attention. The formalized pilot, as described in Chapter 7, includes the use of a skilled cross-functional team, a thorough review strategy, appropriate change and project management, and the implementation of an effective communications plan.

Some pilots lack a strong business focus. Work transformation programs that are implemented for limited business return are typically not taken seriously by either senior or middle management. A weak or nonexistent business program can cause a work transformation program to flounder. Unfortunately, many programs that have evolved based on employee benefits have found that it is very difficult to bring senior and middle management on board when they perceive that the program has few, if any, tangible business benefits.

Many of these pilot-related challenges can be corrected by following the key steps to implementation outlined in Chapter 7. As with many initiatives, putting the effort into doing the front-end work increases the likelihood of achieving the long-run benefits.

Organizational Focus

Another major cause of the failure of work transformation programs to expand is a lack of organizational focus. Many organizations bring together the necessary human, technological, and financial resources to make the pilot a success, only to see subsequent implementations fail. Often this is is because the organization feels it now knows all it needs to know about work transformation and is ready to move on to something new, assuming that organization-wide implementation will somehow build itself on the success of the pilot.

Self-perpetuating implementation with laser-sharp focus, of course, is usually not the case. The change management model described in Chapter 7 shows how change has a longer life than most projects. The key to expanding a work transformation program is to form *another* project to maintain the momen-

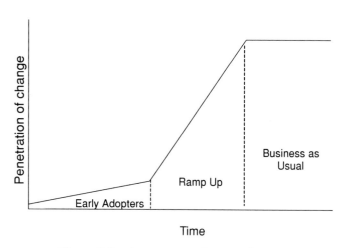

Figure 8-3 Acceptance of major change.

tum. This follow-up project should take work transformation to the next level; it should not be a repeat of what has just been completed. Remember that the goal is to learn and constantly evolve. This renewed focus also sends a strong message to staff and middle managers that the work transformation program is still on senior management's list of important projects and that additional work is still remaining.

The key to long-term success is to recognize that the best approach is to slowly approach the ramp-up phase of change acceptance (Figure 8-3) to capture all of the early adopters in the organization and then to accelerate the program through the ramp-up phase and into the "business-as-usual" phase.

At completion of the first pilot, the organization is likely in the middle of the "early adopter" zone. It is now essential that efforts continue to move the organization into the "ramp up" zone, where full implementation begins. It is important to note that the completion of full implementation does not automatically land the organization in the "business as usual" zone. Continuous effort is required to ensure that the program evolves into a state of "business as usual."

Middle Managers as Obstacles

Another classic challenge is obtaining the support of middle managers. Middle managers tend to be the most resistant to change. Often, this occurs because they equate the loss of space and the loss of visual contact (face time) with employees as a loss of control. They also are concerned about switching their management style to managing by results, preferring the now somewhat outdated 1980s model of management by "walking around." Many of these managers believe that face time is critical. A common response is "How can I be certain that work is really occurring when I can't see my employees?" The corollary to this is how do managers know work is really occurring when they see employees sitting at their desks.

The net result is that these managers feel that work transformation programs are just another way of eroding their control. They have been trained to be the conduit between the workers and senior management—their role is to "direct traffic" and stay the course. All of this can be more difficult under the new work transformation concepts.

To be truthful, the middle managers raise some valid arguments. After all, they are often the ones who are hit hardest in any downsizing, as the organizational hierarchy is flattened (see Figure 1-3) and employees are empowered. Senior management may be tempted to ask, "If employees are allowed to work anytime, anywhere, then why are these middle managers even needed?"

Another challenge is addressing the tendency for middle managers to focus on short-term costs. These managers are usually evaluated on their ability to manage the immediate short-term costs of their departments. In any work transformation implementation, short-term costs may increase before the longer-term benefits are realized. Even then, the benefits may translate as overall corporate cost savings, which may not be reflected in the middle manager's budget. Senior management has to give these managers some latitude with their individual budgets with regard to work transformation to provide the organization with the opportunity to realize the longer-term benefits.

Managers focused on short-term schedules with tight deadlines may also fear the "disruption" posed by the period of adjustment inevitable in work transformation implementation. Even with careful planning, the implementation of alternative space arrangements may incur very real, if temporary, disruptions as changes are made to the office. As with budgetary concerns, senior management would be prudent to address managers' concerns about meeting short-term schedules to realize the longer-term benefits.

The budget management issue is particularly challenging in environments where the manager's budget does not include accommodation costs. In some organizations, the accommodation costs are handled separately and are not allocated to each department. The middle manager is then asked to participate in a work transformation program that will reduce the accommodation costs, but this savings will not be reflected in the manager's budget. The result is that the short-term increase in costs associated with the implementation of the program cannot be offset by the space savings. This scenario makes it very difficult for the middle managers to become supportive of the work transformation implementation. In this type of situation, it is essential that senior management take steps to alleviate this short-term, department-only thinking and get the managers focused on the overall longer-term corporate benefits.

To be successful, the organization must win over this sometimes disgruntled middle management group. Doing so is not an easy task, but it is critical—and possible. The starting point in convincing middle managers of the value of work transformation is to focus on the business benefits:

- How it will impact the effectiveness of their groups
- How they can integrate the work transformation benefits with other business changes to achieve even higher returns
- How they can be seen as being more successful by implementing these changes

Another strategy is to get resistant managers more involved in the process. Have them explain their concerns to the working group and collaboratively develop creative solutions to address these issues. It is hoped that other managers will already be "on board" with the work transformation program. Ensuring that on-board managers are part of the working group will provide peer support and help the concerned manager see that his or her peer has worked through these issues.

Yet another strategy is to make the problem manager part of the solution. If the manager is uncomfortable with telework, suggest that the manager try it for a few months. Virtually every manager could work from home one day a week. Duncan Sutherland Jr., an international business and design consultant suggests that organizations encourage managers to "free up a day of their week to do their mind's best work."[1] Or if managers are uncomfortable with giving up their office for a shared space, have them try it for a few months with the proviso that they can have their dedicated office back if the trial is not successful (make sure that "success" is defined before starting the trial and measure it during the trial period).

Still another interesting strategy is to have senior management make work transformation a critical success factor in evaluating each manager's individual and departmental performance plan. The manager will then have his or her success directly dependent on the success of the work transformation implementation. This should provide ample incentive to help open the manager's mind to these new concepts. A word of caution is necessary with this last suggestion. The goal here is to create a win–win situation for the organization, employees, and manager; not to belittle or punish the manager.

Support of the concerned middle managers is critical to the overall success of a work transformation program. It is well worthwhile to ensure that the "roll-out" team spends enough time coaching these managers to help them be successful.

MOVING FORWARD

It is essential that the organization continue to commit efforts to the further refinement and implementation of work transformation. The concept of continuing to move forward involves reinforcing the business case, updating the key strategies, forming a "roll-out" team, and expanding the work transformation program.

Reinforcing the Business Case

When expanding the work transformation program, it is imperative to remain focused on the business benefits. The realization of the business benefits will, in the end, separate the successful programs from those that are unable to grow.

The business case (described in Chapter 6) was initially developed during the early stages of investigating the work transformation concept. It was based on a series of assumptions that may have been understated or overstated. The completed implementation should provide the organization with better, more realistic data by which to evaluate the business validity.

When the implementation is completed and the final data on achieving the expected business objectives have been summarized, the business case should be updated and the following questions addressed:

- Are the original assumptions still valid?
- Did the expected business benefits materialize? If so, to the level expected? Better than expected?
- What new business benefits were discovered during the course of the pilot?
- How did the actual costs compare to the budget?
- Is the business case still financially viable?

The business case should be updated to reflect these findings and expanded or contracted to more accurately reflect the data gathered in terms of additional benefits—or those that did not materialize at all.

Next, the business case financial analysis needs to shift to an incremental analysis. This explores the business case for the next individual or group that is to implement work transformation. The front-end costs of the first implementation are "sunk" costs and should be excluded from this incremental analysis.

With the incremental analysis, focus is shifted to the next group of employees to be involved in the implementation of work transformation. This "next group" can be any number of employees. The incremental financial analysis examines only costs on the "margin" (the costs to get to that point are not included).

The revised business case and the incremental financial analysis should be broadly distributed throughout the organization. Managers should be empowered to implement work transformation programs within their areas using the incremental financial analysis as a guideline both for justification and for creating their own specific business case.

Again, the key to success is to continue to drive home the business benefits. If the organization cannot deliver on these benefits, the program will be perceived as having limited value.

Updating Work Transformation Strategies

The organization's strategies and plans in the areas of human resources, facilities management, and information technology will have been developed based on the knowledge of work transformation available at the time. After the initial implementation, the organization should have a greater level of knowledge of the concept and, more importantly, how it fits into the culture and style of the organization.

This more "mature" knowledge of work transformation should be used to update the key strategies. In many cases, the original strategies may have supported a small number of employees. If the work transformation concept is growing, then perhaps it is time to upgrade the strategies to handle a larger number of participants.

A good example of this is the information technology solution to remote access. Many organizations will start with a "baling wire and chewing gum" solution to support a small number of remote workers at a reasonably low cost. Most organizations do not want to implement the full and complete remote access solution until they go through the pilot—which is an excellent strategy. However, once the pilot is completed, the information technology group will need to rethink the original strategy and develop a more rigorous remote access solution that will handle the growing number of remote workers.

All strategies should be reviewed, critiqued by the roll-out team, and updated. This will most likely include updating the alternative work arrangement (AWA) policies, guidelines, and procedures; the alternative officing policies, guidelines, design considerations, and implementation strategies; and the remote access, voice communications, and desktop technologies.

Strategic Positioning

The early stages of work transformation involved gaining support from senior management. This support was probably in terms of having them buy a vision of what the work transformation concepts could produce. The vision was supported by a proper business case, but the decision to proceed with the initial implementation also required a "leap of faith."

The executives should review the results and recommendations of the pilot. If they support expanding the use of the work transformation concepts, they will need to reconsider the relative strategic position of this expanded initiative.

In making the decision to expand the number of participants using work transformation concepts, the executives must be reminded of the need for a larger number of participants to ensure that business benefits are derived. They need to remember that some true bottom-line benefits will accrue only if the proper economies of scale exist. For example, the saving on space will not materialize if only 5 people are teleworking and sharing space but could be significant if 500 are teleworking and sharing regular office space.

The executives need to know the size of the critical mass that is required to actually begin to realize some of these benefits. For example, how many square feet does the organization need to free up to be able to sublet the space? How many work transformation participants will be required to free up this amount of space?

The executives should be asked to reexamine to the positioning strategies chart (Figure 8-4) to see where they now want to be positioned on the change continuum. They also need to recognize the need to continue the change process to ensure that adequate resources are allocated to ensure that the roll-out is a success. The project is not over at the end of the pilot; it is, in fact, just beginning.

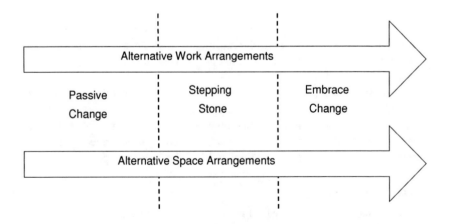

Figure 8-4 Work transformation positioning strategy.

Work Transformation "Roll-Out" Team

When expanding the work transformation program, it would be a critical error to completely disband the work transformation implementation team (described in Chapter 7). To maintain momentum, the organization will need to have some resources that are dedicated to supporting the new concepts and continuing to evolve the strategies and plans to support a larger population of participants.

The original work transformation implementation team will have broken through the initial barriers to introduce and demonstrate the concept to the organization. The roll-out team will be smaller than the original implementation team and will shift its attention to expansion of the concept and supporting/coaching the organization to further successful implementations and refinements. Figure 8-5 shows the potential organization chart for the roll-out team.

A key role for the team will be to maintain the change management process. This will include working through the change management process described in Chapter 7 and formalizing the new desired state for the organization. These functions, formerly performed by a separate change management group, can be picked up by the project manager and the human resources representative(s).

Another key role will be to build a new communications plan and to implement it. Communication is the ultimate key to change management. The revised communications plan should build on the work done in the pilot to show how the organization can now take the work transformation concepts to the next level. In today's organization, there is a constant flow of changes, so it is important to keep information regarding the work transformation concepts in

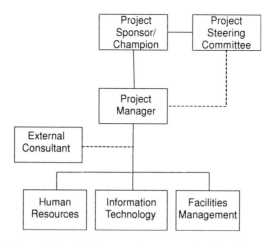

Figure 8-5 Roll-out project organization chart.

front of the organization to maintain the momentum. A newsletter and announced updates on the organization's Intranet site can be effective ways of furthering this communication.

The implementation of work transformation needs to be supported by business cases. The roll-out team will work with managers and staff to develop business cases that identify the potential business benefits and methods for tracking these measures of success. The team must also be prepared to continue to "push the envelope," as this is a journey that needs to constantly evolve. Finally, the team will continue to evolve the human resources, facilities management, and information technology strategies and plans to support the growing number of work transformation participants. This will involve working with resources in each of these groups to ensure that the solutions fit the evolving requirements of the organization.

Program Expansion

Obviously, the key to maintaining momentum is to continue to expand the work transformation program. If the organization took the pilot route, it will now be ready to add more people to the program. The easiest way to do this is to add more people from the same departments and job types currently represented in the pilot. Presumably, the management in these areas is on board with the concept, so some expansion should be possible.

If the organization has still not completely embraced work transformation concepts, it might consider implementing another small pilot using a different group of individuals. These subsequent pilots should be less formal than previous ones in terms of the preparation and the formal review. The goal of the subsequent pilots is to expand the program and to ease the organization into the work transformation program. It is, however, critical that all new groups and/or individuals added to the work transformation program be trained and have specific business objectives that they will be attempting to achieve through the program.

Organizations that feel they are past the piloting stage will want to empower their managers to implement work transformation concepts within their departments. These managers should be given the training and support to develop an appropriate business case, select individuals for participation in AWAs, and work with the roll-out team to design their new work areas. The work transformation roll-out team will support the managers and their employees to ensure that the expected business benefits are achieved.

Organizations that have been most successful in implementing these new strategies have implemented them gradually. This is not to say that the "big bang" approach will not work; just that history suggests that the chances of success are greatest when gradual incremental change is implemented. The change to the work transformation concepts represents a huge organizational, personal, and cultural change; this does not need to be compounded by making an "overnight" transition to the full and complete adoption of these concepts.

The work transformation program will reach the business-as-usual state when management and employees (and, if applicable, the union) can see these alternative concepts as just another obvious way of working. At this point, the expansion of the program will become automatic and obvious. In fact, the program will have reached a logical level of implementation, and undoubtedly the next set of new workplace strategies, driven by ever-changing technologies, will have emerged, and the organization will begin to experiment with them.

SUMMARY

Maintaining momentum for a work transformation program involves reviewing the current progress, looking out for the classic challenges, and moving forward to expand the use of these concepts.

Reviews are critical to maintaining momentum. They help the organization document the successes and failures of the implementation, allowing it to learn from these experiences. The reviews should be a combination of structured data gathered through questionnaires and less structured "anecdotal" input gathered through focus groups. The lessons learned from the reviews should be clearly documented and used as input to the further expansion of the organization's work transformation program.

Many organizations have already attempted to implement work transformation, and many of them struggle with the same challenges. Those that utilize pilots sometimes find that the pilot is not adequately structured, or it appears not to represent an appropriate cross-section of the organization. Others find that the pilots do not have a compelling business driver, which reduces their level of importance for senior and middle management. These classic piloting problems can be overcome by structuring formal pilots that are perceived to be representative of the entire organization and that are based on tangible business benefits.

Another common challenge is a lack of organizational focus on work transformation. The completion of the first implementation can sometimes be seen as reaching the finish line. In fact, this is merely the first step on a long journey towards incorporating work transformation into the culture and operation of the organization.

The most common challenge in implementing work transformation is the support of middle managers. These employees are often skeptical of the proposed new ways of working and the resulting changes to the way they manage. These employees need to be brought on board by focusing them on the expected business benefits.

To move forward, the organization should review and reinforce the original business case. It should consider the results of the first implementation and apply this to the business case. The next level of business case should focus on the incremental costs and benefits—what it will take to implement the next individual or group. The organization should also review and revise the human resources, facilities management, and information technology strategies and plans to reflect the lessons learned to date.

The organization needs to re-visit the strategic positioning model periodically to determine where it should go next. Should it continue to slowly evolve through the stepping stone model? Move to complete implementation? Go back and run some more small pilots?

The organization needs to allocate appropriate resources to maintain momentum. This includes assigning a work transformation "roll-out" team, which will be a trimmed-down version of the implementation team. This team will maintain the organization's focus on work transformation and will continue to move these concepts forward.

The ultimate goal of maintaining momentum is to expand the work transformation program to the point where work transformation becomes "business as usual" for the organization. Only at this stage, should the implementation be considered complete.

NOTE

1. Sutherland Duncan B. Jr. *Technology and the White-Collar Productivity Paradox: Time, Tools, and The Minds Best Work in Knowledge Infrastructure Engineering: An Emerging Community of Practice in Knowledge-Intensive Organizations*. Ann Arbor, MI: Industrial Technology Institute, 1992.

9

Theory to Reality

In providing a framework for the successful implementation of work transformation, this book has focused on the concepts. The real benefit of work transformation is realized only when the "rubber hits the road" in terms of taking the theory and turning it into reality. This chapter provided details of a generic case study and several examples of how a broad range of organizations have implemented these concepts.

GENERIC CASE STUDY

A generic organization will be used to illustrate the primary points of work transformation. This organization is typical of many organizations that I have seen in my consulting practice; it is a composite of companies; not a reflection of any single company.

The Pacific Telecommunications Corporation (PTC) (a fictitious name) is in the business of designing and building high technology components for use in the telecommunications industry. PTC has customers across North America with potential for additional business in the Pacific Rim and Europe. The industry is highly competitive with tight margins and a growing number of new entrants. The key to long-term success is to get new products to the market as soon as possible.

PTC currently has a downtown head office. Sixty employees are occupying one floor of an office tower, with a total of 13,500 ft^2 of usable floor space.

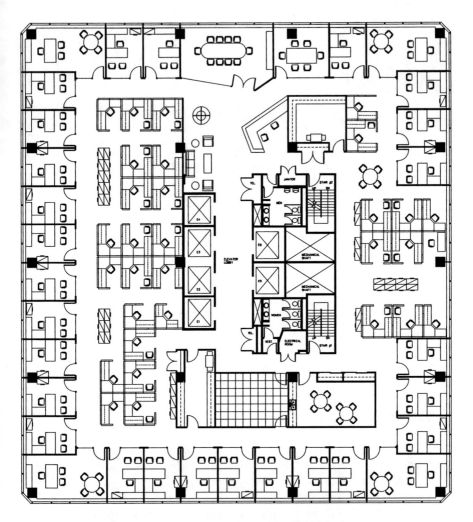

Figure 9-1   Existing floor plan—60 employees.

The current space plan shown in Figure 9-1 is typical of most organizations today. Approximately 225 ft² is allotted per employee, and the space is designed with offices along the outside windows and open areas on the inside. All employees have an assigned workspace.

An analysis of the space shows that there is no room to accommodate the planned 45% growth (27 more employees). The only choices available are to lease additional space using the current space planning standards, to reduce the space per person, or to consider the potential for work transformation. PTC has decided to consider the potential for work transformation while analyzing the costs of expanding its space or reducing the space per person.

The first step in the process for PTC was to do some basic research and to create a work transformation vision within the organization. The executives were very skeptical of these ideas but came on board once they thought through the potential business benefits. The vice president of marketing became the executive champion.

The next step was to educate staff and management about work transformation. Information sessions were held with all staff attending. The sessions helped all employees understand work transformation concepts, the potential benefits, and the process that would be undertaken to determine appropriateness. These sessions were very informal, with a brief presentation by a knowledgeable consultant, followed by an extensive question and answer period. All employees were encouraged to participate in the process, and all questions were answered. Employees left these sessions more knowledgeable of the concepts and thinking about how these ideas would impact their workgroup and themselves personally. The information sessions did not alleviate all fears of work transformation but they did reduce the overall anxiety level of the employees.

Once everyone was aware of the work transformation process, it was time to start collecting information. The first step was to involve the facilities management group to do an inventory of existing furniture and to investigate the cost of acquiring more space in the same building and the cost of shrinking the square footage per person. The facilities manager also arranged to perform a space utilization analysis of all workspaces to determine how effectively they were being used.

The human resources manager was involved to put together a policy on alternative work arrangements (AWAs). Employees at PTC all worked on a regular schedule—Monday to Friday 8:30 A.M. to 5:00 P.M. Managers had in the past not been supportive of any significant variation in the traditional times or location of work. The human resources group set out to involve staff and management in developing a range of alternative work arrangements including telework, modified work weeks, and variable work hours.

The information technology group was involved to determine if the existing technology infrastructure could support work transformation. PTC is highly computerized, with all employees having their own personal computer and access to the local area network. The telephone system was based on assigning specific phone numbers to physical locations but the PBX (phone computer) currently installed could be upgraded to accommodate virtual numbers (allowing employees to share offices). The biggest challenge for the technology group was to establish a facility to allow teleworkers and mobile workers to dial into the PTC network. The existing dial-in facilities were very basic and needed significant improvements in security, speed, and capacity to handle remote workers.

Once the three key strategies (people, facilities, and technology) were in place, it was time to involve all staff in determining how and where they could potentially work. This was accomplished by a questionnaire which asked employees about their current space—what they liked and did not like and how prepared they would be to share. The questionnaire also inquired about the work performed by the employees to determine (1) if they could do any of it remotely and (2) what type of workspace would be most appropriate. Finally, employees were questioned on the technology they used to perform their job.

The final step in gathering work transformation information was to determine the business objectives. This was done by getting a group of employees and managers together from across the organization to discuss the business drivers. The discussion brought out a series of interesting responses, and the group decided on the following key business objectives:

- To improve the communications within the organization (this was particularly critical given the dramatic growth of the organization)
- To reduce the cycle time required to take a product from the conceptual phase to the marketplace—the group felt that this could be accomplished by getting the design and marketing teams to work closer together (they are currently located on opposite sides of the floor)
- To have the sales staff spend more time with the customers—to improve the level of customer service and increase sales
- To improve the productivity of all employees (part of a continuous improvement program)
- To accommodate the 45% growth in staffing within the existing space

The data was collected and analyzed by an external resource which assured PTC employees that the information provided would be kept confidential—thus encouraging them to be open and honest in their responses. The output of this data analysis was quite interesting and provided several surprises to PTC.

The results of the facilities data raised a few eyebrows in the organization. The space utilization data shown in Figure 9-2 indicates that, on average, a workspace is idle 65% of the time, in use by one person 30% of the time, and in use by multiple persons 5% of the time. This data suggests that there was an opportunity for some space sharing. It also shows that there was very little interaction between employees within the work area—most employees tended to stay in their offices rather than walk over to another office.

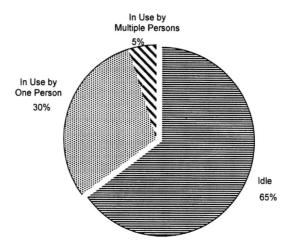

Figure 9-2 Space utilization of workspace.

The space utilization was also performed for meeting spaces. The results, shown in Figure 9-3, indicate that the meeting spaces are in use by multiple people 65% of the time, idle 20% of the time, and in use by one person 15% of the time. This shows that meetings are taking place but that they have to be scheduled in one of the available meeting rooms. The most interesting statistic is that 15% of the time the meeting space is being used by one person. The room is likely being

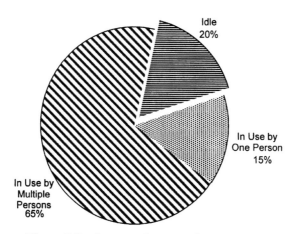

Figure 9-3 Space utilization of meeting space.

used by employees who are looking for quiet spaces to do concentrated work. The use of a medium-sized or large meeting room as a quiet space for one person is extremely expensive and inefficient.

The analysis of work patterns also resulted in some interesting conclusions. It was reported that 20% of the staff were already operating remotely. These people included sales staff, who were out of the office 3–4 days per week, and a few employees who were "guerrilla" teleworkers working from home 2–3 days per week without any type of formal agreement. The number of existing remote workers probably helps to explain the high percentage of idle office space in the office.

The analysis of work pattern data also shows some interesting results regarding the type of work performed by employees. Figure 9-4 shows the response to questions about the amount of time employees spend on various segments of their jobs. The data shows that a large portion of time in the office is spent at their desks doing concentrated work on their personal computers—this probably indicates that some portion of their work could be performed remotely. The low use of ad hoc meetings could be a problem as there is a lack of ad hoc space in which to meet—this coincides with the utilization figures on the meeting rooms.

The work pattern data also suggests that most communication within the office typically occurred in scheduled meetings. The employees tended to spend

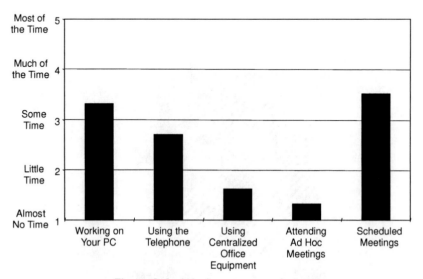

Figure 9-4 Work pattern analysis.

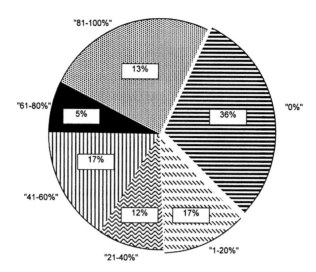

Figure 9-5 Employee responses (in quotation marks) to the question "What percentage of work could be performed remotely?"

their time in their offices or in the meeting rooms. The data confirmed the concern that the level of ad hoc communications was suspect.

The employees were also asked if any portion of their job could be performed remotely. More than half responded that some portion of their work could be performed remotely. The data in Figure 9-5 show that 53% of the employees should be working in the traditional office environment all week. However, 29% of the employees felt that they could be working remotely between 1 and 3 days per week (21–60%)—these employees could potentially be teleworking from home. Finally, 18% of the employees felt they could be working remotely 3–5 days per week (61–100%)—these employees are likely the mobile employees, whose job has them out of the office most of the time.

The questionnaire also inquired about the level of interest in teleworking. Over 80% of the employees were strongly supportive of instituting a formal telework program at PTC.

The information technology data showed that all employees had a personal computer that was connected to the local area network. The remote workers were all using notebook computers (laptops) and cellular phones.

The data analysis shows an opportunity for work transformation. The real selling of these concepts came about when the financial analysis was performed. PTC had three options to consider.

Option #1: Acquire Additional Space

The first option was to acquire additional space to accommodate the 45% growth in staffing. To accommodate the growth, PTC would have had to acquire at least 6075 ft^2 of office space (27 new employees @ 225 ft^2/employee). The facilities people were able to determine that based on current market conditions the cost of establishing this space would be a one-time cost of $350,000 plus an ongoing cost of $150,000 per year. The one-time cost includes the setup, consulting, data/telephone wiring, furniture, and moving costs associated with the new space. The senior management team had established an objective of not increasing the facility operating costs, so this option did not look promising.

Option #2: Squeeze in Additional Staff

The second option was to fit the staff expansion into the existing space using traditional work and space arrangements. This would mean having to reduce the number of ft^2 per person from the current 225 to 155 ft^2 (13,500 ft^2/87 employees). This change would probably have meant moving all employees into much smaller offices, reconstructing the space, and possibly replacing the furniture. The facilities group determined that this could be done for a one-time cost of $500,000, with no change in the ongoing operating costs. The one-time costs would be to move some office walls, rearrange the data and telephone wiring, rearrange the furniture, and acquire new furniture for the extra 27 people, plus the costs of performing the construction after hours to minimize the impact on staff. This option met the business objective of not increasing the facility operating costs but it did not address any of the other business objectives such as improved communications or increased time with customers.

Option #3: Work Transformation

A third option was to reengineer where and when people work. The data shows an opportunity to achieve all of the identified business objectives. The first objective was to improve communication. This could be accomplished by establishing team spaces where logical groupings of employees could interact easily without having to leave their work area. This approach also included the use of more casual meeting space for impromptu meetings and a greater number of smaller meeting rooms (which would double as offices). Reducing the cycle time from design to customer should be enhanced by putting the marketing and design groups into a team space allowing them to easily interact with each other which should help to reduce the cycle time.

The sales staff were already functioning as mobile workers, so the work transformation project would ensure that they would have the right technology and encourage them to work remotely 4–5 days per week. This would allow them to spend more time with customers, which should have a positive impact on sales and customer service. The sales staff would no longer have permanently assigned offices. Instead, they would have shared spaces, probably a carrel-type space, which they would use when they were in the office. This minimal space would work effectively for the sales staff as they would be spending most of their time in the office, interacting with others rather than doing "heads down" work.

The improvement in productivity would be accomplished in several ways. The team spaces should improve overall team productivity, and the use of quiet rooms and phone booths would provide employees with areas where they could work for a few hours at a time on "heads down" activities. PTC would also implement a formal telework program which would allow approximately 12 employees to work from home 2–3 days per week. These employees would be more productive by doing their quiet work at home and would share space at the traditional office.

The work transformation strategy was to be accomplished by reworking the existing space to establish team spaces, more open areas, phone booths, more meeting rooms, and locker storage for remote workers. The one-time cost of these changes was estimated at $400,000. This cost would include removing existing fixed walls, buying some new furniture (existing furniture would be used wherever possible), reworking some of the telephone and data wiring, and the costs associated with implementing AWAs (i.e., policies, procedures, training).

Figure 9-6 shows the financial analysis for PTC's work transformation proposal. Note that when analyzed at a discount rate of 8%, the net present value of the real estate portion of the analysis is almost $600,000. When the intangible benefits are included, the net present value (NPV) soars to just over $1 million. The investment pays back in 2 years. The work transformation (option #3) clearly was the best financial option available for PTC.

The NPV analysis for work transformation looks fairly impressive; however, senior management was convinced of the financial benefit only when the three options were compared over five years, as shown in Figure 9-7.

Figure 9-7 clearly shows the work transformation option as being significantly ahead of the other two options that were being considered. The option of acquiring space on another floor would have had the lowest one-time cost but also would have increased the annual operating costs by $150,000. The option of squeezing more people into the same space by reducing the size of each workstation would have had a one-time cost of $500,000 with no incremental

	Year 1	Year 2	Year 3	Year 4	Year 5	Total
Costs:						
Work Transformation	$400,000					$400,000
Total Costs	$400,000	$0	$0	$0	$0	$400,000
Tangible Benefits:						
Costs Avoided:						
Additional space fit-up	$350,000					$350,000
Office Savings	$150,000	$150,000	$150,000	$150,000	$150,000	$750,000
Total Benefits	$500,000	$150,000	$150,000	$150,000	$150,000	$1,100,000
Net Cash Flow (NCF)	$100,000	$150,000	$150,000	$150,000	$150,000	$700,000
Net Present Value (NPV)	$100,000	$138,889	$128,601	$119,075	$110,254	**$596,819**
Intangible Benefits:						
Productivity	$69,600	$69,600	$69,600	$69,600	$69,600	$348,000
NCF with Intangibles	$169,600	$219,600	$219,600	$219,600	$219,600	$1,048,000
NPV with Intangibles	$169,600	$203,333	$188,272	$174,326	$161,413	**$896,943**
Key Indicators:						
General:						
Discount Rate	8%					
Productivity Improvement	2.0%					
Average Annual Salary	$40,000					

Figure 9-6   Work transformation financial analysis.

operating costs. This option was appealing but it would not have helped to support any of the other business objectives such as improved communications or reduced time to market. The work transformation option had the lowest one-time cost, no increase in operating costs, and the greatest chance of meeting PTC'S real estate and other business objectives.

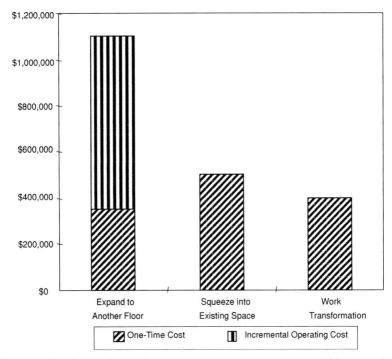

Figure 9-7 Comparison of three options to accommodate 45% growth.

Once the business case was approved, PTC immediately moved to design the new space and implement the AWA programs. The new space was designed by bringing together all staff to have them participate in defining their requirements and to include them in the design process. The result of this consultation was the added support of employees who would have to "live" in the space. This level of commitment and support is possible only when people feel that they have played an active role in the design.

Figure 9-8 compares the new space plan accommodating the 45% growth along with the old plan. It is immediately obvious that the new space plan is more spacious than the old one. This is because all of the offices from two of the four "window" walls and have been replaced with open areas. This strategy really opens up the space while allowing additional staff to be to accommodated.

Figure 9-9 shows a full-size view of the new floor plan. This plan now includes several team spaces. The team space (T) in the middle of the left-hand side is where the design and marketing staff are working. They are able to easily interact with each other across the team space.

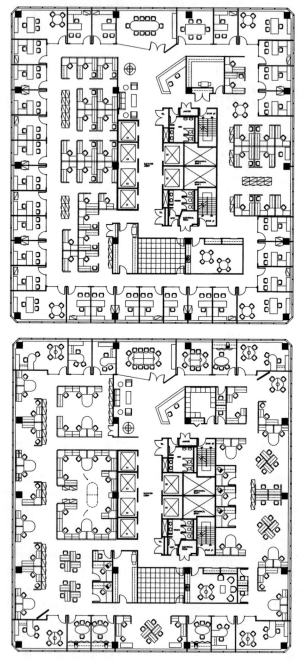

Figure 9-8 Comparison of old floor plan (top) for 60 employees and new floor plan (bottom) for 87 employees.

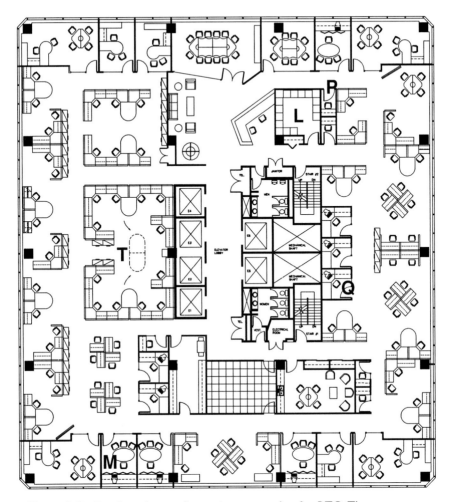

Figure 9-9 Final work transformation space plan for PTC. The new space features team space for design and marketing (T), lockers (L), manager offices/meeting rooms (M), phone booths (P), and quiet spaces (Q).

The sales staff, who are out of the office most of the time, use the carrels located throughout the space when they are in the office. When they return to the office, they first stop in the room (L) behind the main storage. This space contains lockers holding the remote workers' personal items. The locker also houses a "portable pedestal," which the employee can wheel to the workstation at which they will be working that day.

On the days the remote workers are in the office, they will spend most of their day interacting with others. This will be done in the team areas, the formal meeting rooms, the manager/meeting spaces, and some of the casual spaces.

Employees who spend the majority of the week in the office are now using the phone booths and other quiet spaces during the times when they need a high level of concentration. Two of the quiet offices have been designed without a telephone—the ultimate in quiet!

The implementation of work transformation at PTC was a journey of new experiences and constant learning. Along the way, the sales staff acquired new technology for working on the road, and they are now able to be even more productive. The space plan shown does not represent a radical implementation of new officing strategies. It still includes a large number traditional offices. PTC is managing the change to work transformation effectively and is continuing to develop the office space and the way the employees work.

DUN & BRADSTREET

Teaming Space

Dun & Bradstreet's North American Transaction Services Center in Allentown, PA, provides accounting for the corporation's North American business units. The center is a high-tech operation providing financial information services to over 28,000 internal customers and to many more external customers and vendors.

The organizational objective of the center is to provide cost effective operation by reducing costs and improving productivity. According to Jim Malone, team leader of operations,

> Cost efficiency is a goal, but so are speed and quality service. This facility supports the kind of horizontal structure and team focus needed to get there.[1]

The initial plan for the office was to have a core of enclosed executive offices and conference rooms with staff workspaces clustered around the perimeter—a typical design strategy used in many companies today. However, the design team decided to take the concepts a bid further and considered the potential of eliminating the private offices as a way of developing closer links between to the empowered work teams.

The space design effort and the organizational change efforts met when the design started to look like a fully integrated team environment. The decision was made to make the workspaces the same for everyone. The teams were delineated through the use of "streets" and "avenues" within the facility using building columns as signposts along the way. This strategy established work-group neighborhoods with pathways for access and intercommunication.

The design team had some fun in developing new names for the new concepts. Casual break/work areas were called "pantries." These areas were located between group spaces and were designed to enable chance encounters over coffee into informal work sessions. Besides the standard coffee supplies, the pantries were equipped with computer equipment, a whiteboard, and storage towers for supplies.

The space design clearly promotes teamwork and interaction between teams.

CASETEK SOFTWARE FACTORY INC.
Team Rooms Improve Productivity

Casetek Software Factory Inc. is an application development, and component provisioning and reuse management company. Casetek is based in Toronto, Ontario, and works on a worldwide scale with customers primarily in the financial services sector. According to Dragan Kopunovic, Chairman and VP Marketing, "Castek's exclusive focus is the assembly and delivery of software solutions from prefabricated software components."[2]

Casetek's strategy is based around quickly delivering quality solutions to its clients. The focus is on delivering fixed-price solutions on time and on budget—this is in an industry that is commonly plagued by delays and large cost overruns.

Castek's goals in developing its new office space were to be capable of supporting small, high-performance teams while being modular and flexible enough to allow for rapid growth (it has doubled in size every year for the past five years). Faye Wu, Chief Financial Officer explains that "the facility is designed to encourage the transfer of knowledge, which is how we have managed to grow so fast."[3] The Casetek solution includes the use of group work settings in which project managers are linked to their workgroups in settings that encourage frequent interaction and the informal sharing of ideas. There are also project rooms throughout the space which are surrounded with whiteboards for tracking project design and delivery. There is a broad range of furniture and space solutions that can be quickly and easily changed to meet the changing needs of the organization.

Productivity in the software development industry averages 10 to 12 "function points" per developer per month. The Casetek average is *70*, or seven times faster than the industry average. President and CEO, Yung Wu, describes the bottom-line impact of the work transformation at Casetek as follows:

I believe this environment, which is comfortable, functional and conducive to creativity, accounts for fully one third of our productivity advantage.[4]

WALDORF INTELEWORKNET CENTER

Shared Telework Center

The Waldorf InTeleWorkNet Center in suburban Maryland is a project funded by the United States Congress and supported by the Administration's "reinvent government" initiative. The telework center is 2225 feet^2, with 14 workstations, a common area, and a videoconferencing space.

The challenge for this telework center was to provide workstations that would accommodate a broad range of people performing different tasks. This, of course, can raise some significant ergonomic issues for traditional furniture solutions. The result was the implementation of flexible furniture that could be easily adjusted by the individual user without assistance.

People who work in the InTeleWorkNet Center do not have permanently assigned spaces. However, all have a dedicated storage cabinet and a "puppy" (mobile pedestal), which they can move from workstation to workstation. At the end of the day, the puppies are returned to the common storage area. Each puppy has its own luggage tag to identify the owner in case the puppy gets lost!

The ability to quickly and easily adjust the workstations is one of the keys to success at the center. Each workstation includes a height-adjustable work surface with an attached or freestanding adjustable keyboard tray. Each also has a portable screen that can easily be moved within the shared space to provide additional privacy.

According to Eric Blum, InTeleWorkNet project director,

[The center] requires an unprecedented level of innovation and flexibility to create a learning laboratory of alternative work arrangements. The development and operation of this model is intended to clearly establish the direction for future work arrangements for the public and private sectors regionally and nationwide.[5]

SOUTHERN CALIFORNIA EDISON

Beta Site Pilot

The electric utility industry in California is going through the deregulation process. Southern California Edison wanted to ensure that it was positioned to become a leader in the domestic and international markets. To do this, it felt that it was important to create a new office environment that would reflect this strategic change in the company.

Claire Spence, Manager of Facilities Planning and Construction, explains that:

> You can't drive a '70 Chevy into the new millennium. Nor can you face the challenge of a competitive new market without a state-of-the art workplace. We were looking for an environment that reduced facility operation costs and enhanced the culture of our competitive utility business.[6]

Spence adds that

> Our offices were designed for the kind of work we did in the early 1970s, when these facilities were built. But the company and what we do have changed. Now, we have to think differently about our jobs and what our office environment should do for us.[7]

The starting point for Edison was to develop a vision of the new space. This vision included using high-performance workspace; increasing tenancy by using space more efficiently; reducing the costs of moving employees by reconfiguring departments; creating a pleasant, ergonomic environment while helping employees to work more effectively; and encouraging teamwork and "over-the-back-fence" conversation.

The result of this visioning effort was the decision to implement a beta site of 25,000 ft^2 with 124 workstations, 7 conference rooms, 7 enclosed offices, 7 meeting spaces, 8 "hotel" stations, a coffee bar, and a resource library.

Employees can call ahead to reserve a spot in one of the "hotel" workstations that are equipped for immediate use with computers, phones, and basic office supplies. The hotel users all have locker space and use portable pedestals, which can be wheeled to their assigned workstation.

The beta site has been equipped with a universal 8×8 ft workstation that can be adapted to accommodate different work processes and personal preferences. Edison has created informal collaboration spaces in team areas made up of teardrop tables on wheels, which can be moved to meet specific team requirements.

NATIONAL DEMOGRAPHICS & LIFESTYLES/ THE POLK COMPANY

Creating a Sense of Community

NDL/Polk is a database marketing and information resource company comprised of highly skilled database specialists, analysts, marketing executives, researchers, and software designers. In 1991, NDL started getting its employees to work in teams in an attempt to get the organization closer to its customers.

NDL redesigned its new team-oriented work environment to reinforce its image as an innovative and forward-thinking company. It wanted to underscore to employees their value to the company and help them feel good about their work environment and the work they performed. It also wanted to challenge conventional views of space and create an environment that inspired fun. Finally, it wanted to create a strong sense of community within the company and promote team collaboration.

Marilyn Heit, Director of Facility Design and Purchasing Management, reports that

> In working towards these objectives, we started by researching the most cost-effective methods of designing space for flexibility and responsiveness to the many changes taking place in today's business environment—changing organizational structures, changing work force, changing technologies and changing economic conditions.[8]

The new space includes private offices around the core of the building (an atrium) for vice-presidents. These offices use an abundance of glass for high visibility and to allow the natural light to be viewed and shared by the greatest number of employees. Traffic pathways were designed to bypass private team spaces while providing opportunities for team interaction in the natural walkways.

Teams are in spaces called "neighborhoods." For private work, these neighborhoods include 9×9 ft workstations (a size based on functional needs rather than status); project and conference rooms; and "eddy" areas used for team files, reference materials, and shared equipment. The space includes broad use of moveable furniture, walls, whiteboards, and project screens.

"Watering holes" are high-activity areas designed to encourage casual interaction and inspire fun among the neighborhoods. These areas support printing, photocopying, mailing, and faxing while providing great places for casual discussions without disturbing the private work areas. In addition, small telephone booths were built throughout the space for private calls.

HITACHI AMERICA LIMITED

Reducing Facility Costs

Hitachi employs over 330,000 people worldwide, marketing more than 20,000 products. In the United States, Hitachi has over 5,000 workers employed by Hitachi America, Ltd. The western regional headquarters in Brisbane, CA, houses 500 people in 11 sales and marketing divisions.

Hitachi's goal was to reinvent the work environment to support its reengineered team-based approach. The objective of its new business strategies were to develop better products, bring them to market faster, respond more quickly to customer needs, and manage facility costs.

To meet the corporate goals and objectives, the new space had to improve the adjacencies among teammates, provide accessible meeting space, and enhance flexibility within individual space while increasing building occupancy; reducing the cost of moves, additions, and changes; and reusing existing furniture.

The existing space had team members scattered throughout the building, often on different floors. The meeting spaces were also scattered and usually were not conveniently located to those who wanted to use the facilities. Finally, the rectangular workspaces were based on status in the organization, not actual need. Joan Carroll-Newman, Administrative Specialist, explains that

> Previously, there were three or four different kinds of office configurations and certain accouterments which went with certain ones, depending on one's job grade. It would get to be a real slug-fest about who got what office; it took a lot of time, a lot of money, a lot of effort—what is the business benefit of that?[9]

The new space design is a dramatic transformation from the old. First of all, the dividing panels in workstations were reduced in height to provide broader access to breathtaking views of San Francisco Bay immediately adjacent to the building. The rectangular cubes were changed to honeycomb shapes, which better utilized the building's curved shape. Half-round activity tables now reside throughout the team spaces, providing ready spaces for informal discussions or team meetings. "Superman booths" are enclosed spaces scattered throughout the design for privacy. All of this was provided using 60% of Hitachi's existing systems furniture.

The business benefits of the new space are significant. The organization has noticed improved team communication by uniting the teams into contiguous space and by equipping its team spaces with the tools necessary to support ongoing communications. It has also noticed an improvement in morale and productivity. The frustrating, time-wasting search for meeting space has been reduced by placing the meeting facilities right in the team spaces. Basically, collaboration among team members and among teams happens more easily and naturally in the new space. The result is increased productivity and improved quality.

The real estate costs have also been reduced because of the new design. The current building had been "bursting at the seams" with 500 people, but under the new design, it can accommodate 700 people. "Our business overall is growing and we can probably expand within this building for the next three or four years, whereas if we stayed with the old set-up, we would have had to find external space"[10] says Bill Gsand, executive vice president.

The new design has also reduced the costs of moves, additions, and changes. The decision to go to a generic workstation that can be easily customized to meet individual requirements and business needs has reduced the cost of changes. The old scheme of "status standards" made reconfigurations a nightmare.

We often hear about the business benefits and sometimes question the level of staff support. At Hitachi, the staff have been very accepting of the new space. Mitch Bull, Manager of Office Planning and Administration, explained that "when we first put this into effect, we were really hoping for an 80% acceptance rate. We have been pleasantly surprised that we have about a 98% acceptance rate."[11]

NATIONAL CITY BANK

Shedding Traditional Ways

The National City Bank of Minneapolis, MN, has been in the banking business for more than 30 years. Like other businesses, the banking industry is changing. To support a new organizational culture, the $600 million bank decided to move 250 headquarters employees into an all-glass setting in an upscale retail mall—in essence, signaling their commitment to shedding traditional ways.

The bank's goal was to reinvent every facet of bank life, creating a customer-centric organization. This includes working in teams, equipping employees with the right tools, managing workflows, helping employees feeling important and good about the workplace, using technology to keep people connected, and keeping facilities costs in check.

The initial visioning process produced a challenging set of objectives for the new space: facilitate teaming and communication, provide people with the right tools, foster equality, maximize the bank's investment in technology, fit the same-size work force into 12% less space while allowing for 20% future growth, and reduce the costs of change—a tall order if limited to traditional definitions of how work is performed.

Reviewing the current design showed that most people did not understand how they impact each other. The private offices, tall cubes, and lack of meeting space kept people apart. Don Kjonaas, Senior Vice President, Operations Division, explains that "it's important for our employees to feel connected to each other and the outside world. The more our employees know, the better they can perform."[12]

The new design standardized on the same furniture for all employees, including all of the executives. The furniture is available in four generic configurations based on the specific requirements of the job being performed. This has really had an impact on staff morale and created a sense of equity. Trudy Tidwell, Lockbox Coordinator, Transaction Processing Department, likes the arrangement: "I have the same furniture as the president and CEO of this company. That makes me feel special.[13]

The design is very open. Glass walls and low partition screens have put everyone in the open, making it easier for staff to interact, share work, and catch internal and external news on ceiling-mounted television sets. The workstations are organized in team spaces, with casual meeting space in the team area along with nearby meeting rooms.

The bottom-line impact of this new design has been significant. The changes in the work environment along with changes to marketing and business practices have produced a 12% increase in new accounts in the first year after the move. At the same time, staff turnover has dropped 20%, as employees say they feel more appreciated and have grown personally and professionally. Significant savings in real estate have also been realized in moving from the old facility, with 107,000 ft^2, to the new headquarters, with 94,000 ft^2, with room for at least 20% future growth. Lastly, the implementation of four generic types of workstations throughout the company has allowed the bank to move the people, and not the furniture, when changes are required.

DIGITAL EQUIPMENT CORPORATION

Space Sharing

Digital Equipment (DEC) has gone through tremendous changes in the past few years: repositioning products, downsizing staff, and altering marketing channels. DEC has faced these significant challenges and now appears to have turned the corner.

One of the key changes was to the desire to redefine the way people worked. This required rethinking the corporation's definition of where employees work, the technology they need to perform their jobs, hours of work, and the type of physical facilities provided. A few years ago, DEC formed a task force to look for opportunities to change the traditional work environment. The result: the implementation of a new work environment, significantly changing the way DEC staff function.

The goals were to allow sales staff to work anytime/anywhere, spend more time with customers, work independently on administrative items (creating letters and reports), and reduce real estate costs. The new work environment initially focused on the sales force. Changes included equipping all sales staff with notebook computers, cellular phones, cellular modems, and a complete set of office software. Dedicated traditional offices were taken away, replaced by shared workstations available on a first-come, first-served basis. The project started with the Toronto office and made its way across Canada.

Sales staff were required to become mobile workers. The company requested that sales employees purchase their own notebooks. Michael Shove, British Columbia Branch Manager, explained that the company "believed staff would be more responsible with the equipment if they owned it. DEC offered notebooks at cost and provided financing where required." Shove is pleased to report "over 95% of the staff were agreeable to the arrangement."[14]

The net result was an improvement in productivity for sales staff and a reduction in the administrative workload previously required to support these employees. Real estate savings have been realized by having three to four employees sharing a workstation.

The new work environment has grown to include other offices. The program now includes non-sales personnel (administrative, support, and management staff), who represent the typical teleworker. They work from home 1–4 days per week and spend time at customer locations and the traditional office. These teleworkers use either notebooks or desktops and have high-speed modems and separate telephone lines.

The new work environment has created challenges for DEC. While most of the staff have been receptive to the changes and have embraced them, as with any organization, some are skeptical. The biggest hurdle: bringing managers on board. Some are wrestling with how to manage remote workers. The classic question "How do I know my staff are working when I can't see them?" is a challenge. It has brought changes to individual management styles and more effective screening to determine those jobs that are most appropriate for teleworking.

A tour of the DEC offices shows the extent of the changes. The traditional closed offices and paneled cubicles have disappeared. Closed offices are being replaced with open cubicles and small meeting rooms. Open cubicles are being replaced by four-station "pods." In many cases, these pods are surrounded by common areas for shared manual storage and equipment. The pods also come with roll-away pedestals, making it possible for staff to easily move their personal files to any workstation. Employees arrive at the facility, choose an appropriate place to work, bring their pedestal to the station, activate the phone at the chosen desk with their specific phone number, and are ready for business.

DEC has experienced the difficulties of moving people out of their personal comfort zone. For managers, it may mean changing their management style. For employees, it means breaking out of the routine of coming to the same workplace everyday. The concept of sharing office space is also a challenge; a few workers are still trying to lay permanent claim to some of the shared space. Shove feels the move to the new work environment has been a success.

It has allowed individual employees to tailor their day and work schedule around their personal and work environment. The result has been a definite improvement in productivity, an increase in sales, a reduction in staff and overall real estate cost savings.[15]

Shove suggests,

You must burn the bridge. Don't go back. Train management to deal with change; if you don't you will have nothing but problems. You also need to make sure you equip people with the right technology then encourage them to use it.[16]

NEC JAPAN

Telework

There is much doom and gloom in the Japanese market today, with the market having collapsed in late 1997 and the economy still apparently stalled. These changes in market conditions are forcing Japanese organizations to seriously rethink how work is performed. As existing hiring, pay, and work practices come under closer scrutiny, some Japanese firms are beginning to dabble in various work option schemes. Naturally, smaller companies are proving the most nimble here, but NEC is one example of a corporate behemoth that has gone further than many in testing the teleworking waters.

NEC's initial experimentation with remote working dates from its integrated network systems (INS) testing at the Kichijoji satellite office in 1984, but it reached a new level of commitment in the late 1980s and early 1990s with the company's involvement in several joint pilot programs, and the establishment of its own in-house program in 1992. In June 1992, NEC began leasing 33 m^2 in the 1560 m^2 Urawa Hologon facility for its Urawa Flex Office. Situated some 60 minutes from the Tokyo head office, the flex office is, in effect, a satellite office offering considerable commute savings for workers posted there. The facility has five workstations and access to such shared facilities as reception, office administration (OA) corner, lounge, relaxation corner, and fitness room. Starting with 10 participants in Stage 1 (June–October 1992), the pilot progressed to Stage 2 (November 1992 to April 1993, 13 participants) and Stage 3 (May–September 1993, 20 participants). Currently, the facility is used on a regular basis by some 18 workers, two thirds of whom are female system engineers involved in software development.

Around the same time, NEC also established a drop-in facility in central Osaka to facilitate customer servicing by employees based at its Kansai offices in the Osaka Business Park, approximately one hour from downtown Osaka. Use of the 340-m² facility is extremely high, with a monthly average of 519 workers dropping in to use either individual workstations, meeting rooms, or both. While not a satellite office in the strictest sense of the term, this flexible approach to providing employees with diverse kinds of workspace is indicative of NEC's commitment to liberating its work force from static locations.

NEC's telework arrangements are not confined to the company proper; they are also being used by some of its subsidiaries, most notably NEC Computer Systems. This company has a long-standing work-at-home program, professionally managed and with close checks on work conditions and worker satisfaction for its off-site staff, usually drawn from the ranks of ex-NEC employees to obviate training requirements.

NEC Chairman and Vice President of the Keidanren, Tadahiro Sekimoto, places NEC's interest in telework against a backdrop of advances in multimedia and changing workstyles. By making it increasingly possible to work remotely, multimedia is promoting both telework and the virtual office. Secondly, changing workstyles, mainly in the form of discretionary work systems and flex offices, are being driven by diversifying worker mentalities and the need for greater productivity. According to in-house surveys, both the Urawa and Osaka flex offices have been successful, although use of the Urawa facility has been hampered somewhat by sudden meetings and other unforeseen developments, preventing certain workers from teleworking on their scheduled days. Efficient management of the available space to ensure full occupancy is an issue that remains to be solved, but the productivity gains registered (150–200% reported increases) guarantee the continued existence of these facilities. In an encouraging move, NEC has expanded its program by opening a new facility in Machida, a suburb of Tokyo, with 8 individual work booths and some 65 employees registered. Partially to overcome the space allocation problems experienced at Urawa, an e-mail space reservation system is currently being tested as a way of improving facility occupancy.

All in all, traditional Japanese management practices are further entrenched than their North American or European counterparts. This has been exacerbated by the slow uptake of information technology in the typical Japanese workplace. NEC's efforts, however, show that it is not impossible to start the telework ball rolling. As in other companies around the globe, the key seems to be a firm commitment on the part of top management and a willingness to experiment with the new.

BENEVIA

Radical Change

Benevia, a subsidiary of Monsanto, is in the business of producing and selling coffee/tea sweeteners. Recently, Benevia went through the process of dramatically changing its corporate culture. It used the design of its new workplace in Chicago, IL, to demonstrate this new culture.

The Benevia business was expanding, but the focus was to "think big and act small," with the goal of doubling the size of the business in five years. The support for work transformation came directly from the top. The CEO was fully supportive. The new design (35,000 ft^2) has everyone, including the CEO, working in an open office of approximately 7.5 × 7.5 ft (56.25 ft^2). The office spaces are acoustically private but visually open. The degree of honesty and openness is shown in the simulation of cracked glass that can be found throughout the office—the concept is to show the breaking down of glass barriers reinforcing the corporate cultural changes.

The workplace also includes some very creative spaces. There is a pool table room, which is heavily used during lunch and break times; grocery store shelves in the office, which show staff how their product is displayed to consumers; and a meditation room, where employees can listen to a stereo, meditate, or have a nap. There are also 24 enclosed spaces, which are shared by all staff for "concentrated" work. There are also project rooms, where the teams can customize the space to meet their specific requirements. The bottom line has been a 20% reduction in the amount of space used per person.

Tammy Skelton, Director, Human Resources, notes that "the space looks different and people are changed from the moment they walk in the door.[18] She also explained that Benevia has increased the level of informal communication, improved creativity, and improved the level of collaboration/team focus. The key for Benevia has been its ability to turn space into an asset, to use changes to the workplace to drive cultural change.

NORTHERN TELECOM LTD.

Old Factory Converted to Corporate City

One of the most exciting examples of work transformation can be found at the world headquarters for Northern Telecom Ltd. (Nortel) in Brampton, Ontario. Prior to moving to its "new" facility, Nortel had 1300 employees spread across 3 buildings in the Greater Toronto Area. These 1300 people would typically fit into a 20-story building, but Nortel decided instead to recycle its old (circa 1963) digital-switching manufacturing plant in Brampton into a new-look office for its headquarters.

Initially, the decision to move to the old factory was a financial one. Nortel had three leases in Toronto area towers that were due. There was a strong desire to consolidate the offices, but the costs to build a 20-story office tower were approximately $10 million more in capital costs than renovating the old factory. In addition, Nortel switched to leased, moveable furniture and compressed the amount of space per employee to save about $22.6 million per year.

The financial numbers certainly showed a significant benefit to moving to the renovated factory, but it soon expanded into an opportunity to reinvent the company. David Dunn, Nortel Real Estate's Director of Global Planning and Design, explained that "at first, it was a financial question but then we went further to help facilitate the reinvention of Nortel."[19]

The resulting design is truly impressive. The 1963 factory has now been converted into a corporate city, housing the Nortel world headquarters staff. The space looks more like a design by city planners than by office architects. The Nortel planners

> perceive the working environment of the 1990s as a community of teams, with greater emphasis placed on people working together without artificial barriers to separate them. The goal is to create a sense of interdependence, like citizens in a community who need the co-operation and support of one another.[20]

The space is designed like a city. A main street runs through the middle of the space, with side streets delineating the various corporate communities within the organization. The design includes several amenities for employees such as a bank, credit union, doughnut shop, gourmet coffee bar, fully equipped cafeteria, computer store, and travel agency. There are ample areas to interact throughout the space, with "oasis" spots for coffee, photocopying, and supplies distributed throughout the space; numerous casual interaction spots; and a main courtyard that includes enough space for all staff to gather for corporate functions. The main courtyard also contains a large bank of monitors that can be used to connect the headquarters staff with other Nortel locations throughout the world.

Nortel took the concept of work transformation a step further than most. The company created an environment in which employees not only feel very comfortable in the office but actually enjoy their time there. Nortel also made a major commitment to telework, with a large portion of its staff working from home 2–3 days per week. The commitment to telework is shown by a mock-up of a home office which demonstrates how to set up a home office—using the latest in Nortel equipment, of course.

SUMMARY

Each of these examples shows how organizations have transformed the way employees work and the place(s) they can work from. They have all shown that the best solution for their organization was to think outside of the traditional definitions and to look for new and creative ways of having the workplace reflect the culture of the organization.

In late 1997, *Business Week* published the results of the first annual *Business Week* Architectural Records Award, which is sponsored by the American Institute of Architects (AIA). This competition showed that all the winning teams

> rethought the work process. The architects spent long months on each project examining how people do their jobs. Work in the information age is complex and often involves speaking with team members inside the organization; having extensive dialogues with clients, customers and the outside world; and doing individual, creative work in private. The winning projects contained spaces for both kinds of collaboration [internal and external] as well as privacy.[21]

The road to work transformation is not an easy one. The pioneers discussed in this chapter show that business objectives can be realized while delivering personal value to employees. The most important lesson to be learned is to invest the time and energy to explore new ways of thinking about where, when, and how work is performed. These implementations did not happen overnight; but if you are careful not to rush this process, you will stand a much better chance of succeeding.

NOTES

1. Steelcase Inc. Case Study. Dun & Bradstreet http://www.steelcase.com/studies/dunbrad.html
2. Castek Software Factory Inc. http://www.castek.com/outlook/business.htm
3. Steelcase Inc. Case Study. Casetek Software Factory Inc. http://www.steelcase.com/studies/casteck.html
4. Ibid.
5. Herman Miller Inc. Waldorf InTeleWorkNet Center "reinvents" the workplace. http://www.hermanmiller/research/case_studies/waldorf.html
6. Herman Miller Inc. Southern California Edison drives into the future. http://www.hermanmiller/research/case_studies/edison.html
7. Ibid.
8. Haworth Office Journal. Case History: Creating a Team Environment. http://www.haworth-furn.com/teaming.html

9. Steelcase Inc. Case Study. Hitachi America, Ltd. http://www.steelcase.com/ studies/hitachi.html

10. Ibid.

11. Ibid.

12. Steelcase Inc. Case Study. National City Bank. http://www.steelcase.com/studies/ncbank.html

13. Ibid.

14. Robertson, Ken. Alternative Officing at DEC. *Telework International*, *3*(3), Fall 1995.

15. Ibid.

16. Ibid

17. Spinks, Wendy. Telework in Japan: NEC's Approach. *Telework International*, *3*(3), Fall 1995.

18. Robertson, Ken. Alternative Officing: BTV Update. *Telework International*, *5*(1), January/February 1997.

19. Nussbaum, Bruce. Blueprints for Business: Recognizing Architecture's Ability to Solve Corporate Problems, Increase the Productivity of Workers, and Boost the Bottom Line. *Business Week*, November 3, 1997.

20. Levitch, Gerald. Zen and The New-Age Art of Workplace Design, *The Ottawa Citizen*, February 22, 1997, p. E5.

21. Nussbaum, Bruce. Blueprints for Business: Recognizing Architecture's Ability to Solve Corporate Problems, Increase the Productivity of Workers, and Boost the Bottom Line. *Business Week*, November 3, 1997.

10

The Future

Many people who have read about work transformation concepts feel that these concepts represent the future, that having adopted them, we can then stabilize our work environments for the next 20 years. After all, it took us over 50 years to change to our current traditional definition of the office, so presumably our new definitions will hold for at least 20 years. Wrong!

The world is in the midst of the greatest series of changes experienced since the Industrial Revolution. All of our "traditional" definitions are being overturned and changed. We are developing new and creative methods of dealing with today's and tomorrow's challenges. The switch to the Information Age is happening, so be prepared for even more changes.

For the past 25 years, Francis Kinsman—author, thinker, professional crystal ball gazer, clairvoyant, prophet, guru, and futurist—has looked to the future, writing, thinking, and imagining our world as it could be in years to come. In 1987, he wrote *The Telecommuters*, the first book in Britain to examine the concept of remote working.

Kinsman explains:

> I think there will be far fewer people traditionally employed by 2020. Society will be highly mobile with much flexible working. People will be "chunking" their jobs, working remotely when they can work that way but then coming together with others when they need to. And work will no longer be a nine-to-five pastime; future bosses/contractors will have to inspire rather than rule. Finally, watch out for virtual reality—a new dimension not only in entertainment, but in every aspect of life, especially work. Once holographic virtual meetings are possible, probably some time after 2035, everything will change.[1]

Nicholas Negroponte, Professor of Media Technology at MIT, discusses the switch from atoms to bits in his book *Being Digital*. Negroponte describes atoms as the traditional products we can physically put our hands around, while bits represent the digital transmission of information. In his book, he describes the future of work in the following terms:

> As the business world globalizes and the Internet grows, we will start to see a seamless digital workplace. Long before political harmony and long before the GATT talks can reach agreement on the tariff of atoms, bits will be borderless, stored and manipulated with absolutely no respect to geopolitical boundaries. In fact, time zones will probably play a bigger role in our digital future than trade zones. I can imagine some software projects that literally move around the world from east to west on a twenty-four hour cycle, from person to person or from group to group, one working as the other sleeps.[2]

Negroponte's comments reminds us that the new information-based economy does not fit within our traditional definitions of work. The transmission of information will have no geopolitical boundaries; we may well be working for companies located in other countries—being able to perform the majority of our work from a telework center, traditional office, or from home.

Negroponte's suggestion about working "around the clock" by teaming with individuals in other time zones has been raised by several other prominent consultants and futurists. The potential to transform our definitions of who performs the work, when the work is performed, and from where it is performed are all up for grabs. Imagine the competitive advantage that a software vendor would have if new product development could be completed in 50% of the elapsed time by using three shifts of workers from different time zones. Certainly these types of organizations would hold a tremendous competitive advantage over competitors that were still using a traditional model of working only one shift in one time zone.

FUTURE FACILITIES

Until recently, most organizations have treated their facilities as merely a cost of doing business. The concepts presented in this book suggest a move to making the facilities much more of business tool and to expand the definition of the facilities from just the traditional corporate locations to the employee's home and distributed telework centers.

The future direction for facilities will evolve towards making the right facilities available on an as-required basis. This means further expansion of the nonterritorial concepts to accommodate the evolving needs of workers. The future office will likely be a broad combination of locations, styles, and practices—which would seem totally outrageous today. However, teleworking three days a week from home would have been seen as impossible in 1970.

The new type of office facilities will have an impact on the organization's overall real estate portfolio. Today, most office real estate is located in a central business district or in areas designated as industrial or commercial nodes. The future real estate holdings for offices will include a broad range of satellite offices, telework centers, shared facilities, and downsized central locations.

The broad range of real estate holdings will require more effort than managing a single centralized facility. In addition, the new real estate holdings will be in locations that are very different from those of today. You may have a neighborhood telework center in the middle of a community, far from the central office. This telework center may, or may not, be owned by the organization. The use of offices shared with other organizations will become more common.

An example of the changes in real estate is the emergence of telecottages in Australia and the United Kingdom. Telecottages are neighborhood-based offices which can function both as telework centers for employees who live in the neighborhood and as a vital link in the virtual office operation of small entrepreneurial ventures. The UK has an entire network of telecottages that are used by small businesses as a location for meetings, an informal office environment, and a place to interact with other small businesses and home based business operators. Some of the UK offices even offer "in house" daycare facilities, technology training programs for the community, and other "community center"– type services.

The Australian telecottages are similar to those in the UK, although some of them are designated heritage (landmark) buildings. Like many countries, Australia is trying to save its heritage buildings but is having difficulty in raising the funds necessary to retain them. The Australian government has tried turning a few heritage sites into telecottages by renovating the inside to accommodate office workers while retaining exterior and key interior historical architecture. The buildings are put to good use during the workday, and the funds raised from the telecottage are used to support their ongoing maintenance. This has created a win–win situation for the teleworkers, taxpayers, and the community in general.

Landlords will also see changes in what tenants expect in their buildings. Most organizations will revisit their traditional office designs and will likely move to some form of alternative officing. This will likely result in the elimination of large, infrequently used conference rooms and an increase in requests for more facilities the can be shared among the tenants. This could include building-based conference rooms that can be booked by any tenant, soft seating areas, high-end coffee bars, fitness/health facilities, and so forth.

Organizations will also become involved in the ergonomics of the home office. Today, many organizations are ignoring the home office. They suggest that if employees want to work from home, the employees will be responsible for providing their own furniture. This is a seen as a practical short-term solution but one that may cost the organization in the long run if there is an increase in the number of workplace injuries occurring in home offices that are not ergonomically sound.

Supplying furniture for the home office will be a significant challenge. Facilities managers will have to develop guidelines for home ergonomics and be prepared to offer a range of solutions that will match the employee's desire in terms of interior design. This will be far more challenging than providing the same furniture system to everyone in the traditional office building. Ensuring a continuously safe working environment at the employee's home will be another significant challenge for the facilities management group.

The continued evolution of more portable technology will also impact the number of mobile workers. It will become more common for facilities groups to start looking at true mobile offices as a solution. This is, of course, already happening today. For example, one of the top real estate agents in Calgary, Alberta, has a customized vehicle that she uses as her "head office." The vehicle has been equipped with a desk, cellular phone, notebook computer, cellular modem, and cellular fax to allow her to work anytime, anywhere. The agent has been able to justify the cost of the upgrades to her vehicle, plus the cost of the full-time chauffeur, with the increase in revenues generated by this increased flexibility.

Another example is a hospital servicing a large rural community. Studies have shown that many of the people who attend the hospital for treatments live a significant distance from the hospital. For many of these geographically dispersed individuals, the journey to the hospital is long and difficult. So the hospital decided to invest in a motorhome, which is equipped with basic examination facilities, and sent medical staff out on the road to care for a large percentage of these individuals.

The continued move to mobility will mean that facilities management groups will have to start to consider a much broader range of potential work-spaces—some of which will be motorized!

The amenities included in these newly designed offices are also changing. Recall from Chapter 4 that Procter & Gamble's new $280 million, 1.3 million ft^2 building in Cincinnati, OH, includes a dry cleaner, a shoe-repair shop, and a cafeteria that prepares food that employees can take home at night.

The P&G example shows a recognition of the increased demands on families when both partners are working or when families consist of one parent. P&G realizes that balancing work and family is a challenge at the best of times.

The amenities included in their new facility help employees deal with these challenges.

Another example of a more common amenity is the fitness center. The fitness center may become a common place for holding either formal or impromptu meetings as employees attempt to get some physical recreation while still meeting their business objectives.

Facilities managers will see their role change dramatically. No longer will the facilities group be just an order taker and provider of standard furniture and space; it will now have to work very closely with the human resources and information technology groups to ensure that all aspects of the work environment are covered.

Dr. Ahden Busch, Director of Alternative Officing Strategies with RNL Design, suggests that

> Facilities groups will have to take some risks and design space with fewer rules, in essence, to step outside the box. They need to understand the human interactions as much as they understand blueprints.[4]

Busch realizes the extent to which facilities managers will need to readjust their current skills to be affective in this new environment. She has been working directly with the University College of the University of Denver (CO) to develop an extensive graduate program called New Work Processes for the New Economy. Like all other professionals, the future will hold constant change and therefore the need for regular educational upgrading to meet the requirements for continuous improvements.

The changes in facilities are not limited to changes at the central office. There will also be the development of telework centers or satellite offices and changes to employees' homes. A 1995 research study by the Canadian Mortgage and Housing Corporation (CMHC) reports an increase in the amount of home renovations due to the increasing number of people who are working from home (fueled by home-based businesses and teleworkers).[5]

In addition to the increase in renovations to support home offices, we are also seeing a few changes in the architectural design of some homes. The initial architectural changes are in the form of including home office space in new designs. In addition to including the home office in the plan, architects and home designers are also starting to recognize the need to place the office at the front door to accommodate deliveries and meetings, while minimizing the interaction with the remainder of the house—thus separating work and family more effectively.

Future home changes will likely include the design of better individual room heating and cooling solutions to allow teleworkers to function effectively all year long and lighting solutions that provide for good viewing of desktop and notebook screens without creating an institutional look. In addition, the concept of separate structures for home office workers may become common.

FUTURE TECHNOLOGIES

In the 1970s, when I started to work in the information technology area (data processing as we called it then), I was amazed at the advancements we were able to make by moving from punch cards to an on-line terminal. This was a terrific but somewhat expensive step. When we first moved to terminals, the company I worked for installed 10 terminals to support the needs of a group of 150 technologists. Can you imagine your job today if you had to share your PC with 15 other employees? How would you get anything done?

The reason for this reminiscence is not to explain why I now have gray hair but rather to illustrate the tremendous change we have seen in the world of technology. In the past 20 years, we have moved from punch cards and paper to notebook computers, personal digital assistants, and high-speed cellular phones and modems. We are certainly on an exponential curve that is climbing steeply.

In my opinion, the biggest developments in the technology arena in the past decade have all been related to telecommunications. First, there is the Internet. The Internet has existed for a long time, but only in the past few years has it exploded in terms of the number of people who are using it. It is now expected that individuals will have at least one Internet e-mail address and that organizations will have some sort of presence on the World Wide Web (WWW). The interesting aspect of the Internet is that it has brought the concept of exchanging information electronically to anyone, anywhere, at seemingly little or no cost.

It is clear that the penetration of technology is increasing dramatically. The Gartner Group's Bob Hafner suggests that "by the year 2000 more than 30 million people in the United States and 55 million world-wide will work away from the traditional work-place.[6]

The use of technology is no longer limited to work. There is now widespread speculation that we will experience an increase in interactive experiences with our home computers and a decrease in our passive watching of television. The integration of computers and television already exists with the latest in "Web TV" devices.

The use of technology for work, home, education, and pleasure is decreasing the uncomfortable feeling a lot of people have about technology. In essence, we are seeing technology in all facets of our lives, and we are growing to accept it everywhere.

One example that clearly illustrates our personal level of acceptance is the use of automated teller machines (ATMs). In the early days of ATMs, many people were hesitant to use them, as they were more comfortable dealing with the teller, a real person who could be counted on to meet all your needs. However, as the ATM technology became more widespread, they realized that it allowed them to do a large portion of their banking at distributed machines anytime they wanted. If they were at the shopping mall and needed some cash, they didn't need to drive to their local bank branch (which probably wasn't open at the time you really needed the money.) Instead people became very comfortable with the distributed technology—ATMs, in fact, being networked to powerful computers, constituted many people's first "on-line" experience—and today the removal of ATM technology (without a better replacement) would be met with a huge outcry by the bank's customers.

It is hard to predict with any confidence what the key new technologies will be in the next decade. I would, however, suggest that a few telecommunications-related technologies that should be watched carefully. The most important advancement will be the delivery of high-bandwidth, high-speed voice/data/image communications to the home. This will come from one or more of many sources and will likely be reasonably affordable. The options, as I see them, include: broad-scale implementation of ISDN or ADSL or some future variant; developments in compression technologies that allow full motion video to be compressed to the point where it can be transmitted over slower-speed lines; the introduction of high-bandwidth, high-speed wireless communications; and the emergence of cable technology to support the high-speed transmission.

Advancing the telecommunications infrastructure is clearly the key to success in the future.

FUTURE EMPLOYEES

The facilities and technology are certainly changing. The expectations regarding future employees will also be significantly different from where they are today. The main issues in considering future employees will include balancing work and family, "technology enabled" children entering the work force, and baby boomer knowledge workers retiring.

A major problem faced by most employees today is trying to balance work and family pressures, and this problem will become only more exacerbated in the future. Employees are being pressured from both sides: they are being asked to do more with less at work, which normally translates into longer hours. Families are also pressuring employees to spend more time with them, to attend family events—which may occur shortly after business hours—and to care for both young children and aging parents.

These pressures are stretching people, in many cases, to their limits. They are looking for ways to relieve some portion of these pressures. Implementing alternative work arrangements is one such solution. Employees of the future will expect, and in some cases demand, the flexibility to perform their job while still being able to spend time with their families. Though organizations may want employees to put the organization first in terms of dedication and involvement, the reality is that most people will want to put their families first, with their work a close second. The work and family commitments are somewhat in conflict under the traditional work model.

People are also seeing their work changing. The traditional job market is designed around working in the office Monday to Friday, for 35–40 hours a week. This arrangement can be reasonably successful when only one spouse is working. However, today the reality is that there are many couples in which both partners work. The issue becomes how to organize the working time and nonworking time so that a family can spend time together.

William Bridges, in his best-seller, *Job Shift—How to Prosper in a Workplace Without Jobs*, suggests that

> Everyone is a contingent worker, not just the part-time and the contract workers. Everyone's employment, that is, is contingent on results that the organization can achieve.[7]

Bridges reminds us that the old rules of a job are gone, that the new world includes much more variety and the inherent flexibility along with a lack of traditional security that many have come to know in the past.

This issue becomes even more dramatic when you consider that our traditional mode of Monday to Friday, 9:00 to 5:00, is no longer valid for many jobs. We have seen a tremendous shift in North America from production-oriented jobs to service jobs. The service jobs must be worked during the hours that best fit customer demand. This, in many cases, is outside the traditional working window.

For example, consider the situation of a family with three children and both spouses working full-time (a necessity for many North American families). One spouse's working hours are the traditional Monday to Friday, 9:00 to 5:00, while the other spouse's job is in the tourism industry and involves working Wednesday to Sunday from 2:00 P.M. to 9:00 P.M. It is readily apparent that the window of opportunity for any family get-together is extremely limited (Saturday or Sunday morning or Monday or Tuesday evening). This obviously is less than ideal. If it were possible to apply some of the work transformation concepts, the family might be able to adjust the schedules to free up at least one day when everyone could be together.

The entrance of today's "technology enabled" children into the work force will have a dramatic affect on the future employees. The average employee today has gained the majority of technology expertise on the job. Today's children are learning about technology at an extremely young age, making them totally comfortable with the technology.

If you doubt the assertion that today's children are technologically advanced, then chat with your child, visit a friend's, or drop by a school. Today's children are definitely computer literate. A few years ago, when CD ROM drives first came out, my niece and nephew (then ages 6 and 8) knew more about this new technology than I did. They knew how to fire up the computer, load the CD drive, and use the software. In fact, my six-year-old niece's only problem was opening the plastic case containing the CD (her hands weren't quite big or strong enough).

Many children are extremely active on their computers. They use the Internet to "chat" with other children around the world. They have absolutely no fear of the technology. Today's generation treats the PC like an appliance—unconcerned with how it works, just knowing that it does. The same way we don't try to figure out all the technical ins and outs of our televisions or video cassette recorders—we merely turn them on and use them.

Children who are communicating with others around the world are going to seriously question why they would have to leave home, enter an overly congested road system, and crawl to work. They will expect to have the ability to work from home—with clients in other cities, regions, or countries—and work whenever they are at their peak. They will not accept our traditional definition of where and when we work, as they know the technology can overcome most of the arguments for commuting to work at the centralized office.

The baby boomers have had an impact on almost everything in the past 30 years, and they will again with the future of work. The baby boomers (defined as those born between 1945 and 1965) will be retiring or near retirement during the next 20 years. Many futurists and economists have expressed the concern that there will not be enough employees left in the highly skilled knowledge worker category to fill the positions left vacant by the retiring baby boomers.

This statement may be hard to swallow, given the current state of employment and apparent lack of jobs in some regions today. However, these highly skilled knowledge workers will be leaving the work force en masse, and there do not appear to be enough new graduates to replace them. Companies that analyze their resourcing strategy over the long run will have to compensate for this.

The problem will also be compounded as many of these baby boomers inherit family estates. The baby boomers are the first generation of North Americans who will, on average, inherit significantly more than previous generations. The input of additional personal funds will likely encourage many employees to consider early retirement. They will be financially secure and will be positioned to retire early.

The retiring of baby boomer knowledge workers will definitely impact an organization's resourcing plan. The implementation of work transformation may be used to help keep these valuable knowledge workers on for a longer period of time. This could be accomplished through the phased retirement option, whereby employees can scale down the hours they work to eventually be fully retired. This strategy also allows the organization to enable that adequate skills transfer is occurring so that the experienced gained by the retiring employee is passed on to younger knowledge workers.

FUTURE BUSINESS

Business itself is also changing. It seems that every company has reengineered, right-sized, and repositioned to make itself more effective and competitive. These changes have included getting closer to the customer, working longer hours, redefining customer service, and becoming more service oriented.

The "getting closer to the customer" approach is common in many organizations. Some companies, such as IBM, have taken the strategy of implementing work transformation concepts to get its staff out of the office to spend more time with customers. The net result for IBM has been significant savings in real estate costs and improvements in customer service and sales.

In the future, businesses will be getting closer to the customer by positioning distributed facilities and information technology–based kiosks, and/or using telecommunications technology to deliver services to clients. The distributed facilities might include the development of telework centers in local neighborhoods, where a "street front" facility can be integrated into the telework center. Information kiosks might be placed in shopping malls, airports, hotel lobbies, and so on to provide information to customers. These kiosks could be supported by "live" operators, who would be available for telephone calls or video conferences from customers at the kiosk. The level of support required for this could dramatically stretch the regular work day.

The ultimate way to get closer to your customers is the use of electronic commerce. This concept will continue to grow as the Internet, or some variation on the Internet, becomes more widely utilized and the security available for transferring credit card information becomes more ubiquitous. This will allow organizations to provide information services directly to their customer's businesses and/or homes. Again, like the kiosks, support must be available during a more extended day than is common today.

The future of business will likely involve providing longer hours of service. This is starting to happen today and will become more predominant in the future, when a standard definition of a work day or work week will no longer be in place. For example, banks have begun to notice that being open from 9:00 A.M. to 3:00 P.M. is no longer enough. To stay competitive with credit unions and other financial institutions, they must extend their hours and consider being open on the weekends.

Even government organizations are starting to change their hours of operation. Several municipalities are now offering "counter" service for building permits, plan inspections, etc., in the evening or on the weekend. These hours are more appropriate for the large number of customers who are working during the "regular" working day and cannot afford to take time off to stop by the local municipal hall or county clerk' office.

The concept of extended hours brings up several staffing issues, all of which are likely to be contentious with labor unions. The greatest challenge will be staffing to meet peak periods without incurring substantial additional labor costs. Many organizations that are providing telephone services and/or support for customers are finding that the peak periods of the day probably do not match with the work shifts.

For example, consider an organization that has a customer service group to field calls. The peak periods are from 6:00 A.M. to 9:00 A.M. and again from 4:00 P.M. to 7:00 P.M. To accommodate the peak periods, the organization will have contract two shifts of workers to cover the extended hours or consider split shifting. The cost of hiring two shifts of workers is likely to be more than the value of the additional hours of customer service. The additional staff will not be very busy during the hours between the peaks, but the organization will need the staff to meet an expected level of customer service during the peak periods.

The concept of split shifting workers is attractive to employers but usually not attractive to employees. Consider the split shift in our example. The employee would start at 6:00 A.M. and work to 9:00 A.M. and then return to work at 3:30 P.M. and work to 7:00 P.M. If the employee has a 45-minute commute to the office, then the employee will have spent 3 hours (4 trips × 45 minutes/trip) commuting. This is not going to be popular.

The solution to this dilemma is to use work transformation concepts. Firstly, the peak periods could be partially staffed with part-time workers, those who want to work only 3–4 hours per day. Secondly, the split shift concept could work very effectively if the employees could perform the job from home. A split shift that provides the employee with 9:00 A.M. to 3:30 P.M. off will likely be very attractive to teleworkers who would like to be with their children during the day, go golfing, do gardening, and so on. When the commute is eliminated from the equation, the split shift takes on a new perspective.

The future strategies will use the telecommunications technology available to provide higher levels of customer service and to make it easier for customers to get information and make purchases. The key to enhancing service will be longer hours of support, being closer to the customer, and providing customer-friendly ways of interacting with the organization.

POSITIONING FOR THE FUTURE TODAY

When pondering the future, we tend to think it is a long way away. Of course, it is not. The future is coming at us at a fast and furious pace, and to survive, we need to recognize the changes that are occurring and reposition ourselves and our organizations for long-term survival.

This book has suggested numerous strategies for starting, growing, and supporting work transformation concepts. These concepts will be the norm in the future. Those who have their heads down today, hoping for the return of the "good old days" will be sadly mistaken. Those days are not coming back— and whether they were good or not depends on your memory.

Technology is opening up an entire new world for us. To take advantage of it, we must ensure that our organizations can maximize the value it receives from the technology. This involves starting to develop work transformation strategies. This should be done by using the information technology and your facilities as effective business tools. If you integrate the human resources, facilities management, and information technology strategies as suggested in this book, you will be on your way to developing and nurturing a work transformation strategy to move your organization into the future.

The key is to position your organization today to start taking advantage of these opportunities. If you do, you will be able to gradually grow your program and keep pace with other changes. If you choose to ignore these concepts, you will face the potential of placing your organization in jeopardy of not staying competitive, loosing market share, or even worse, going out of business.

Work transformation is the wave of the future. You need to position your organization today along the path of change to take advantage of these new ways of working in the new work anytime, anywhere world of the future.

The work transformation concepts presented in this book are not an end in themselves. They are the beginning of an exciting journey that will lead to even greater changes. As you come to embrace change, you should keep in mind that you will be involved with change activities at various stages: rolling out some changes, piloting others, and doing the initial research and analysis on others. While the individual paths themselves may be bumpy and tortuous, the continuum of change will move inexorably forward.

Start your work transformation program today. Take a small step and move forward. This stepping stone approach will take you, one step at a time, into the future.

NOTES

1. Phillipson, Ian. 2020 Vision, *Teleworker: The Magazine of The Telecottage Association* , 5, October–November 1994 (United Kingdom).
2. Negroponte, Nicholas. *Being Digital.* New York: Alfred A. Knopf, 1995, p. 228.
3. Office of The Future. *Business Week,* April 29, 1996.
4. Ahden Busch. Quoted from Steelcase/IFMA Business Television broadcast. May 22, 1996.
5. Gurstein, Penny. Planning for Telework and Home Based Employment: A Canadian Survey on Integrating Work into Residential Environments. Produced from Canada Mortgage and Housing Corporation and the Center for Future Studies in Housing and Living Environments, March 1995.
6. *ComputerWorld Canada*, March 1, 1996.
7. Bridges, William. *Job Shift.* Addison-Wesley, 1994. p. 50.

Website Bibliography

The following is a list of some of the websites that have been used in research for this book. Information available electronically is extremely fluid. To obtain the most up-to-date list of research information on work transformation, you are encouraged to visit the KLR Consulting Inc. website (www.klr.com), where this list will be updated on a regular basis.

HUMAN RESOURCES

Americans with Disabilities Act	www.doj.gov/crt/ada/adahom1.htm
Distributed Work force Solutions	www.awelynx.com/about.html
European Community Telework	www.agora.stm.it/ectf/ectfhome.html
European Telework Forum	www.telework-forum.org
European Telework Online	www.eto.org.uk
Flexibility (UK)	www.flexibility.co.uk
Information Society disAbilities Challenge	www.isdac.org
International Flexwork Forum (Japan)	www.iff.org
International Homeworkers Association	www.homeworkers.com
International Telework Association	www.telecommute.org
Labour Telematics	www.poptel.org.uk/LTC/
Models of Industrial Relations in Telework Innovation	www.iess-ae.it/mirti

HUMAN RESOURCES (continued)

PacBell Telecommuting Guide	www.pacbell.com/lib/tcguide
Smart Valley Telework Guide	www.svi.org
Telecommute America	www.att.com/Telecommute_America
Telecommuting Review	www.gilgordon.com
TeleTrends	www.graphex.com/langhoff
Telework & Internet Cyberworkers (France)	www.cyberworkers.com
Telework in Italy	www.mclink.it/telelavoro
Telework International	www.klr.com
Teleworxs (Germany)	www.iwtnet.de/teleworx

FACILITIES MANAGEMENT

Alternative Officing	www.altoffice.com
Building Owners and Managers Association (BOMA)	www.boma.org
Chiat Day	www.chiatday.com/factory
Future @ Work	www.future-at-work.org
Haworth Inc.	www.haworth-furn.com
Herman Miller, Inc.	www.hmiller.com/hmi.html
International Development Research Council (IDRC)	www.idrc.org
International Facilities Management Association (IFMA)	www.ifma.org
International Workplace Studies Program (Cornell University)	iwsp.human.cornell.edu/default.htm
Neighborhood Telecenters Program (California)	www.engr.ucdavis.edu/~its/tccenters/tc.stm
Philips: Vision of the Future	www-eur.philips.com/design/vof/toc1/
SMED	www.SMEDnet.com
Steelcase, Inc.	www.steelcase.com
Telecottage Association (UK)	www.tca.org.uk
The Office	the-office.com/office
Virtual Office	www.virtualoffice.com

INFORMATION TECHNOLOGY

ADSL Forum	www.adsl.com
Ascend Corporation	www.ascend.com
AT&T	www.att.com
Bell Atlantic	ba.com
Bell Canada	www.bell.ca
Cable Datacom News	www.cabledatacomnews.com
Cisco Systems	www.cisco.com
Ericsson	www.ericsson.se
Internet Telephony	www.internettelephony.com
ISDN Reference Page	www.informatik.uni-bre-man.de/~henken/dank.html
MCI Workplace Alternatives	www.mci.com
MCK Communications, Inc.	www.mck.com
Motorola	www.motorola.com
Northern Telecomm	www.nortel.com
Pacific Bell	www.pacbell.com
Security Dynamics	www.securid.com
Shiva	www.shiva.com
Symantec	www.symantec.com
Teltone Office Link	www.teltone.com
3 Com	www.3com.com:80/
V Technologies (hoteling software)	www.vtic.com/default.htm

Index